Heavenly Gems

Written and Compiled

By

Rayola Kelley

Hidden Manna Publications
P.O. Box 3572
Oldtown, ID. 83822

Heavenly Gems
Copyright © 2016 by Rayola Kelley

ISBN: 978-0-9864066-0-7

Except where otherwise indicated, all Scripture quotations in this book are taken from the King James Version of the Bible.

The (*) signifies a word whose definition can be found in the glossary located in the back of this book.

Dedication:

I want to dedicate this book of
spiritual wisdom to some special
couples,
Jim and Gloria Craft,
Fred and Elzo O'Brien,
and
Pastor Phil and Donna Skoog.
Thank you for your
example, friendship, and support
through the years.
You are gifts from heaven.

Acknowledgements

Special appreciation goes to my tireless, enduring co-laborers in the Gospel: Jeannette Haley and Carrie Seaney. You all have been supportive in various ways: Jeannette, you have been my constant source of inspiration to reach for the impossible, and Carrie, you are the one who brings a smile and song to the uncertain plateaus of drudgery and mediocrity of my life, as well as help me wade through the challenges of modern technology.

I also want to thank Faye Moore for providing me with the past newsletters from the Laclede Community Church of Laclede, Idaho, and Nyla Ray for providing me with funny stories from the Internet.

Contents

Introduction

I have always appreciated the wisdom from above. There is something about it that is so practical in presentation and so simple in meaning, yet is highlighted with deep profundity. Due to its truth, there can be a sharpness about it, but at the same time a gentleness that can serve as a means to knock off and sand the rough edges to make such wisdom pliable and precious once it makes the necessary impact.

For years I have collected what I consider to be those precious gems from heaven. It seems that at times, like the manna of old, it actually fell out of heaven, while at other times it was acquired in deep places of obscurity and adversity. It is for this reason that such priceless nuggets can prove to be surprising.

One of the surprising aspects about heavenly wisdom is that it has fallen on the most unlikely people. Some of these individuals might have questionable backgrounds or possible heretical beliefs, yet they have spoken truths that only could be associated with heaven. Years ago I learned that the real test is more about the message than the vessel. After all, God used a Balaam's jackass to speak the truth.

This brings me to another aspect about heavenly wisdom--it will always be found to be the truth. As long as a vessel speaks truth, it is up to me to discern it as so and receive it in a proper way. God has used some unlikely vessels in my life to speak some tough truths. I recognize truths as being a test to see whether I love the truth and would receive it in a right spirit regardless of how it came to me.

Once again, I found these treasures within different sources. Some gems came from the internet and prized books, some which have been accredited in the Bibliography in the back of this book, along with Church and ministry newsletters. There are those nuggets that came from those whom I am personally involved with.

Every book that contains the treasures of heaven has its own flavor and emphasis. For instance, in *More Nuggets From Heaven,* there were legends, while in this book evangelism and the persecuted Church has been highlighted. However, each book contains those statements, examples, poems, or stories that show that heavenly wisdom has been mixed in the equation to bring greater depth or meaning to a Scriptural truth and principle.

The other thing I have learned about wisdom from above is that it is passed down like a priceless heirloom. I recognize how much of the investment of others have influenced the nuggets I now openly share. I do not believe I can solely lay claim to any heavenly gem. The reality is that all heavenly wisdom originates from the throne of God. As Christians we can only pass such heirlooms down to the next generation. It is for this reason Jesus told His disciples that not only would they do greater works, but their works would follow them. In the end, all the heavenly nuggets obtained in this lifetime will be cast at the feet of the One who is Wisdom Personified. Clearly, it will all belong to the Lord Jesus Christ.

Each person who presented the spiritual gem is identified, along with the known source when available. Intertwined in the text are both Scriptures and prayers. As in the previous books, I have composed the stories recorded in this book and use my initials, RJK, to identify my own statements or thoughts. I also tried my hand at a bit of poetry, one of which starts this book off, and I discovered that one can almost condense an entire book into a poem.

I have received positive feedback from my first nuggets book; therefore, it is my sincere hope that as with the previous two books, *Heavenly Gems* will once again touch people's hearts and minds with special treasures from above.

Heavenly Treasures

I've search the world through,
  For treasures not yet found.
I've explored amid worldly trinkets,
  Alas, no lasting success to know.
Still left a pauper in my plight,
  With no hope in sight,
Languishing in the deep ditches of despair,
  Consumed by the waters of anguish.

In darkness I grope in restless desperation,
  Till it was parted by a light of inspiration.
There before me the Word of God I found,
  Revealing the map to riches untold.
Its very route highlighted by heaven unfolding,
  Illuminating gems of beauty to behold.
Marked by mileposts divine,
  Encased in promises so fine.

Heavenly paths paved by sapphire so blue,
  With numerous treasures not yet secured,
Transparent beryl pointing to majesty,
  Of pure holiness yet to unfold,
Divine gold sheathed in precious stones
  Not yet uncovered.
Sparkling diamonds reflecting the glory from above
  Not yet obtained.

The Bible revealed,
  At last, heavenly treasures dotted the terrain.
Some lay openly on the trodden paths
  Of wisdom from above,
Other treasure ran in veins,
  Rich with truth eternal,
Some hidden,
  Deep in shadows and canyons of obscurity.

Ah, each treasure proved great,
  Ready to be possessed by a heart so tender,
With the light of the hope of salvation,
  Each treasure illuminated.
With the spade of faith,
  Each nugget uncovered.
Obtained by the shovel of love,
  Secured by the abundance of grace.

Now counted among the richest,
 A clay jar, possessing great treasures within,
Packaged in unmistakable fashion,
 Their beauty radiates heaven above.
Clothed with heavenly splendor,
 Enfolded in grace and meekness;
The Pearl of heaven taking on glorious form,
 After being hidden and veiled from the beginning:
 The Lord Jesus Christ!

-RJK

Prayer: Lord, You and I have been on a lot of adventures together. Some experiences may have lasted for only a season, but there were so many treasures I discovered along the way. Thank You for dotting my path with valuable nuggets that have enriched my life. Amen.

A Matter of Salvation and Redemption

~

The Cost of the Soul

During the great reformation of the 18th century, there was a great preacher by the name of Roland Hill. One day he was preaching in the streets, which were gathering a large crowd. An aristocrat by the name of Lady Ann Erskine was passing by in her carriage when she heard that Hill was preaching. Since she had heard much about the preacher, she decided that she wanted to join the assembly. However, when the preacher saw her and realized she belonged to the elite aristocracy, he suddenly stopped in the midst of his preaching, and said, "My friend I have something for sale."

The hearers were amazed at Hill's statement. "Yes, I have something for sale; it is the soul of Lady Ann Erskine. Is there any one here that will bid for her soul? Ah, do I hear a bid? Who bids? Satan bids. Satan, what will you give for her soul?

"I will give riches, honour, and pleasure.

"But stop! Do I hear another bid? Yes, Jesus Christ bids. Jesus what will you give for her soul?'

"I will give eternal life.

"Lady Ann Erskine, you have heard the two bids—which will you have?"

And Lady Ann Erskine fell down on her knees and cried out, "I will have Jesus."

R. A. Torrey used this story to drive home an important point in one of his revival messages. He put forth this plea to the hearers. "Man and woman, two are bidding for your soul tonight. Satan and Jesus. Satan offers you the world, the world that does not satisfy, and that does not last. Jesus offers you life, real life, eternal life. To which will you listen? 'What shall it profit a man, if he gain the whole world, and lose his own soul?'"

God put a cost on your and my soul. It costs His only begotten Son. However, if we do not accept His bid and receive the gift of His life, we might gain the temporary world, but we will forever lose our soul in the end. (RA, pg. 111)

For God so loved the world, that he gave his only begotten Son, that whosoever believeth in him should not perish, but have everlasting life (John 3:16).

♦ God spares no cost, nor thinks anything too costly for those who are truly His. When He spared not His Son for the World's salvation, He parted with the best of Heaven for the worst of earth.

-Herbert Lockyer
(DP, pg. 270)

♦ Men are not sinners because they sin. They sin because they are sinners.

-H. A. Ironside
(CBO, Jun. 25)

♦ Anything that fails to deal with sin cannot be taken seriously as a cure.

-William MacDonald
(ODT, Jan.18)

♦ Had men not been lost no Savior would have been required. Had they been abandoned no Savior would have come.

-A. W. Tozer
(AG, Aug. 15)

♦ Shedding the "wrongs" of my life at the foot of the cross is a liberating exercise that allows me to discover my "rights" as a child of God in His kingdom.

-RJK

♦ Have you ever thought of it in the light of the context, that when God, in infinite condescension, the great and infinitely holy God, sent down His own Son to proclaim pardon to the vilest sinner, if you and I neglect this salvation we are pouring contempt upon the Son of God, and upon the Father that sent Him?

-R. A. Torrey
(RA, pg. 90)

Prayer: Lord, neglect of our spiritual lives can cause so much damage. Forgive me for my complacency towards spiritual matters. Stir me up to love You more, pursue You in truth and holiness, and to become more pliable in Your hands. Amen.

♦ To stop at the cross is to preach but a half gospel. It is the truth of the resurrection that completes it. . .There can be no salvation apart from the raising up of the Son of God from the dead.

-H. A. Ironside
(CBO, Aug. 1)

♦ The good news is that God knows the problem that besets humanity and He has provided the solution through His Son—a solution that will change the heart of every human who will turn to Him and accept His offer.

-T. A. McMahon

That if thou shalt confess with thy mouth the Lord Jesus, and shalt believe in thine heart that God hath raised him from the dead, thou shalt be saved. For with the heart man believeth unto righteousness; and with the mouth confession is made unto salvation (Romans 10:9-10).

♦ The Gospel is not a "get out of hell free" card or a message of self-improvement. Jesus didn't die to improve self. He died to replace it. Self, sinful at its core, must be put to death and replaced with the nature and character of Christ.

-Anna Alden-Tirrill
(SP, Aug. 10)

♦ The devil, not God, is your father, unless your hearts are purified by faith and you are born again from above. It is not merely being baptized by water, but being born again of the Holy Ghost that must qualify you for salvation; and it will do you no service at the great day, to say unto Christ, Lord, my name is in the register of such and such a parish.

-George Whitefield
(GW, pg. 107)

Jesus answered, Verily, verily, I say unto thee, Except a man be born of water and of the Spirit, he cannot enter into the kingdom of God (John 3:5).

♦ I need the Cross of Christ to strike at the root of my capacity to sin. The Blood of Christ has dealt with my sins, but only the power of his death and resurrection is sufficient to deal with me... To us who believe, the Cross of Christ is central; central to all time because it is central to the whole work of God.

-Watchman Nee
(WN, May 25)

♦ In the cross the sin question has been settled in a righteous way, and so God can now save all who come to Him in faith.

-H. A. Ironside
(CBO, Apr. 22)

Even as the Son of man came not to be ministered unto, but to minister, and to give his life a ransom for many (Matthew 20:28).

♦ Where can we look in all the vast creation around us to find anything as beautiful—as utterly, awesomely, deeply beautiful—as the Incarnation? God became flesh to dwell among us to redeem us, to restore us, to save us completely.

-A. W. Tozer
(AG, Jul. 8)

♦ Jesus did not survive the Cross. He conquered it. He did not merely survive his ordeal; he triumphed. He returned in his resurrected body to deliver the news to his disciples who would soon tell the world. Jesus died saving others so that they could live. Yet he is now alive, back from the dead, offering salvation to the world.

-Extreme Devotion
(ED, pg. 312)

♦ Sentimental theology says that we are saved by admiring Jesus. This makes about as much sense as saying that when the whitewashed gable of a house reflects the glory of sunlight, the sun is shining inside the house.

-Oswald Chambers
(DL, Feb. 18)

♦ Christ's death on the cross was the highest exhibition of His holiness and victory over sin.

-Andrew Murray
(AP, Sept. 14)

Prayer: Lord, we have been ransomed by You. We belong to You, have purpose and hope because of You. However, we must come to You as our truth and hope to gain Your life from above. Amen.

♦ When Jesus came as a Savior, he came as a revelation of the mind of God, because He was slain before the foundation of the world. God provided a remedy before the disease.

-Hebert Lockyer

******

Are You In A Burning Building?

What would you do if you were in a burning building? Why, you would look for a way of escape. However, imagine for a moment, there was only one way to escape and that is by way of a fire escape. Would you take it? Most people would think it foolish not to take the fire escape.

The truth is the fires of judgment are burning before those who are in the arena of the world. God has provided a fire escape through the cross of Jesus. Granted, it is not a very pretty one and even appears a bit uncertain and scary because people are not sure where it will lead them.

Sadly, many people are not aware of the pending destruction of the fire that is getting brighter on the horizon. If they are slightly aware, they are looking elsewhere for an escape other than to the one that is marked by heaven itself. There are even those who are aware of the fire, but they live in a state of "wishful thinking" that someone will come in at the right time and save them in their uncertainty. However, the fire escape is the only provision and all the wishful thinking will not change the scenario.

R. A. Torrey best summarized man's plight. He clearly laid out before a congregation that there is only one way of escape: that is, by Christ. It is either salvation in Christ, or it is no salvation at all. He made this statement to a congregation, "But when the great King of Glory, the King of Kings and Lord of Lords, the great eternal Son of God comes to you and me, in our filth and rags and sin and wants to take us out of our filth and sin and rags of unrighteousness, and says, 'I want to adopt you into my family and make you an heir of God and a joint-heir with me,' there are some of you to-night who, by your actions are saying, 'go away with your salvation, go away with your adoption into the family of God; I would rather have the crust of the world's pleasure and the rags of my sin than all the royal apparel of righteousness and glory which you offer me.' Oh, the daring, daming guilt of any man or woman who neglects so great salvation! (RA, pg. 93)

For all have sinned, and come short of the glory of God;...For the wages of sin is death; but the gift of God is eternal life through Jesus Christ, our Lord...How shall we escape, if we neglect so great salvation; which at the first began to be spoken by the Lord, and was confirmed unto us by them that heard him (Romans 3:23; 6:23; Hebrews 2:3).

♦ God may have not been the children of Israel's first choice when it came to service and worship, but He would ultimately be their only choice when it came to salvation.

-RJK

♦ Remember there was a Joseph with us in prison, a Jeremy in the dungeon, a Daniel in the den, a Peter in chains, a Hezekiah upon the brink of the grave: and they all found the help of God most faithfully protecting them, and saving them in all their troubles.

-John Flavel
(RR, pg. 124)

♦ In modern day evangelism, this precious doctrine [of regeneration] has been reduced to nothing more than a human decision to raise one's hand, walk an aisle, or pray a "sinner's prayer." As a result, the majority of Americans believe that they've been "born again" even though their thoughts, words, and deeds are a continual contradiction to the nature and will of God.

-Paul Washer

******

The Million Dollar Question

Like most people, I am a creature of habit. I am comfortable with what I know, what I believe, and what I understand about matters. It is for this reason I have my standby Scriptures that I always run to depending on the subject or matter. The problem with my standby Scriptures is that I fail to discover the nuggets in other Scriptures. I must avoid glossing over the less familiar Scriptures and take time to meditate on them.

For example, take *Psalm 20:6, Now know I that the LORD saveth his anointed; he will hear him from his holy heaven with the saving strength of his right hand.* The million dollar question is, "What must I do to be saved?" The truth of the matter is the Bible tells us how to be saved, what salvation looks like, and how to make sure it is being worked in and out of our lives.

The real question should be, "Just how serious or desperate am I when it comes to salvation?" Most people embrace the idea of salvation, but not the life or responsibility of it. In this Scripture, we are told that the Lord saves those who are anointed. As believers, we know that we are anointed by the Spirit of God, and that such anointing comes from above through the life of Christ being established in us.

It has been made obvious that to be saved, I must have the presence of the Holy Spirit in my inner tabernacle. To have the Holy Spirit present in me verifies that I have been born again from above with the new life of Christ, which was planted by the seed of the Gospel and watered by His eternal Word *(John 3:3, 5).*

Prayer: Lord, I thank You for the means of feeding my mind with Your Word, disciplining my body with godliness, and nourishing my soul with the ways of righteousness. I praise You for providing an abundant life through the presence and work of Your Spirit. Amen.

♦ God's Gospel is perfect. It never needs to be changed, modified, altered, upgraded, or made more palatable as is increasingly being done by some who parade as Bible teachers. The pure and simple truth of the "old-fashioned" Gospel is the only cure for man's sin.

-Marv Rosenthal

♦ When a man is converted, not only are his present and future transformed, but also his past. He is changed into a man who has always been elect and righteous in God's eyes…God can heal our past, thus time is "reversible" for the faithful. We sing the songs of ascents and ascend and descend freely on the steps of time.

-Richard Wurmbrand
(AWG, pg. 84)

♦ The first condition of salvation is not knowledge, but meeting Christ.

-Watchman Nee
(WN, Jan. 17)

♦ The experiential knowledge of God is eternal life.

-A. W. Tozer
(AG, Feb. 19)

And this is life eternal, that they might know thee the only true God, and Jesus Christ, whom thou has sent (John 17:3).

****

In the Sights of Glory

Ira Sankey was a famous songwriter who traveled with Dwight Moody to conduct evangelistic meetings in the mid and late1800s. In one particular story, it was recorded that his musical abilities actually saved his life. He was in the union army standing guard duty when a Confederate rifleman had him in his sights. However, when the soldier heard Sankey singing, he lowered his rifle and did not shoot. God not only used Sankey's musical gift to save his life at that time, but to later reach into the dark souls of men and save them from His wrath to come. (PCK, pg. 185)

♦ The Church exists with the divine purpose and promise of conversions.
-Andrew Murray
(AP, Jun. 24)

♦ Our sins should have crushed us. We deserved eternal death, but the load fell on God's Lamb; He was crushed, and we are free!
-Hebert Lockyer
(MP, pg. 285)

♦ There is only one ground upon which man may meet God with joy and not with despair. That ground is the atoning blood of Jesus Christ.
-R. A. Torrey
(RA, pg. 15)

♦ Like the blood from the Passover lamb of old, the blood of Jesus on the doorposts of our hearts serves as a reminder that we are not part of the curse of rebellion or the fierce judgment on disobedience that is yet to come.

-RJK

Prayer: Lord, there is no greater display of heavenly wisdom outside of the salvation and spiritual maturity of a person. Lord, I pray Your wisdom will penetrate the foolish heart and the corrupt understanding of the lost so they can see their need to be saved and established in, and brought up according to Your Lordship. Amen.

♦ Marvel not at my asking you what you think about Christ being formed within you. For either God must change his nature or we ours. For as in Adam we all have spiritually died, so all that are effectually saved by Christ must in Christ be spiritually made alive.
-George Whitefield
(GW, pgs. 94, 95)

******

My life, a voyage o'er a tempestuous sea
In a frail bark, draws near the common end
Of all men, I, as others, must descend
Into the grave. What profit now to me
Pencil or chisel? Where the gain to be
In highest art a monarch? Can I bend
God's sin-avenging justice to befriend
My helpless soul that would of guilt be free?
Nor saints nor angels can my ransom give

From the two deaths that are before mine eyes—
The first at hand: the twain my righteous doom—
But on the cross, the sinner to receive,
God's Son spread out His hands. He hears my cries;
To Him I look and triumph o'er the tomb.

-Robert Chapman
1803-1903
(RC, pg. 19)
(Translation of a sonnet by Michelangelo)

♦ Broadly speaking, salvation was **planned** by the Father, **purchased** by the Son, and **processed** by the Holy Spirit.

-Marvin Rosenthal

♦ A clear conscience is never based upon our attainment; it can only be based on the atoning work of the Lord Jesus in the shedding of his Blood.

-Watchman Nee
(WN, Sept. 13)

♦ Repentance is simply giving up to stop fighting against God and to stop attempting to gain your own salvation through your own works; to literally give up and fall upon Christ. That is salvation.

-Paul Washer

♦ Jesus came in the likeness of sinful flesh. In other words, He was fashioned as man so that He could become sin for us by offering Himself as a sin offering. This was the way sin was condemned. It was condemned in Jesus' flesh as He became the essence of sin for us.

-RJK

For what the law could not do, in that it was weak through the flesh, God sending his own Son in the likeness of sinful flesh, and for sin, condemned sin in the flesh (Romans 8:3).

♦ There is no question about man's sin—therefore, there is no question about him being lost. A man is lost if he is not converted—overwhelmed in the vast darkness of emptiness. He was created to know God, but he chose the gutter.

-A. W. Tozer

******

The Entrance

What does it mean to be saved? The Bible talks about the way to life. It entails the entrance of redemption, the door of growth and service, and the veil of fellowship. These three entrances can be found in the study of the Old Testament Tabernacle. Each entrance served as an opening to the three compartments that were separated by the activities that took place in their confines. All of these entrances were in line with one another. The reason there are three entrances is because we have been saved through *justification* (the gate of redemption), we are being saved through the work of *sanctification* (the door of service), and we will be saved through *glorification* (as our flesh gives way to the complete work of redemption).

Heaven has framed the altar of the cross that leads each of us to salvation. Its work of death stands at the entrance of our life to God. Hebert Lockyer made this comparison about the single gate into heaven in His book, *All the Messianic Prophecies of the Bible*, "The gate of salvation is strong because it is the creation of the Trinity for the whole of mankind. Redemption is not for angels, but for men and women, lost and ruined by the Fall."

The narrow entrance points to the hard way of suffering. The gate simply opened to the altar that loomed in front of everyone. In the Old Testament, each individual had to bring their offerings to the altar that stood before the gate in the outer court to make atonement, but for those of the New Testament, they must personally embrace the sacrifice that was offered on the altar of the cross. It was on this rugged altar that Jesus did take away sin to bring reconciliation between God and man, as well as complete healing of the soul and restoration of the spirit.

We know the gate points to the work of redemption, but the door points to the person of Jesus. Jesus paid the price of redemption, but it is the essence of who He is that opens the greater life to us. Coming by way of who Jesus is shows there must be consecration on our part. Consecration and devotion from the first altar must constantly light our prayer life represented by the Altar of Incense. We must seek the inspiration for our prayer life at the table of shewbread and the subject of our prayer life at the candlestick.

The Bible is clear that there is only one way to heaven by which man can be saved, that there is only one true God who man must be reconciled to, and that this God alone is the source of all life.

This brings us to the message. The Gospel message that is the power of God unto salvation reminds us that Jesus is the promised Son who came by way of a handmaiden in the manger. He was sent by the Father, and is also the only begotten Son who will establish an everlasting government. The Bible clearly unveils Him in His attributes, ways, and works.

The beauty about redemption is that the way to God has been opened by Jesus' work on the cross. In Him we have all wisdom made available to us, we stand in complete righteousness and sanctification, knowing that in the world to come we will realize the fullness of His glorious redemption *(1 Corinthians 1:30).*

For I am not ashamed of the gospel of Christ: for it is the power of God unto salvation to every one that believeth; to the Jew first, and also to the Greek (Romans 1:16).

♦ In reference to the fact that an Israelite could not enter the tabernacle except through the only gate, Hebert Lockyer made this statement, "Yet, how many there are who are trying, like Cain of old, to please God, not in God's way but in their own. They are seeking to climb over the high curtain by self-righteousness and self-effort, or by religion, but says our Lord of such, 'He that...climbeth up some other way, the same is a thief and a robber.'" (MP, pg. 366)

♦ Entering in the narrow gate is allowing Him to define your life, and not in general terms. See, there's your problem. "Oh, Jesus is everything to me, and Jesus is Lord." Okay, specifically though, explain to me what that means: what has it cost you, how have you changed your life from the course the rest of the world is walking in?

-Paul Washer

♦ God has weighed the whole world in the balances and found it wanting, and in Christ He provided salvation for a wanting world.

-R. A. Torrey
(RA, pg. 46)

♦ When Peter first encountered Jesus, he fell at His feet and cried, "Depart from me." In reference to this situation, H. A. Ironside made this statement, "It is those who own their sinfulness who find mercy. Peter had joined the goodly fellowship of Job, David, and Isaiah, all of whom, when consciously in the presence of God, took the place of self-judgment and found forgiveness and cleansing. The place of confession is the place of blessing."

♦ We should never judge God's love for us by our circumstances, but by the Cross where He died for us.

-Micca Campbell

In whom we have redemption through the blood, the forgiveness of sins, according to the riches of his grace (Ephesians 1:7).

♦ The cross of Christ may be behind us but because of redemption its work is ever before us.

-RJK

♦ The one great desire of God that moved Him in the work of redemption was that His heart longed for us to dwell with Him and in Him.

-Andrew Murray
(AP, Nov. 17)

♦ The work of God in salvation is a supernatural work, but in the United States of America and among Baptists, it's been reduced down to a few evangelical hoops that if we can get someone to jump through, we declare them popishly to be saved…it has been the pulpit that's sending more people to Hell than any liberal organization on the face of the earth.

-Paul Washer

******

Being Witnesses of Salvation

It is interesting to study those who now serve as a cloud of witness concerning the Christian life. One of the people I read about was Samuel Chadwick. He had a simple philosophy about evangelism. He believed that to draw men to Christ, all you had to do was raise up a Lazarus from the grave of depravity, spiritual ruin, and imminent death.

It is true there are many walking dead among us. It takes a vision for the lost and an abiding confidence in the power of God and His Word to witness the raising of those who are dead in sin to a new life. God used Chadwick to "raise many from the dead" to become a witness of His incredible power to save those who are indeed far away from Him.

Chadwick also stood for righteousness and truth. He went to court to oppose licensing new pubs in popular places. There was an incident where the attorney for the brewers did his best to deride the preacher in court. He even went as far as to remind Chadwick that he had sheep to tend to. At which time Chadwick jumped to his feet and replied, "Don't you trouble about my sheep! I'm after the wolf today!"

In another incident there were some intellectual young pastors who tried to bring a "new gospel" into the Methodist movement. Chadwick opposed it. He told them to go down to the coalfields in South Yorkshire and try out their new gospel on those individuals. He exhorted them that until they have a gospel that they know will work, they need to shut up. He then concluded with this statement, "This is not an age for twiddling your thumbs!" (PCK, pgs. 246-252)

And when he thus had spoken, he cried with a loud voice, Lazarus, come forth (John 11:43).

♦ God is love—an ever-flowing fountain out of which steams the unceasing desire to make His creatures the partakers of all the holiness and the blessedness there is in Him. This desire for the salvation of souls is God's perfect will, His highest glory.

-Andrew Murray
(AP, Nov. 18)

♦ There is only one highway between Earth and Heaven, God built it, and it is His Son.

-Marvin Rosenthal

Neither is there salvation in any other; for there is none other name under heaven given among men, whereby we must be saved (Acts 4:12).

♦ The 4 spiritual laws and sinner's prayer is not the gospel of Jesus Christ, and that methodology and evangelism has done more to hurt this country than every heresy introduced by every cult combined. Millions of people in this country whose lives have never been changed believed themselves born again because we have so reduced the gospel of Jesus Christ that it means now nothing more than simple decision that will only take five minutes of your time.

-Paul Washer

♦ He who was with the Father from all eternity, became man that He might qualify as the Mediator of our redemption. It was necessary that He partake of our nature apart from sin, that He might represent us before God and pay the penalty that we deserved.

-H. A. Ironside
(CBO, Jan. 26)

♦ Christians think of eternal life as a free gift. It is, but it is also a promise of God. It was promised back in the Garden of Eden when God promised that a Redeemer would come forth from the seed of woman. It was promised to Abraham in the form of a covenant and blessing that would be made available through the nation that would come out of his loins. It was promised to King David in the form of a coming King and Messiah who would set up an eternal kingdom. It was promised, and God kept His promise. Jesus came from the seed of woman via Abraham's descendants through the royal lineage of King David. And then, He died on the cross to redeem us.

-RJK

******

The Unnerving Reality

There is a humorous story about a pastor who was paying a visit to one of the homes of his parishioner. Even though there was no reply to his repeated knocks, he sensed someone was home. Therefore, he took out a business card that he had printed with "Revelation 3:20" on the back of it for just such an occasion, and stuck it in the door.

That Sunday when the offering was processed, he found that his card had been returned. Added to it was the Scriptural reference of "Genesis 3:10." Reaching for his Bible to check out the reference, the pastor broke up in gales of laughter. Revelation 3:20 begins, "Behold, I stand at the door and knock." Genesis 3:10 reads, "I heard your voice in the garden and I was afraid for I was naked."

In some ways we can all relate to this humorous story. Every one of us has been caught in embarrassing situations. However, what happened in the Garden of Eden is no laughing matter. It is a story of great tragedy. For it was in the Garden of Eden that the first man had the freedom to walk in the garden with his Creator. It must have been a glorious environment. However, something within man caused him to cease to value the intimacy and freedom he had with his Creator. He risked it all by eating of the forbidden fruit and breaking not only God's commandment but his fellowship with his Creator.

When man fell from fulfilling his potential and becoming base in his thinking and being, he was stripped of all innocence. In his physical and spiritual nakedness of shame, he chose to hide from his God instead of face the unnerving reality that he was no longer in the state of being presentable before his holy Creator. He not only had to hide because of his indecent state, but he would not have the freedom to make himself known to God.

Even though a great tragedy took place in the garden, a great promise was given: that a Redeemer would come to right the tragedy. Jesus died on the cross to restore back to man what was lost in the garden: his relationship with his God. And, today He walks our way and even knocks on the door of our hearts to once again fellowship with us. Sadly, there are still many hiding behind the fig leaves of shame, in the coverings and shadows of man-made religion, and behind the walls of the fear of unbelief.

24

If you are such a person, cease to hide and come out into the light. Know that the Lord is calling you and that there is forgiveness, freedom, reconciliation, and restoration waiting on the other side of your hiding place.

And the LORD God called unto Adam, and said unto him, Where art thou (Genesis 3:9)?

♦ The reason we sense that God is remote is because there is a dissimilarity between moral characters...The Bible has a word for this moral incompatibility, this spiritual unlikeness between man and God— alienation.

-A. W. Tozer
(AG, Apr. 29)

♦ We have *justification* as we are seen in Him. We have *sanctification* as He is seen in us. We have increasing glory and ultimate *redemption* as both of these divine works of grace combine in the sovereign purpose of God.

-Oswald Chambers

♦ Redemption comes in three parts. To be born again means I was spiritually saved. However, I am presently being saved in the soul area, and will one day be physically saved and given a new glorified body.

-Jeannette Haley

♦ Remembering our humble beginnings at the cross of Jesus will establish our lives as living memorials for our Lord and Savior in light of the present, as well as serve as living testimonies of the future that is yet to come.

-RJK

Prayer: Lord, my faith can prove to be fickle depending on where I put it, but if I remember to put it in You, I can be assured of salvation being brought forth in the challenges of life. Amen.

♦ The true convert does not receive the gospel as an addition to his previous life, but in exchange for it.

-Paul Washer

♦ When once Christians realize that salvation means a vital union with Jesus Christ—an actual sharing of His life working in us, and the consecration of our whole being as a royal priesthood—the Church will prove how truly the likeness and the power of Christ dwell in her.

-Andrew Murray
(AP, Nov. 21)

♦ We may all start out trying to avoid being caught by God, but if we do not allow the Holy Spirit to attract us, the Gospel to snatch us, and the Word of God to become a net that captures our very soul, we will prove to be useless in taste, foolish in our resistance, and doomed to die in our vain state.

-RJK

♦ We are saved by the death of Christ. The antitype of the unrent veil is seen at Bethlehem, at Nazareth, and all the life long of the Christ of God. The miracles of grace wrought during His ministry were like the swaying of the folds of that veil before men's eye; and so were His words of grace from day to day.

-Herbert Lockyer
(MP, pg. 463)

Having therefore, brethren, boldness to enter into the holiest by the blood of Jesus, By a new and living way, which he hath consecrated for us, through the veil, that is to say, his flesh (Hebrews 10:19-20).

♦ The Gospel provides God with the cords to gently draw us to the redemption wrought by His Son on the cross.

-RJK

♦ As believers we appropriate that great work of redemption when we pray, "Your will be done in heaven as on earth."

-Andrew Murray
(AP, Nov. 4)

♦ As we consider deliverance from sin, we can see how we were delivered from sin on the cross. We are being delivered from sin by the righteousness of Christ reigning in us, and we will be delivered by our hope in Christ. Obviously, our deliverance from the slavery of sin through Jesus' redemption will be complete.

-RJK

When Jesus therefore had received the vinegar, he said, It is finished: and he bowed his head, and gave up the ghost (John 19:30).

♦ Concerning our decision to receive Jesus Christ, we surely would have been ill advised to go out and try to get a second opinion! Jesus Christ is

God's last word to us. There is no other. God has headed up all of our help and forgiveness and blessing in the person of Jesus Christ.

-A. W. Tozer
(AG, Sept. 3)

♦ We cannot know what freedom is unless we have experienced the benefits of it. For Christians, they come to an understanding of liberty because of what Jesus Christ did for them on the cross. Everything attached to the work of redemption produces liberty.

-RJK

******

Our Portion

What does it mean to inherit eternal life? Inheritance comes from outside of any personal means or activity. Others who have already paid the necessary price have secured it for those who will benefit from it.

If we have been truly born again from above, we are children of God. As children of God, we must come to terms with what we are actually inheriting. For example, in relationship with worldly inheritance, we think in terms of money and worldly possession. Our perception is that these inheritances are to add value or worth to our present lives.

When it comes to inheriting our spiritual inheritance, we must conclude it will not be money or physical possessions. However, since the inheritance is from God, it must be considered priceless and eternal.

To most Christians' surprise the portion of their inheritance is God Himself. Sadly, many do not see any value or worth in possessing God. After all, to such individuals, Christianity is all about benefiting from the best both worlds have to offer. Subsequently, due to worldly influence, the misdirected conclusion that many children of God draw is that our Father's main desire is to see us happy.

This is not true. Our Father's main desire is to see us saved from sin and its consequences. To accomplish this, He had to send forth His Son who secured redemption on the cross. As a result, God has bought us back from the slavery of sin to restore us back into His kingdom.

When we receive salvation, we have simply received the life of Jesus. This life serves as our portion and identification to the eternal inheritance of heaven that now awaits each of us.

The LORD is the portion of mine inheritance and of my cup: thou maintainest my lot (Psalm 16:5).

A Matter of the Eternal And Unseen

~

The Mystery of Godliness

What is the mystery of godliness? According to the Apostle Paul, it was the incarnation, prophetic fulfillment, and work of Jesus Christ *(1 Timothy 3:16)*. Jesus, who was fully God and became fully man, and until His entrance into the world, was veiled in the Old Testament, but was brought forth as a living manifestation of the Godhead in bodily form in the New Testament *(Colossians 2:9)*. As *Hebrews 1:3* tells us, Jesus was the image of His very person. In other words, even though He became lower than the angels in creation to take on humanity, He still retained the fullness of His deity. He never ceased to be God and maintained His divine personage even in His humanity.

Part of the mystery of godliness was hidden in the predominate colors of the temple: blue, purple, and scarlet. Blue points to the heavenly, purple to royalty, and scarlet to man who was formed from the red dust of the earth. The color blue came from a shellfish, purple from snails, and scarlet from an insect, a worm. Purple is a combination of blue and scarlet.

Jesus came from above and was injected into humanity when He took on human form. In His humanity He would be a fulfillment of the promise of a king (purple) coming out of the lineage of David. Also in His humanity (scarlet) He became a worm (lower than creation) to become the instrument of God. Like the color of purple He bridged the stark contrast between blue (heavenly) and scarlet (of the earth) through reconciliation.

The union of Jesus' humanity and undiminished deity is referred to by Bible Teachers as, "the **hypostatic union**". Sadly, this union has caused much controversy even among Christians. There are those who deny that Jesus was God or deny the reality of His humanity. Yet, it is because of Jesus in His human form that He became the Lamb of God who could serve as the ultimate sacrifice, and because of His deity He was part of raising Himself from the grave, proving victory over death *(John 2:19-21; Philippians 2:6-8)*.

29

For some individuals the idea of humanity and deity being a reality in one person seems ludicrous. Whether it is making God too small to accomplish such a task or deeming Him foolish for conceiving and bringing forth such a union in light of their intellectual understanding is speculative on my part; but, the reality is that these people perceive those who believe it as being a bit "touched" or deceived. However, to me to not believe this fundamental Scriptural truth is a grave product of unbelief. It means that the veil is still upon the minds and hearts of these people. This veil is only taken away by the Lord when faith embraces the complete truth about Him *(2 Corinthians 2:14-16; 10:3-5)*.

The Bible is clear that Jesus had dual natures. It was because of who He is as God that salvation has been obtained and offered to all of those who will believe, and due to His humanity He served as the supreme sacrifice on the cross to suffice the holy Law, but due to His resurrection, He now serves as our High Priest and intercessor in the courts of heaven. Clearly, His dual nature allows Him to carry out dual positions and responsibilities.

We cannot intellectually dissect or separate Jesus from who He is. We cannot receive certain truths about Him while rejecting others because they do not fit within our intellectual understanding. We must believe and receive by faith the whole matter of Jesus in regard to His incarnation as being true.

This is why faith plays a vital role in salvation. We must approach the Bible to believe all of it whether it makes sense or not. We must cast aside any intellectual arrogance by ignoring the pride of our carnal logic and the vain imaginations that exalt themselves against the knowledge of the one true God. We must trust that the real teacher of all spiritual matters, the Holy Spirit, will make the Christ of the Bible a living reality to our spirits. In the end, we will know without a doubt that He is indeed the God-Man.

For in him dwelleth all the fullness of the Godhead bodily (Colossians 2:9).

♦ The mystery of godliness or as it might be rendered, the secret of piety, is deity enshrined in humanity in the Person of our Lord Jesus Christ.

-H. A. Ironside
(CBO, Nov. 15)

♦ Twenty centuries ago God took on the form of man. Glory from above came to rest on Him, majesty manifested itself through His miracles and deeds, and honor was expressed when He received due worship. That man was Christ, the Son of the Living God.

-RJK

♦ If you have God in a box, it is time to release Him and let Him be all that the Bible portrays Him to be. A mature understanding of Who God is will more likely lead to a healthy relationship with Him.

-Anna Alden-Tirrill
(SP, Mar. 16)

♦ John commences his Gospel like a piercing laser beam with seventeen words. John writes, "In the beginning (any beginning of which the mind can conceive) was the Word, and the Word was with God, and the Word (logos) was (face to face with) God" (John 1:1). "In the beginning was the Word: proclaims the eternality of Jesus. "And the Word was with God" proclaims the equality of Jesus with the Father. "And the Word was God" proclaims the identity of Jesus. In John's Gospel, Jesus is declared as **God.**

-Marvin Rosenthal

♦ When you look in *Vine's Expository Dictionary of Biblical Words,* you will find that the term, "Son of God" means that Jesus was a reflection of God, identifying Him to God in the position as the Messiah, in nature as deity, and in purpose as Savior. It is the combination of Jesus as Messiah, deity, and Savior that makes Him the only Son of God. As the Messiah, He was the reflection of God's power and anointing, as deity, a visible reflection of His eternal attributes, and as Savior the reflection of the Father's heart of love towards mankind.

-RJK

Prayer: Lord, thank You for putting nuggets about You in Your Written Word. Give me the heart to seek out such treasures and the eyes to see them. Amen.

♦ If ever a man appears like a consummate idiot, it is when he tries to tell you how God ought to act. God is infinite, and no number of finites will ever equal the infinite, and the Infinite God is of immeasurably more importance than the whole race of infinitesimal men who inhabit this little globe.

-R. A. Torrey
(RA, pg. 13)

♦ Hope without God's promises is empty and futile, and often even presumptuous. But based on the promises of God, it rests upon His character and cannot lead to disappointment.

-Woodring

♦ "The foundation of God standeth sure." Providences serve, but never frustrate; execute, but cannot make void the decree; so that you may say

31

of the most afflicting providences, as David doth of the stormy winds. "Thy all fulfil his word."

-John Flavel
(RR, pg. 144)

♦ We fear men so much because we fear God so little.

-William Gurnall

♦ Man can deem all as being relative because his time on earth fades like the flower, but what God declares is not only absolute, but will stand as supreme, ageless, immovable, and eternal.

-RJK

Prayer: Lord, we are so limited as to what we see on the horizon of our lives. However, You have eternity before You. We can trust You to do all things well. Amen.

♦ Jesus Christ will destroy every peace and every love that is not based on the disposition of holiness.

-Oswald Chambers
(DL, pg. 11)

♦ Jesus Christ has done more than die for you on a tree; He told you how you're supposed to live and you have no right to live any other way. I'm sorry, that's discipleship…this Lord, He's Lord of absolutely everything… How much of your life is defined by what the word of God says, by what Jesus says, and how much of it is defined by culture?

-Paul Washer

♦ The Son of God died instead of us for our forgiveness; he lives instead of us for our deliverance. So we can speak of two substitutions: a substitute on the Cross who secures our forgiveness and a Substitute within who secures our victory.

-Watchman Nee
(WN, Jan. 7)

♦ If God is glorified, His people will be edified.

-RJK

♦ A sanctified self is a poor substitute for a glorified Christ.

-Unknown

♦ Adam, the second, was tried in a wilderness among the wild beasts, with all nature apparently arrayed against Him, yet He stood like a rock— invulnerable and impeccable—because He was God revealed in flesh.

His temptation was like exposing the gold to the acid test—not to find out if it is a precious metal, but to prove that it is really gold and not base metal gilded.

-H. A. Ironside
(CBO, Nov. 25)

But we see Jesus, who was made lower than the angels for the suffering of death, crowned with glory and honour; that he by the grace of God should taste death for every man (Hebrews 2:9).

♦ Religious foes tired to destroy Him (Jesus) but He was preserved until His task was completed. Down the ages deliberate efforts have been made to extinguish Him from the minds of men. Today, Communism, Atheism, Humanism, modernism, and materialism are combined to put out His fire, but on He burns and is still a living, bright reality in the lives of millions around the earth. Our blessed Lord is the fire on the divine altar that can never be quenched.

-Hebert Lockyer

******

What think ye of Christ? Is the test
　To try both your state and your scheme.
You cannot be right in the rest,
　Unless you think rightly of Him.

-John Newton
(1725-1807)

♦ The evangelical rationalism which tries to explain everything takes the mystery out of life and the mystery out of worship. When you have taken the mystery out you have taken God out, for while we may be able to understand Him in some measure, we can never fully understand God.

-A. W. Tozer
(AG, pg. Dec. 16)

♦ The gospel, as a glass (mirror), should be kept clean and clear in the pulpit, that the hearers may see the glory of Christ and be changed to the same image.

-Christmas Evans

♦ Jesus was a solitary figure. Hidden away in obscurity, most of His life pointed to preparation. Even though His light would only shine for three years, He would temporarily be once again veiled in the obscurity of a grave, only to rise three days later. In her devotional book, *The Secret Place,* Anna Alden-Tirrill made this observation about solitude, "People often confuse solitude with loneliness, but they are different. Loneliness is the pain of being alone. Solitude is the glory of being alone."

♦ That Triumphal Entry into Jerusalem at Passover was only a dimly prescient foreshadowing, a mere misty *adumbration of the ineffably marvelous and glorious Triumphal Entry to come.

-F. Ellsworth Powell
(KG, pg. 62)

♦ We think more loftily of God by knowing that He is incomprehensible, and above our understanding, than by conceiving Him under any image, and creature beauty, according to our rude understanding.

-Michael de Molinos

♦ The history of mankind will probably show that no people has ever risen above its religion, and man's spiritual history will positively demonstrate that no religion has ever been greater than its idea of God.

-A. W. Tozer

Prayer: O' Lord never let me take a detour away from finding You! Let me always see You as that glorious shining star that must daily dawn within my heart and upon my life to cause the dark night upon my soul to flee. Amen.

******

Glimpses of Glory

The Apostle Paul stated in *1 Corinthians 2:9,* "But as it is written, Eye hath not seen, nor ear heard, neither have entered into the heart of man, the things which God hath prepared for them that love him." Obviously, we cannot imagine the glory that adorns heaven. It probably possesses sights that would be indescribable in any language. No doubt the description would be highlighted with awe that would turn into a worshipful type of silence.

However, man has had a few glimpses into heaven. In the Old Testament, you have Jacob who encountered the ladder of God at Bethel, connecting heaven and earth, and he saw the Lord standing at the top of it *(Genesis 28:12-13)*. There was the time that the elders of Israel encountered a bit of heaven on earth when the Lord walked in their midst on a paved work of sapphire stone, and it appeared as if His very body was reflecting heaven itself *(Exodus 24:10)*. Then there was Moses who reflected the glory of heaven from his face, but had to veil it with a covering because of how it affected others *(Exodus 34:29-35)*.

We are told that in Christ all of the fullness of the Godhead dwelled in bodily form *(Colossians 2:9)*. Although the glory of heaven was veiled in Jesus, the Father would draw the curtains of heaven to confirm and verify His Son's identity at different times. You have the angels at His birth revealing the glory of heaven to mere shepherds. The heavens parted as the Holy Spirit came down upon the Lord when He was baptized by John, the Baptist. You have the incident on the Mount of Transfiguration, where the outer veil of Jesus' flesh parted for a short time to reveal His deity. Then there was the triumphal entry where Jesus was being recognized for who He was: King. Even though Jesus was led to the cross, heaven once again made an appearance in His resurrection, when He was raised in a new, glorified body. After resurrection, the heavens parted again to receive Him, but in the near future they will part once again when He comes back as the great Judge and Ruler of all.

The truth is people are always looking for a bit of heaven on earth, but it will elude them if the presence and glory of Christ is not present in their earthly tabernacles. As believers we are formed to reflect His glory, but if sin reigns in our lives we will reflect the brokenness of hopelessness, the darkness of delusion, and the destruction of the present age we live in.

The challenge of every Christian is to realize that each of us have been formed to bring a bit of heaven to earth by reflecting its glory. It is only as we reflect the heavenly that people will begin to consider the reality of their present situation. It is clear that the world is digressing down to complete ruin, and there is only one hope and way. Heaven has declared it, the heavens have parted to highlight it, and the thin veil of the flesh has given way to its very light and glory. The one hope and way is the Person of Jesus Christ.

But we all, with open face beholding as in a glass the glory of the Lord, are changed into the same image from glory to glory, even as by the Spirit of the Lord (2 Corinthians 3:18).

♦ Where God's glory rests we need not ask the way.

-Watchman Nee
(WN, Jan. 21)

♦ We can always be awed by the heights of the mountains, but in light of the heights of the glory of God, they are nothing more than His insignificant, little upward pointers and footstools.

-RJK

♦ Men are in one mind today, and another tomorrow; the winds are not more variable than the minds of men: but God is in one mind, the purposes of his heart never changes.

-John Flavel
(RR, pg. 134)

♦ If you look at the world, you'll be distressed. If you look within, you'll be depressed. If you look at God you'll be at rest.

-Corrie Ten Boom

♦ Believing God is glorious, waiting on the Lord is trying, relying on God is blissful, and knowing God is satisfying. Therefore, I choose to believe in God, knowing the end will be glorious. I surrender to waiting on God to know that He will be faithful in His dealings. I rely on God because He is the safest place. I pursue to know God because He is the present reality that makes my life a surprising gift.

-RJK

♦ God's work done in God's way will never lack God's supplies.

-J. Hudson Taylor

♦ It is possible to do work *for* God that may not be the work *of* God. Such work does not carry the promise of His power.

-William MacDonald
(ODT, Jan. 13)

******

The Maker of the universe
As Man, for man was made a curse.
The claims of Law which He had made,
Unto the uttermost He paid.

His holy fingers made the bough
Which grew the thorns that crowned His brow.
The nails that pierced His hands were mined
In secret places He designed.

He made the forest whence there sprung
The tree on which His body hung.
He died upon a cross of wood,
Yet made the hill on which it stood.

The sky that darkened o'er His head
By Him above the earth was spread.
The sun that hid from Him its face
By His decree was poised in space.

The spear which spilled His precious blood
Was tempered in the fires of God.
The grave in which His form was laid,
Was hewn in rocks His hands had made.

The throne on which He now appears
Was His from everlasting years,
But a new glory crowns His brow,
And every knee to Him shall bow.

-F. W. Pitt
(1797-1843)

He was in the world, and the world was made by him, and the world knew him not. He came unto his own, and his own received him not (John 1:10-11).

◆ You can study Nature in the minute, or you can study Nature in the vast, it makes no difference; everywhere you find the marks of intelligence and creative design.

-R. A. Torrey
(RA, pg. 6)

Prayer: Lord, Your creation reveals so much about You. Give me the eyesight to see You in it, the ears to hear it praise You, the smells that speak of Your heavenly fragrance, the touch to feel Your presence, and the means to taste Your goodness. Amen.

◆ All things are through Jesus – He is the **Creator.** All things are from Jesus – He is the **Sustainer.** All things are to Jesus – He is the **Consummator.** All things have their origin, movement, and completion in Him. He alone upholds all things by the word of His power.

-Marvin Rosenthal

******

Making God Small?

We often minimize the power of our eternal God. We allow that which exerts its power on us in this present age to affect our reality about Him. However, we are told that the Lord has spoken things into being, mainly creation. Can you begin to imagine the power that God possesses? To speak creation into being gives us a slight glimpse into His power.

As believers, we must remember that our Lord is the Almighty and that all things are under His control. He is the one who calls for the sun to rise in the east and to set in the west. He directs the stars in a symphony, as the moon highlights the artistry of His abilities to produce beauty even in the darkness.

This beauty may be hidden by darkness, but in time the dark curtain will be pulled back to reveal how that which proved priceless was first conceived and formed in darkness. This is also true for every Christian. Our life in Christ is conceived in darkness and formed in obscurity, but once the light is turned on the handiwork of it, God will be revealed.

And the light shineth in darkness; and the darkness comprehended it not (John 1:5).

♦ But go back as far as the human mind can think and we come right up against *God*. The universe is not the result of blind chance or of certain unexplained laws of nature. It is the product of a master mind. A personal God brought it into existence. "He spoke, and it was done; He commanded, and it stood fast."

-H. A. Ironside
(CBO, Jan. 1)

♦ We need a dead Saviour to meet the claims of a guilty past, and a living Lord to keep us saved. And we have both in Him who died and rose again.

-Herbert Lockyer
(MP, pg. 473)

♦ When you refuse to teach on the radical depravity of men, it is an impossibility that you bring glory to God, His Christ, and His cross, because the cross of Jesus Christ and the glory thereof is most magnified when it's placed in front of the backdrop of our depravity!

-Paul Washer

Prayer: Lord, we must love who You are, value what You have done, and seek what is real in light of eternity to possess You as our Truth. Amen.

♦ The God of the modern evangelical rarely astonishes anybody. He manages to stay pretty much within the constitution. Never breaks over our bylaws. He's a very well-behaved God and very denominational and very much one of us, and we ask Him to help us when we're in trouble and look to Him to watch over us when we're asleep. The God of the modern evangelical is a God you could have much respect for. But when the Holy Ghost shows us God as He is we admire Him to the point of wonder and delight.

-A. W. Tozer
(AG, Dec.11)

♦ Christ's highest glory is His Cross...One reason why we may find it so difficult to expect and enjoy His abiding presence is because we do not glory in the cross.

-Andrew Murray
(AP, Mar. 29)

♦ And now, why should it be thought a breach of charity to affirm that those who deny the divinity of Jesus Christ, in the strictest sense of the word, cannot be Christians? For they are greater infidels than the devils themselves, who confessed that they knew who he was, "even the holy one of God." they not only believe, but, which is more than the unbelievers of this generation do, they tremble.

-George Whitefield
(GW, pg. 86)

♦ It is one thing to read the Bible, choosing something that suits me (as is shamefully said), and another thing to search it that I may become acquainted with God in Christ. (If I do the former) I turn the Gospel of Christ into the law of Moses without knowing it, and instead of paths of pleasantness and peace, the Gospel of Christ becomes bands of iron.

-Robert Chapman
(RC, pg. 166)

♦ There are four symbols that point to Jesus' universal leadership: the lion, the man, the eagle, and the ox. As the lion, He rules in royalty. As man, He serves as the visible manifestation of God, and as the eagle He soars above the entanglements of this world to bring the reality of heaven down to man. As the ox, He offered up His life as the ultimate sacrifice.

-RJK

As for the likeness of their faces, they four had the face of a man, and the face of a lion, on the right side; and they four had the face of an ox on the left side; they four also had the face of an eagle (Ezekiel 1:10).

♦ The book of the Revelation is the unveiling of the *apokalupsis,* of Jesus Christ... John's remedy for our ills is not a matter of so many seals and trumpets and vials. It is not in fact designed to satisfy our intellectual curiosity at all, but to meet our spiritual need by revealing Christ Jesus himself in fullness, that we may know him. For Christ is the answer to all our questions. Get clear first about him, and we shall know all we need to know about "things to come."

-Watchman Nee
(WN, May 19)

♦ The word "holy" is more than an adjective saying that God is a holy God—it is an ecstatic ascription of glory to the Triune God.

-A. W. Tozer
(AG, May 6)

Prayer: Lord, I can see in my life with You, there will only be the light of great promise after the reality of great darkness has first taken hold of my soul. Lord, You will make a division between the light and darkness as you pass in-between the darkness and light to bring insight to your servants about the matters and promises of heaven which will reveal Your majesty and power to reign in the midst of both. Amen.

♦ To an unregenerate person temptation cannot cause pain of a heavenly or spiritual kind; to one born of God it does. The more like God His child is, the more keenly he feels temptation to sin.

-Robert Chapman
(RC, pg. 172)

♦ (Jesus) knew that the nation would reject Him as *prophet,* crucify Him as *King,* and that thereafter His perpetual ministry would be *priestly.*

-Hebert Lockyer
(MP, pg. 268)

For there is one God, and one mediator between God and men, the man Christ Jesus (1 Timothy 2:5).

******

The Historical Jesus

Jesus is a historical fact. The historian Josephus wrote about Him, along with other Roman historians such as Tacitus and Suetonius. Pliny the Younger, a distinguished philosopher wrote about Jesus in a letter to Emperor Trajan. Trajan reply to Pliny was that Christians should not be sought after for following another universal rule, but if they are apprehended, they need to be punished.

In spite of the historical records of Jesus' existence, many have tried to renounce it. There was the great German rationalist, David Strauss who put a great effort in abolishing the life of Jesus, but when his work was subjected to criticism, it went to pieces until there was nothing left.

Renan was another man who with rare subtlety and literary deftness took up the cause of Strauss, but in the end failed completely. The reason why is that no matter how one tries to wipe out the reality of God, it has been maintained by an unseen hand of such supernatural force that all such attempts end up laying in shambles.

However man in his foolishness refuses to concede that there is a God. He rages against the idea that this God is personal and that He stepped out of eternity, out of glory, into time and history. His entrance was noted and recorded because He turned the world upside down by turning it right side up with a message that since its conception many have carried and paid dearly for, even with their lives.

Today Jesus is dressed up with many titles. Each presentation demotes His character. The results are devastating. Underneath a veneer of so-called "faith" towards God what these individuals display is a deep abiding "unbelief" towards the truth of God. The god that has been erected in their minds is a god of their own liking and has no resemblance to the God of heaven.

The unbelief has created agnostics. As Kenneth Wuest stated, "Where knowledge enters agnosticism flees. Indeed, the very word "agnostic" is simple Greek for 'one who has no knowledge.'"

R. A. Torrey summarized the existence and reality of God in this way, "I have risked my life, reputation, work, everything upon the fact that the God of the Bible is. And friends, I risked and won. THERE is a GOD. Therefore the man who says that there is no God is a fool; for any man who denies a fact is a fool. He who denies the supreme face is a supreme fool. Not only is there a God; but He is the supreme face of nature, of history, of science, of philosophy, of personal life." (RA, pg. 11)

Torrey goes on to point out that God is in the beginning of all things that are true and lasting. Therefore, all truths concerning the matters of life and the working of the world around us will always bring us back to the beginning, back to God, and ultimately it will also end with Him.

Assemble yourselves and come; draw near together, ye that are escaped of the nations: they have no knowledge that set up the wood of their graven image, and pray unto a god that cannot save. Tell ye, and bring them near; yea, let them take counsel together: who hath declared this from ancient time? who hath told it from that time? have not I the LORD? And there is no God else beside me; a just God and a Saviour; there is none beside me (Isaiah 45:20-21).

♦ God shows His power through great miracles, but His faithfulness is revealed in Him taking care of the little personal details of our lives.

-RJK

♦ Every promise is built upon four pillars: God's justice and holiness, which will not suffer Him to deceive; His grace or goodness, which will not suffer Him to forget; His truth, which will not suffer Him to change, which makes Him able to accomplish.

-Unknown

♦ Saul, Hebrew of Hebrews and Pharisee of Pharisees, knew beyond peradventure of doubt, that all God's inspired revelations of Himself and His Glory to the children of men, are, and of necessity **must be**, centered and sublimated in the Person of His Son.

-F. Ellsworth Powell
(KG, pg. 122)

******

Ere God had built the mountains,
Or raised the fruitful hills;
Before He filled the fountains
That feed the running rills;
In Thee, from everlasting,
The wonderful I Am
Found pleasure never wasting,
And wisdom is Thy name.

And couldst Thou be delighted
With Creatures such as we,
Who, when we saw Thee, slighted
And nailed thee to a tree?
Unfathomable wonder!
And mystery divine!
The voice that speaks in thunder
Says, "Sinner, I am thine!"

-William Cowper
(1731-1800)

♦ Time is one of the main standards to measure value. The time we give is proof of the interest we feel. We need time with God—to know His presence and to wait for Him to make Himself known.

-Andrew Murray
(AP, Jun. 8)

Prayer: Lord, all that is associated with You is unseen and eternal. They are the treasures of heaven that not only add to our earthly life, but will follow us into the next life. Thank You for such treasures. Amen.

♦ So let men turn their telescopes on the heavens and their microscopes on the molecules. Let them probe and search and tabulate and name and find and discover. I can dare to say to them, "I know the One who made all this. I'm personally acquainted with the One who made it."

-A. W. Tozer
(AG, Feb. 22)

♦ If you want to follow Jesus because He'll fix your marriage, if you want to follow Jesus because He'll give you a better life, that's idolatry. Follow Christ for the sake of Christ; He is worthy!

-Paul Washer

♦ I simply want to say to you that the evidence for the resurrection of Jesus Christ is so overwhelming that it is impossible for any honest man to sit down and thoroughly sift the evidence, and come to any other conclusion than that Christ did rise from the dead.

-R. A. Torrey
(RA, pg. 51)

And if Christ be not risen, then is our preaching vain, and your faith is also vain (1 Corinthians 15:14).

♦ The Christ we manifest is too small because in ourselves we have grown too big. May God forgive us!

-Watchman Nee
(WN, May 22)

******

If asked what of Jesus I think,
Though still my best thoughts are but poor,
I say, He's my meat and my drink,
My life and my strength and my store;
My Shepherd, my trust and my friend,
My Saviour from sin and from thrall;
My Hope from beginning to end,
My Portion, my Lord and my All.

-J. Newton

♦ Man's extremity was God's opportunity.

-Hebert Lockyer
(MP, pg. 291)

♦ In Christ we have a love that can never be fathomed, a life that can never die, a peace that can never be understood, a rest that can never be disturbed, a joy that can never be diminished, a hope that can never be clouded, a light that can never be darkened, and a spiritual resource that can never be exhausted.

-Unknown

♦ Strength comes from believing God's words, while courage comes from trusting God's faithful character to bring forth a matter that He has clearly promised.

-RJK

But without faith it is impossible to please him: for he that cometh to God must believe that he is, and that he is a rewarder of them that diligently seek him (Hebrews 11:6).

♦ Heaven is the abode of Glories impossible for mortal man to describe, and of utterance that human lips cannot repeat.

-F. Ellsworth Powell
(KG, pg. 16)

♦ The soul feeds on Christ, not on teachings about Him.

-Richard Wurmbrand

♦ Our greatest danger comes from sin: guilt is a fountain of fears; a pardoned soul only can look other troubles in the face boldly: as guilt breeds fear so pardon breeds courage; and God's faithfulness in the covenant is as it were that pardon-office from whence we fetch our discharges and acquittances.

-John Flavel
(RR, pg. 113)

♦ The world may offer temporary beauty, but there is none as beautiful as Jesus. The world offers its own form of light and glitter, but Jesus is the true light that leads to God. The world offers worldly riches, but Jesus offers eternal riches. The world around us gives us occasional glimpses into the reality of heaven, but it proves to be fading at best or a counterfeit at worst. For me, I desire the reality of heaven (Jesus) over the false reality of the world (false promise, light, and happiness).

-RJK

******

Passing the Test

An ancient sage sent his son to a Bible teacher. When the boy returned, the father asked him, "What did you learn?' The son told him all the subject matter. "This is nothing," the father replied. "Go and learn more." The son returned one year later. This time he boasted of having learned other disciplines. The father sent him back a second time. When the son returned again, his face shone. The father embraced him. "You knew theology before. Now you know God."

Yea doubtless, and I count all things but loss for the excellency of the knowledge of Christ Jesus my Lord: for whom I have suffered the loss of all things, and do count them but dung, that I may win Christ (Philippians 3:8).

♦ In some mysterious way He (Jesus) combined both natures in His own when He took upon Himself the likeness of sinful flesh. And this blending of deity and humanity is seen in everything connected with the words and works of Him who was "the Word made flesh."

-Hebert Lockyer
(MP, pg. 371)

♦ Discovering the heavenly life (Jesus), points to possessing the quality of the eternal. Prepared and anointed, He would touch and forever change lives. In simplicity He would offer man a way out of his oppression. In compassion He would touch man with healing virtue. In sacrifice, He would redeem man from his terrible plight.

-RJK

******

The Dawning of the Light

We all start out unknowingly hiding from God because we are afraid to face the wretchedness of our own spiritual condition. In the darkness of deception we all think we are a certain way when in reality we have no idea as to the darkness that engulfs our souls and blinds us to our need to be saved. Granted, we may sense there is something terribly amiss in our lives, but in darkness we have a tendency to believe such a condition will eventually pass.

However, the darkness consuming our souls will not pass. It must be extinguished by the dawning of the bright and morning star of Jesus arising in our souls with the truth of His salvation, reconciliation, and restoration.

Has the light of heaven graced your dark soul with the hope of life?

Prayer: Lord, I spent many years hiding from You. To me it might have been a clever game, but it revealed how foolish I was in my delusion. Lord, You found me when I least expected it. I praise You for Your penetrating light that seeks and finds those who are lost and searching. Amen.

♦ "God is"—two short words. Tremendous significance! "God is" If that simple truth gets hold of your mind and heart it will move and *mould your entire life.

R. A. Torrey
(RA, pg. 5)

♦ We shall get nowhere with "God can" and "God will" if we stop short of "God is."

-Watchman Nee
(WN, Nov. 5)

♦ Noah's ark was not large enough to represent (Jesus') great heart of love. Jacob's ladder was not wide enough to reveal the breadth of His compassion. No paschal lamb was ever pure enough to portray His sinless nature; and, in like manner, no angels' food was sweet enough to express the perfect sweetness of the grace of Him who angels worship and obey.

-Herbert Lockyer adaptation of the lines of Issac Watts
(MP, pg. 305)

♦ God is the mountain out of which everything springs, and He is the foundation upon which everything rests. God is all in all.

-A. W. Tozer
(AG, Feb. 23)

♦ God's gifts put man's best dreams to shame.

-Elizabeth Barrett Browning

♦ To receive the gospel is to receive an entirely different view of reality where Christ is the epicenter of all things. ... He becomes the center of our universe, the source, the purpose, the goal, and the motivation of all that we are and do. When a man receives the gospel, his entire life begins to be lived out in a different context, and that context is Christ.

-Paul Washer

♦ I am persuaded that God's happiness is inseparably linked in with His holiness.

-Robert Murray McCheyne

Having therefore these promises, dearly beloved, let us cleanse ourselves from all filthiness of the flesh and spirit, perfecting holiness in the fear of God (2 Corinthians 7:1).

♦ Your attitude towards life is determined by your perception of God.

-RJK

♦ So God has, or will soon have, in glory, what He could never have had apart from Calvary, namely a vast multitude bearing the same likeness and image as His Son. God gains more by Redemption than He lost by the Fall. Through the cross He reaps a richer harvest.

Herbert Lockyer

Prayer: Lord, thank You for revealing Yourself in surprising ways. We can be blessed by Your promises, but we can only be changed by Your presence. Thank You for being the ladder that connects me to heaven and the cornerstone that lines me up to Your throne. May Your presence bring forth the anointing in my life as I sojourn towards my heavenly destination and home. Amen.

♦ You must first find your life in God before He can bring forth His life in you.

-RJK

♦ I don't think you will ever be strong until you know how utterly weak you are. And you will never know how utterly weak you are until you have stood in the presence of that great plenitude of strength, that great fullness of infinite power that we call God.

-A. W. Tozer
(AG, Mar. 29)

******

God is Missing?

There is a humorous story about two little boys, ages eight and ten. They were mischievous and always found themselves in trouble. In fact, their parents presumed that if there was trouble in town they would find their sons to be right in the middle of it.

In desperation the parents approached the clergyman in town who had a reputation of being successful in disciplining children of the past and requested that he speak to them. The clergyman agreed but asked to see them individually. The eight year old was the first to meet with him. The clergyman sat the boy down and asked him sternly, "Where is God?"

The boy made no response, so the man of the cloth repeated the question in an even sterner tone, "Where is God?" Again the boy made no response, so the clergyman raised his voice even more and shook his finger in the boy's face, "WHERE IS GOD?"

At that stern inquiry the boy bolted from the room and ran directly home, slamming himself in the closet. His older brother followed him into the closet and asked what happened. The younger brother replied, "We are in BIG trouble this time. God is missing and they think we did it."

Even though this story is humorous to consider, there is also another side of it that has a point. God is missing in many people's lives. He is in a sense lost to them and them to Him. It is not that He does not know where to find them; rather, He is separated from them because of sin.

God becoming lost to people has caused them to become blind; therefore, they cannot see to find Him. They do not have ears to hear; therefore, they cannot hear what the Spirit is saying. Since their light is darkness they are groping in the shadows of what they do understand. However, God and His truth remain missing.

And, whose fault is it that God is missing? It is the person's fault who refuses to come to terms with his or her spiritual plight. God has provided the means in which He can be found. He can be found in Christ, and those who seek Him with their whole heart will be given the sight to see Him.

God is holy. He must turn His face from sin to avoid judging it. He must hide Himself in a dark cloud so that His glory will not consume the unregenerate. But, ultimately, He resides in humble hearts so that He can be glorified.

Is God missing in your life? If so, you need to know that you are in BIG trouble. Today is the day of salvation. Receiving God's provision is the only way to avoid the wrath that abides on those who refuse His gift of eternal life.

(For he saith, I have heard thee in a time accepted, and in the day of salvation have I succoured thee; behold, now is the accepted time: behold, now is the day of salvation) (2 Corinthians 6:2).

♦ Deny your weakness, and you'll never realize God's strength in you.
-Joni Eareckson Tada

♦ The faithfulness of God is not necessarily proven in His ability to calm the storms of life, but in the fact that He will actually meet us where we are at in such contrary times of our lives.

-RJK

♦ In explaining how the sovereignty of God can bring such calmness to the believer, A. W. Tozer made this comparison, "The world has no such 'blissful center' upon which to rest and is therefore constantly shifting about, greatly elated today, terribly cast down tomorrow and wildly excited the next day." (AG, Jun. 12)

♦ "God's little while" often proves man's long while, and especially when events are seen in *perspective* as in prophetic vision. We must not stumble over the difficulty of delay. "Long" and "short" are relative terms: everything depends upon the scale.

-Dr. A. T. Pierson

♦ Religious people have a tendency to wrap faith up into a nice theological box to "understand it" rather than activate it by walking it out to discover what is living, unseen, and eternal.

-RJK

Now faith is the substance of things hoped for, the evidence of things not seen (Hebrews 11:1).

♦ True spiritual power does not reside in the ancient cross but in the victory of the mighty, resurrected Lord of Glory...Our power as Christians does not lie in the manger at Bethlehem or in the relics of Golgotha's cross. Our power lies in the Eternal Christ who triumphed over death.

-A. W. Tozer
(AG, Jul. 21)

♦ Since Jesus ascended from earth to His throne above well-nigh two millenniums ago, His dominion has not been recognized though "the mightiest of Empires have gone like visions in the night. We see on the shores of time the wrecks of the Caesars, the relics of the moguls, and the last remnants of the Ottomans. Charlemagne, Maximillian, Napoleon, and Hitler, how they flit like shadows before us! They were but are not; but Jesus forever is. Many rulers have their hour: but the Son of David has all hours and ages as his own."

-Herbert Lockyer
(DP, pg. 244)

♦ It is only upon experiencing the Lord in a personal way that hope is able to blossom into a beautiful bouquet of expectation that will emit the very fragrance of godly love from our innermost being.

-RJK

♦ It is not simply the heart; it is the whole man that makes the theologian.

-A. M. Fairbairn

♦ The Lord is our strong tree in the storms of life, our immovable Rock in the tremulous waves, and our wings of protection in the challenging winds. He is the only One who enables us to weather any element, for He alone serves as our place of refuge.

-RJK

♦ Read the man himself. Don't read *about* the man, or what some writer says about the man. Read the man himself.

-A. W. Tozer

♦ Jesus is the ladder that connects the work of heaven with the matters of earth.

-RJK

******

My Odyssey

As a believer, I have been aware that I am on a spiritual odyssey, a journey. However, I cannot take a journey unless I have a destination. I cannot venture through this world unless I have landmarks.

As a new Christian, my initial journey began with me heading towards the destination of heaven. However, through the years the different landmarks of experience and the guidelines of the Word of God changed my goal.

Do not get me wrong, heaven is still my destination, but my goal is to discover God, to seek Him in the midst of uncertainty, to find Him in darkness, to know Him in spite of the worldly terrain of deception and ignorance, to serve Him regardless of the lures of other masters, and to love Him in spite of the vanity that tugs at my heart to come aside and taste of its empty, deadly fruits.

I walk in confidence in light of this goal. In the end I know it will lead me into a relationship with God that will be marked by excellence and satisfaction. I will be able to come face to face with Him without fear: I will be able to meet Him as my friend.

Meanwhile I must wait for that wondrous time of complete deliverance when I will finally meet my Lord face to face. It does not matter how close the world's tidal wave of destruction is to me, I must wait for His instruction to properly walk through this age. It does not matter how much the water of anxiety is rising, I must wait. It does not matter how the current of urgency is prompting me to move, I must wait. God's timing is perfect. He knows how to deliver me in and through the storms of life.

While I wait, I must keep the goal that in whatever circumstance I am in this present age, I must discover God. There is so much to discover about God, but if I can indeed end up developing a sweet friendship with Him in my journey, I can be assured that there will be no discomfort in our meeting on the other side in glory.

Henceforth I call you not servants; for a servant knoweth not what his Lord doeth: but I have called you friends; for all things that I have heard of my Father I have made known unto you (John 15:15).

A Matter of Spirit And Truth

~

Discerning Error In Today's Wave of Delusion

Discerning error in the midst of great deception in this present day is the gravest of all challenges in Christendom. The greatest attack has always been directed at the truth and intent of the Word of God. There are three ways in which error can occur when it comes to the Word of God. People can err in how they handle it. This means they are handling the truth in unrighteousness according to some other unacceptable agenda. They can err in their interpretation of the Word. In essence, they can adjust it to their own view of a matter. Finally, they can err in their attitude towards it. This simply means they do not perceive it to be the final, infallible authority of God. They do not tremble before it nor do they see it as being absolute in what has been said and established as truth.

Prayer: Lord, have mercy on Your poor sheep. They desire what is pure but are plagued with hireling shepherds and wolves who do not care for their souls. Revive them with the pure water of Your Spirit and feed them with Your life-sustaining Word. Amen.

♦ There is a subtle deception that attending meetings, conferences, and seminars is doing the work of God. We listen to messages and talk about what we know we should be doing, and the delusion creeps over us that we are accomplishing His will. What we are actually doing is increasing our responsibility and deceiving ourselves. We deceive ourselves that we are spiritual when actually we might be quite carnal. We deceive ourselves that we are growing, when the truth is that we are stagnant. We deceive ourselves that we are wise when we are pathetically foolish.

-William MacDonald

♦ Falsehood of every kind is hateful to Him. There is nothing that so manifests the alienation of the natural man from God as his tendency to falsehood.

-H. A. Ironside

♦ How do we get nourishment from God's Word? We need to bite it—take a portion in. We need to chew it—think about what it means. We need to swallow it—make it part of our life. We need to digest it—choose to obey it. When we do, we are nourished spiritually and the end result is spiritual growth.

-Anna Alden-Tirrill
(SP, May 26)

♦ But perhaps you have no taste for this despised Book: perhaps plays, romances, and the books of polite entertainment suit your taste better; if this is your case, give me leave to tell you, your taste is *vitiated, and unless corrected by the Spirit and Word of God, you shall never enter into his heavenly kingdom: for unless you delight in God here, how will you be made meet to dwell with him hereafter?

-George Whitefield
(GW, pg. 204)

♦ Too much mental exercise makes the body weak, while bodily exercise revives the body, but not the spirit. There are different things needed to maintain the different aspects of your person. However, as believers we need spiritual food to feed the mind, godly discipline to keep the body in subjection to the ways of righteousness, and communion with God to revive the soul.

-RJK

For every one that useth milk is unskillful in the word of righteousness: for he is a babe. But strong meat belongeth to them that are of full age, even those who by reason of use have their senses exercised to discern both good and evil (Hebrews 5:13-14).

******

Ah, the Word of God,
  spiritual food to behold,
Presented on a tablecloth
  of grace so fine.
Served on the silver platter
  of redemption so great,
Ready to be imparted
  by the Spirit of the Living God.

There is the pure milk of doctrine
  So sweet to the taste,
The eternal bread in abundance,
  To freely partake,
Among the sweet dainties of truth,
  The meat rests in juices of righteousness,
Chew I must to receive its benefit,
  To know the will of God.

Tis I know, my thirst will
  be quenched,
At last my hunger
  satisfied,
At the heavenly banquet table,
  established on the promises of God.
E'er reminded that we surely,
  "Live by every word that flows from heaven's storehouse."

-RJK

♦ It's the blood that makes us safe; it's the Word that makes us sure.
-George Cutting

♦ You mark my words: Whenever a cult attacks Christianity, the first place they're going to go to is to attack the deity of our Lord and Savior Jesus Christ; is that not true?...Throughout 2000 years of Christian history, we have had to build walls to keep them out. We have had to fight, we have had to amass arms, we have had to do apologetics, we have had to do it all. It is our purpose and our responsibility to proclaim that Jesus Christ is God.
-Paul Washer

♦ More often than we probably realize, apostasy has its roots in moral failure.
-William MacDonald
(ODT, Feb. 19)

♦ In these days of compromise and apostasy, when it is so hard to distinguish many professing Christians from the ordinary men and women of the world, may the Lord make the Outer Court of our separation more distinct and apparent.
-Hebert Lockyer
(MP, pg. 360)

Prayer: Lord, You have given us the sword to use against the wolf, the rod to use against the hireling, and the Spirit to expose their wicked agendas. Help me to learn how to use Your arsenal in the fight against all that affronts Your truth. Amen.

♦ It is important to note that the sowing of doubt followed by the denial of the truth of God's Word has been the Adversary's tactic in his quest to destroy mankind ever since. His chief strategy is to undermine the Scriptures.
-T. A. McMahon

♦ The truth that's told with bad intent beats all the lies you can invent.

William Blake

******

Irony

If anyone knows how to turn something that was intended for evil to good, it is God. There is much irony that surrounds the work of God. It is not that He mocks man in his foolish attempts to undermine Him and destroy the authority and power of His Word; He simply uses such attempts to bring about a desired result that often causes a smile to come to His kingdom.

In the sixteenth century there was a great persecution directed at the group we now know as the Mennonites. At the time they were referred to as Anabaptist. One such martyrdom happened to a man by the name of Joriaen Simons. His crime besides being an Anabaptist was that his residence was a place that housed books written by famous Anabaptist leaders. He was taken to prison and sentenced to death along with another martyr of his faith. They were to be strangled and then burned on the stake.

After the atrocities had been committed against these two faithful individuals and the fires were dying down, the bailiff called for the attention of the people. He wanted to make a greater example by burning the books that they had confiscated at Simons' house.

The carts of boxes were brought forth as a public display. Box after box full of books were brought out from the city hall and discarded upon the ashes. The crowd had been silent during the martyrdom of the two men, but now the people began to become restless and cry out in anger as they watched the affront being made against the books. One courageous person actually slipped between the guards and began to madly toss the books in all directions into the crowd. Before the guards could remove the bold man, the crowd surged forward, and with a shout they pushed the guards almost into the fire. The officials began to scattered and run for shelter as the mob bore down upon them.

The people quickly snatched up the books from the flames and passed them around till almost everyone had a copy. Instead of silencing the truth, it was distributed in a way that would have surpassed even Joriaen Simons' attempts and expectations. One person who received one of those books was Simons' young son who not only held a prized letter his father had written to him from prison in one hand, but in the other hand held the book that contained the words of truth. As Ecclesiastes 11:1 states, *"Cast thy bread upon the waters: for thou shalt find it after many days."* (DW, pgs. 193-199)

In another such incident, there were books put out by the Communists to present their so-called "proof" on why the Bible was a fallacy. In order to prove their point, they used many Scriptures to supposedly show how ridiculous the written Scripture was. Keep in mind, it was illegal to own a Bible, but here were books full of Scriptures that were authorized by the Communist Government. They had printed million of these books.

The irony was that members of the underground church snatched up the copies of these books so that they could read and be edified by the Scriptures. Not only did the believers buy up all the books, but they sent thousands of letters to the publishers to ask for reprints of the books in order to distribute the priceless material to other underground members.

It was stated that in relationship to this event that, "Bible verses remain true, even if the devil quotes them." (ED, pg. 307)

But as for you, ye thought evil against me; but God meant it unto good, to bring to pass, as it is this day, to save much people alive (Genesis 50:20).

♦ The most dangerous thing any nation faces is a citizenry capable of trusting a liar to lead them.

-Andy Andrews

♦ Our Lord says to abstain from critical judgment of others. This sounds very strange, because one characteristic of the Holy Spirit in a believer is His way of revealing things that are wrong and sinful. But the discerning power of the Holy Spirit is not for purposes of criticism; it is for the purpose of conversion.

-Oswald Chambers
(DL, Dec. 10)

♦ The man to be trusted is the man who rules himself and holds all his appetites in subjection. In spiritual things the same rule applies. He who purposes in his heart that he will not "defile himself," but yields to the control of the Holy Spirit, is the one who will be most used of God on earth, and some day will stand before the King to be rewarded in the day of revelation.

-H. A. Ironside
(CBO, May 4)

I therefore so run, not as uncertainly; so fight I, not as one that beateth the air: But I keep under my body, and bring it into subjection: lest that by any means, when I have preached to others, I myself should be a castaway (1 Corinthians 9:26-27).

♦ Alas, many of us think it quite enough if we are orthodox in doctrine and give unqualified mental assent to the Word of Truth. But unless that truth is taking effect inwardly, there may really be no great difference between assent to it and dissent from it. The difference only comes when it begins to play a vital transforming part in life.

-Watchman Nee
(WN, Mar. 16)

♦ Our hearts were assured of the fullness of the Word of God...While colour can be found in it for well-nigh any false doctrine....no error can abide the test of the whole Scripture.

-Robert Chapman
(RC, pg. 165)

******

Tempting the Lord

God's Word possesses simple truths, as well as lasting life. We must live by it. After all, it is the light of His Word that will lead us out of darkness towards the light of the world, Jesus Christ.

The problem is we often tempt the Lord to speak to us other than through His Word, or prove that He means what He says according to our selfish whims. How often is it that we in our arrogance attempt to humble God by insisting He first bows before our insidious, selfish demands to prove something that in our fickle, unbelieving hearts, we have already decided not to believe is true, in spite of it being in His Word. At such a stage we are looking for entertainment, not truth. At such a level, we will never have the pure heart to truly see the Lord for Who He is, and with childlike faith believe His Word.

The Lord will never entertain us, but He will set us free with His unadulterated truth. I will and must choose the latter if I am to ensure that I never become barren in the knowledge of Him.

Jesus said unto him, It is written again, Thou shalt not tempt the Lord thy God (Matthew 4:7).

♦ When I think of the rivers of water in relationship to the kingdom of God, I know the water points to the unending flow of the Spirit from the throne of God. He is that presence within the believer that flows upward, opening each of us up to the endless treasures of heaven. He is the presence around us that enfolds us into the protection and ways of God as He guides us to the treasures of truth. He is the presence that flows down from the throne of God that connects with the water from within and emerges with the water around us, totally immersing us with and into a new, powerful, abundant, and fruitful life.

-RJK

♦ In our day, we must guard against dictating to the Holy Spirit what He can and cannot do. We know that He will never do anything that is sinful. But in other areas He can be counted on to do the extraordinary. He is not limited to a certain set of methods. He is not bound by our traditional ways of doing things. He has a way of protesting against formalism, ritualism, and deadness by raising up new movements with reviving power. We should therefore be open to this sovereign working of the Holy Spirit and not be found sitting on the sidelines, criticizing.

-William MacDonald

♦ The unpardonable sin involves even more than saying a final "No" to God. It is also making a final spiritual decision to attribute the entire testimony of God, by His Spirit through His Son, to be the work of Satan. It is labeling the ultimate good as evil. This is such a blasphemy that the Spirit of God no longer deals with such a person.

-Dr. Gary Cohen

♦ That is the way people become infidels, by resisting the Spirit of God. Show me a hundred infidels, and I will show you ninety-nine cases of men who were under conviction of sin at some time or other, but who have resisted the Spirit of God.

-R. A. Torrey
(RA, pg. 209)

******

A Cracked Vessel

One of the long-time friends of Robert Chapman was a man by the name of William Hake. They had a friendship much like King David and Jonathan had in the Bible. They both loved the Scriptures and were devoted to obeying them. As a result of their hearts towards God, they were knitted together in fellowship of the Spirit. In fact, Hake was an exceptional teacher of Scripture and had much influence on Robert Chapman's thinking.

Even though Hake and Chapman did not always agree on some of the non-essential doctrines, they always walked in agreement when it came to service because they agreed on what was important to the heart of God.

These two men were also much alike, including their sense of humor. Hake's mother-in-law remembered William's reply when she told him, after he had seceded from the Church of England, that he was cracked. His reply brings a whole new light to the idea of being a cracked or broken vessel before the Lord. Hake replied, "Yes, Mother; the crack lets in the light." (RC, pgs. 129-130)

But we have this treasure in earthen vessels, that the excellency of the power may be of God, and not of us (2 Corinthians 4:7).

♦ Henry Thorne best described the shadow (of Christ) that was cast by the Old Testament in this way, "There are clouds, but they are the dust of the Saviour's feet. No type of the Redeemer could be perfect that was destitute of the element of mystery. Think of the mystery of His Birth, of His Cross, of His vacated Tomb!"

♦ The Bible is a Book of preparation for the service of God. It is not a book simply for thrilling us with happy feelings and bringing us peace and joy...We were saved that we might serve. We were sprinkled with the precious blood of Christ, but we were first bought with it, and we are bond-salves of our Lord and Saviour Jesus Christ. The great motive of our Christian life should be, not that we may be happy, or peaceful, or joyful, or even saved; the compelling force of our religion should be full consecration to the Lord.

-Hebert Lockyer

Prayer: Lord, we look for the army, You send Your Word. We look for victory, You brought us to a large place of liberty. You never do it the way we think. Rather, You do it according to Your Word and Spirit. Amen.

♦ The Bible is Christ portrayed; Christ is the Bible fulfilled. One is the Picture, the other is the Person, but the features are the same and proclaim their identity.

-Dr. A. T. Pierson

♦ And so I say, read not only what the Bible records in black on white, but read its white spaces. Listen to its silences. They are eloquent.

-Richard Wurmbrand
(AWG, pg. 35)

♦ How tragic to have a vast knowledge of the Bible, yet little inward experience of its working.

-Watchman Nee
(WN, Mar. 16)

♦ The biggest battle over the Word of God is not what is in it, but whether one is going to believe it is true. People must choose to believe that the Bible indeed answers all of these important questions concerning God, life, and death.

-RJK

So then faith cometh by hearing, and hearing by the word of God (Romans 10:17).

♦ If you have made the good profession, if you claimed to have passed through the gate, if you have received baptism in a public declaration of your faith, and you begin to walk—it doesn't matter how long it appears you're walking in that path—if you step off that path and there's no discipline and you continue on that path, you can have no assurance whatsoever of your salvation. And it is not that you lost your salvation, it's that you're showing now that you never had it. If we would only preach these truths!

-Paul Washer

♦ We do much without the aid of God. We accomplish much with money, advertising, man power, programs, and entertainment. Often the crowds come to be entertained and to laugh at a funny story told by the pastor. This is where we miss the opportunity to have fruit that multiplies from God's perspective! We don't need the Holy Spirit in our churches today, because we are doing just fine without Him!

-E. A. Johnston
(NTB, pg. 12)

♦ Satan does not switch Christians onto a sidetrack that is wrong; he switches them onto a track that is one-railed. Numbers of people today are enamored with one special doctrine, such as healing or holiness or the Second Coming...These hobbled Christians distort God's truth so that His law is not distinctly understood. Our Lord insisted that the only thing that would draw all people to Him was the uplifting of Himself. This should be our supreme attraction.

-Oswald Chambers

And I, if I be lifted up from the earth, will draw all men unto me (John 12:32).

♦ If a believer is relying on a Sunday sermon and perhaps a mid-week Bible teaching of his intake of the Word of God, his spiritual health level is likely comparable to someone who only eats one or two meals a week. Satan and his minions, the cheerleaders of confusion, love to step into the ring with spiritually undernourished and anemic believers—they are easy prey.

-T. A. McMahon

******

Be Not Mistaken!

The problem that must be confronted today is the attitude people have towards the Word of God. They do not believe its authority; therefore, they do not tremble at its warnings and instructions. They do not believe it is applicable for today; therefore, they become flippant and mocking towards it.

Obviously, these individuals have fallen for the lie that was first proclaimed in the garden by the Father of Lies, Satan, "Has God said." If God said it He means what He says and will not move from what He has established as truth. Therefore, it is not up to us to mentally amend, adjust, ignore, or discredit His Word. It is up to us to approach it as truth and with the proper attitude believe, respect, and obey it. In fact, we need to tremble before its admonitions, cling to its promises, and obey its instructions. We need to have a right attitude towards it that will result in a right response.

A right response can be best summarized by a humorous story. There was an elderly woman who had just returned from being at a religious service. She was startled to realize there was an intruder in her home who was robbing her of her valuables. She yelled, "Stop—Acts 2:38!" (…turn from your sin…).

The burglar stopped dead in his tracks. The woman calmly called the police and explained what she had done. As the officer cuffed the man to take him in, he asked the robber, "Why did you just stand there? All she did was yell a scripture to you."

"Scripture?" replied the burglar, "She said she had an AXE and two 38's!"

Even though this robber misunderstood what was being said, we must not be mistaken. We must take heed, listen, and respond accordingly to God's Word. The Word is clear that it carries a big sword and hammer with it. In the end, it will not only judge those who have mishandled it in unrighteousness, but the fiery wrath of God presently abides on such people.

Is not my word like as a fire? saith the LORD; and like the hammer that breaketh the rock in pieces (Jeremiahs 23:29)?

♦ I know that the Bible is the recorded voice of God, His Spirit is His still small voice, His Son His living, visible voice, and creation His active voice. The truth of the matter is He is speaking all around us, but how many of us really hear Him? How much do we hear when He does speak through these avenues?

-RJK

♦ The Holy Spirit intercedes within that we might not sin. The Saviour intercedes, and pleads His blood above, if we do sin.

-Herbert Lockyer
(MP, pg. 458)

♦ We also quench the Spirit when we have services so over-organized that he is effectively in a straitjacket. If arrangements are made in prayerful dependence on the Holy Spirit, then no one can object. But arrangements that are made on the basis of human cleverness have the effect of leaving the Holy Spirit as a Spectator instead of as the Leader.

-William MacDonald
(ODT, Jul. 5)

******

Jesus instructs us to hear what the Spirit is saying. To hear the voice of the Spirit, you must:
1) Bring all thoughts into obedience of Christ.
2) Wait upon the Lord to gently intrude into your silence. However, waiting is hard.
3) Cause your heart to be still so that you can properly realign your affections. Affections must be heavenward in order to fine-tune your ears to hear. God must become your center focus.
4) Examine yourself. It is only when your heart is still that you can examine yourself to see if you will even be receptive to God's voice. So many times we want to hear God's voice, but we fail to because we want to hear matters according to our agendas and preferred ways.

Take heed therefore how ye hear: for whosoever hath, to him shall be given; and whosoever hath not, from him shall be taken even that which he seemeth to have (Luke 8:18).

♦ I stand as a small candle in this dark world. If my candle fails to cast the light, I must question where I am in my life before the Lord. Is my wick charred by indifference? Is the wax of my strength reduced to ashes by lifeless activities? Obviously, there are so many times my relationship with the world has caused my flame to lose its luster. I need to return and position myself as close to the fire of the Spirit and the igniting power of my Lord's life in order to become the candle that once again shines through the darkness of this present age.

-RJK

Prayer: Lord, You are my source of light, Your Spirit is my oil, and Your Word is my flint. Lord, I submit my life as Your wick. Set it ablaze with Your power and glory so others may see You. Amen.

♦ The book of God is a store of manna for God's pilgrim children.

-Robert Chapman
(RC, pg. 166)

♦ The Bible is simply God's love story, the story of the love of a holy God to a sinful world: That is the most amazing thing in the Bible.

-R. A. Torrey
(RA, pg. 18)

♦ The Bible that is falling apart usually belongs to someone who isn't!

-Church Newsletter

♦ There is one "holy anointing oil": The Spirit of God himself. And the flow of oil is down not up! In other words, his anointing is not directly on the members, but upon Christ the Head. The Spirit finds rest and satisfaction in Christ and nowhere else. Hold fast the Head, obey him in all things, and you will be found walking in step with all who do the same.

-Watchman Nee
(WN, Apr. 4)

Prayer: Lord, thank You for Your Spirit. I need His dew to fall upon the dry areas of my soul, the water to flow through the desert places of my spirit, and fresh wind to blow through the different chambers of my mind. Amen.

♦ So many times we try to fit God in a place, rather than allowing Him to be our place. When God is our place every aspect of His heart, ways, and purpose will impact, influence, and eventually consume our lives. Clearly, if God does not have a place in which He is properly honored, His Spirit will withdraw.

-RJK

♦ Pentecost added nothing to the doctrine taught by Jesus Christ or believed by the disciples. What did Pentecost do? Pentecost made the disciples what they preached.

-Oswald Chambers
(DL, Oct. 30)

♦ Who can measure the work of the Spirit of God upon a human soul? How wonderful, mysterious, unfathomable, and immeasurable are His ways! Why, they are past finding out. Yet some would seek to confine Him to creeds, dogmas and organization. But He is without measure. With our little tape measure of human wisdom we try to measure the ways of God and confine Him with certain prescribed bounds. What folly it is to limit the Holy One of Israel.

-Hebert Lockyer
(MP, pg. 389)

For my thoughts are not your thoughts, neither are your ways my ways, saith the LORD (Isaiah 55:8).

******

A Matter of Conviction

The strength of our conviction towards truth will be determined by whether we love the truth, mainly, the Person of Truth, the Lord Jesus Christ. I sometimes wonder how strong my convictions toward the Lord are. It is easy to talk with great conviction because we can back it up with sentimental passion at the right time, but can we live with great conviction, especially when tested. Will we be able to stand because of them?

There is a story about Bernhard de Palissy. His name may hold no real meaning to most, but he is the one who invented porcelain. He was a believer who had endeared himself to the French King, Henry III. The king was Catholic and one day he posed this threat to Palissy, "I will be compelled to give you up to your enemies unless you change your religion."

Palissy responded with great conviction and resolve, "I pity you for having given utterance to the words 'I will be compelled.' What unkingly words! No power in the world can compel me, a manufacturer of earthenware, to change my convictions because a mob wills it."

Those who are truly compelled by that which is true, honest, righteous, and eternal cannot be compelled by that which is inferior. The strength of all conviction rests on whether it becomes an all-consuming reality of what has ultimately been deemed the absolute truth to a matter. Palissy knew the truth about what he believed and nothing that was inferior to it could move him from what had clearly been established by heaven itself.

Whosoever therefore shall confess me before men, him will I confess also before my Father which is in heaven. But whosoever shall deny me before men, him will I also deny before my Father which is in heaven (Matthew 10:32-33).

♦ When stagnation occurs in the world of a believer, it often calls for inward transformation of the Spirit and not outward cosmetic surgery.

-RJK

♦ Baptism by water is an external sign of inner renewing and purifying through regeneration. The Spirit and the blood are spiritual expressions, working together in regeneration: the blood for the forgiveness of sins, the Spirit for the renewal of the whole nature.

-Andrew Murray
(AP, May 18)

******

On thee at the creation, The light first had its birth;
On thee, for our salvation, Christ rose from depths of earth;
On thee our Lord victorious, The Spirit sent from heaven,
And thus on thee most glorious, A triple light was given.

-C. Wordsworth

♦ We are in a life partnership, thou, Lord Jesus, and I, and the Father has promised us two things: glory for Thee, and the Spirit for me. Thou hast received the glory; it is unthinkable, therefore, that I have not receive the Spirit. Thank you, Lord, for this wonderful gift.

-Watchman Nee
(WN, May 6)

♦ In these days of so-called modern advance and enlightenment when music, art, literature, science are exerting their powerful influence upon religion, let us beware of a religion that is bloodless and Christless.

-Herbert Lockyer
(MP, pg. 494)

******

A Matter of Truth

When it comes to the truth of God, there are just a few things we must remember about it.

1) Truth is eternal. When all other beliefs, philosophies, and theologies lie in utter judgment and ruin, truth will remain standing. In fact, it will judge all other realities that prove to be contrary to it, as being fallacy.

2) Truth is trustworthy. Granted, it may be sharp for it is meant to circumcise the heart. It is blunt for it is meant to awaken our spirits, and it is like a hammer that will shatter what is faulty in order to nail down what is right.

3) The truth is also a fire that purges, cleanses, and liberates a person's soul from bondage. But, in the end it will prove to be the only trustworthy stake or standard that one can trust.

4) Finally, truth is simple. It is summarized in two words: Jesus Christ. Truth is not an intellectual notion, a religious stance, or a philosophy; rather, it is a person. Jesus is God in the flesh. As a result, nothing can silence or do away with the truth. All one can do is stand on it, stand for it, and withstand with it.

Buy the truth, and sell it not; also wisdom, and instruction, and understanding (Proverbs 23:23).

♦ Your children will go to public school ... and they will be trained for somewhere around 15,000 hours in ungodly secular thought. And then they'll go to Sunday school and they'll color a picture of Noah's ark. And you think that's going to stand against the lies that they are being told?

-Paul Washer

♦ A child of God who neglects the Scriptures cannot make it his business to please the Lord of Glory.

-Robert Chapman
(RC, pg. 166)

♦ I don't accept as my religion anything apart from union between the bride and bridegroom. All other religion is fornication, idolatry. I will soar where the Truth, which sages on earth call by different names, is One.

-Richard Wurmbrand
(AWG, pg. 48)

♦ Views from propagandist teaching are borrowed plumes. Teaching is meant to stir up thinking, not to store with goods from the outside.

-Oswald Chambers

♦ Truth never limps. If it needs a crutch, it's a lie. Our government and our mainstream media limp so badly they need more than a crutch, they need an ambulance.

-Marv Rosenthal

And for this cause God shall send them strong delusion, that they should believe a lie: That they all might be damned who believed not the truth, but had pleasure in unrighteousness (2 Thessalonians 2:11-12).

♦ Let me state in the briefest manner possible what I want to impress upon the mind of those who are contemplating Bible teaching, by declaring that the Bible never yields itself to indolence. Of all literature none demands more diligent application than that of the Divine Library.

-G. Campbell Morgan

♦ The Holy Spirit came to do a confirmatory work and he raised (Jesus) from the dead and since this mysterious witness is come, Jesus Christ is no longer on trial. It is no longer a question of "What, Jesus the Son of God?"

-A. W. Tozer
(AG, Jul. 5)

♦ When Christ died upon the cross He made our redemption *possible;* and now as the Holy Spirit works through the message of the Gospel, he makes that same redemption *actual* in our lives. On Calvary, we see the ashes; at Pentecost we see the running water, and both are gloriously combined for the cleansing of our sinful lives.

-Hebert Lockyer
(MP, pg. 381)

♦ Remission of sins is not based on my merit but on his Crucifixion, regeneration is not based on my merit but on his resurrection, and the endowment with the Holy Spirit is not based on my merit but on his exaltation.

-Watchman Nee
(WN, Aug. 12)

♦ As Christians, the flow of God's living water (His Spirit) has the capacity of causing newness or revival to our lives. In a way, the pulse and movement of the water from heaven will reinvent the person we are becoming. Therefore, let the storms come and the dams be opened to let the water from heaven have its way in my soul.

-RJK

♦ And the reason why we do not receive larger effusions of the blessed Spirit of God is not because of our all-powerful Redeemer's hand is shortened, but because we do not expect them, and confine them to the primitive times.

-George Whitefield
(GW, pg. 131)

♦ The relation of the Paraclete to the Pentecostal gifts is therefore the relation of quickening to the endowment; the one answers to the power of the resurrection; the other to the power of ascension. The one to victory; the other to sovereignty.

-Oswald Chambers
(DL, Nov. 16)

******

The Cost

It is hard to value something that does not personally cost you. That which is to be valued must first have a price put on it before there is the passion and endurance to possess it. This has been especially true where the Bible is concerned.

It was believed that common man could not understand God's Word, but there were those who did not agree with this perspective. Men such as Wycliffe and John Haus lost their lives because they dared to do what they could to make sure the common man had the opportunity to read God's Word.

In America, we have an array of Bible versions and do not know the bitterness of being deprived of our spiritual bread and meat. As a result, I fear many of us do not value the Word of God. We do not know how precious it has been deemed by those who have been denied it or who have been persecuted because of it.

There is another man who understood there was a cost to that which concerned the Word of God. His problem was not the absence of the Word; rather, it was the desire to develop a reference Bible where people could cross-reference Scriptures as well as provide other valuable insights.

This man was born in 1843. He abandoned his pursuit of a legal career and became a pastor of a new Congregational church in Dallas in 1882. He later became Moody's pastor. However, his desire to provide a reference Bible caused him to drop most of his ministry activities including any pastoral duties. This man endured many challenges before he would see his work completed. For instance, on several occasions he was too ill to work on it. On two occasions his work was almost destroyed. While shipping his work from Europe to America the boxes were lost. After much prayer they were located among the baggage of immigrants who had come on the same ship. In another situation the tent he was living in caught on fire. However, the wind shifted, taking the fire away from the shed that all the information was stored in.

It would have been so easy for this man to forget his dream. However, his dream was an overwhelming passion that would not let go of him. Today his name is attached to the Bible and well known. Perhaps you have heard of him and his work. His name is C. I. Scofield. (CPK, pg. 206)

For which of you, intending to build a tower, sitteth not down first, and counteth the cost, whether he have sufficient to finish it (Luke 14:28).

♦ All spiritual experience derives from the shedding of divine light upon eternal truth. Preached without light from God, truth remains but doctrine.

-Watchman Nee
(WN, Aug. 23)

♦ Those who would send out thousands of questionnaires asking the unconverted what they would desire most in a worship service should realize that ten thousand unanimous opinions of carnal men do not carry the authority of one jot or tittle of God's Word.

-Paul Washer

♦ Today there is a lot of talking going on in the world, but there is not much communication. We often speak to *propagate our personal reality, not to confront a matter to ensure truth and integrity. Therefore, there is much propaganda, but little truth being expounded.

-RJK

♦ Forcible revolution is not the Bible way to correct social evils. The cause of man's inhumanity lies in his own fallen nature. The gospel attacks the root cause, and offers a new creation in Christ Jesus.

-William MacDonald

♦ Christianity is not a philosophy. But Christianity has a philosophy—the best and the brightest of all philosophies.

-Alva Jay McClain

♦ Many can do the work of God, but no one can imitate the fruit of the Holy Spirit.

-Oswald Chambers

But the fruit of the Spirit is love, joy, peace, longsuffering, gentleness, goodness, faith, Meekness, temperance: against such there is no law (Galatians 5:22-23).

♦ If the Bible be used aright by anyone, it will be to him the most pleasant book in the world.

-Robert Chapman
(RC, pg. 166)

♦ Stand according to steadfast faith towards the Lord, withstand with the sharp sword of truth, and continue to stand according to the promises of God.

-RJK

♦ Get your texts from God—your thoughts, your words, from God. In great measure, according to the purity and perfections of the instrument, will be success. It is not great talents God blesses so much as great likeness to Jesus. A holy minister is a powerful weapon in the hands of God.

-Robert McCheyne

♦ In regard to the Word of God, Hebert Lockyer said this, "Like Joseph's sheaves of old, it lifts up its proud head and compels all other books to bow in obeisance before it. It is the anvil that has worn out many hammers! It is the impregnable rock that never moves! Like the three Hebrew youths, it had passed through not one but countless fiery furnaces, and it always emerges without even the smell of fire about it, for the simple reason that it comes from and presents to all the divine Person whose form "is like the Son of God." (MP, pg. 392)

Being born again, not of corruptible seed, but of incorruptible, by the word of God, which liveth and abideth for ever (1 Peter 1:23).

♦ The New Testament is enfolded in the Old Testament and the Old Testament is unfolded in the New.

-F. Ellsworth Powell
(KG, pg. 182)

♦ The Word of God tells us that God seeks those who are seeking Him with their whole heart. The reality is few of us seek for Him. Granted, we may seek knowledge about Him, we may seek some form of religion to connect with Him, and we may seek out those who are considered experts in their religious field to answer our questions about God, but few seek Him.

-RJK

♦ Phillips Brooks identified four different kinds of hearers: Pillars of the church, the skeptical, the habitual, and the sincere seeker after truth.

******

Peering Through the Lattice

In *Song of Solomon 2:9*, it talks about the shepherd coming to the girl, but he is behind her wall as she has to peer through the lattice at him. Due to various influences in our lives, most new believers begin to peer at Jesus through a lattice. This lattice represents their limited or unrealistic perception of Him. Although each of us may think that our understanding of Jesus is lovely, it is also boxed in by various influences such as family, religion, and culture. Our initial notions about Him can prove to be nothing more than sentimental hogwash.

Perception determines how we view all matters of life. It was said of Voltaire, the infidel, that when he read a book, he made it what he pleased, and then would write against what he had concluded (DP, pg. 48). Clearly, nothing was sacred to him because there was no standard of truth. Voltaire had his own lattice of perversion and insanity that would swing with whatever impressed him at the time.

It is for this reason that we, as believers, must beware of how we interpret and perceive the Word of God. Our whole goal must be to come to a place of purity in heart so that we can clearly see Jesus in His Word for who He is and for whom He must be to us. In order to come to such purity, the Lord must remove the lattice. It takes the powerful instruction of the Holy Spirit through the Word to dissipate this trellis.

Sometimes revelation will break down the lattice, while at other times the power of the Word will cleanse us of the perversion in which we consider a situation. Sometimes wishful thinking or exaggeration will add to the circumstance or try to adjust the reality of it; but, if by faith we allow God to providentially move through a matter, He does so in such a practical way that the impossible is finally realized with such sweet awe. The impossible turns out to be better than any exaggeration.

We need to let God's Word stand and always remember that we know in part. We must never try to fill in the blanks of what we think we understand. We must be patient, knowing that in the end, the truth will turn on the light, and what we need to understand will become clear in due time.

Admittedly, we do think we know about a matter, when in reality we do not. We complicate the obvious, while sometimes maintaining the ridiculous. In our spiritual immaturity and limitations, we can hold onto such notions because of what we don't know or what we presume to know.

There is a cute story that can somewhat illustrate this point. While working for an organization that delivered lunches to elderly shut-ins, a

71

woman used to take her 4-year-old daughter on her afternoon rounds. The curious four-year-old had much to be intrigued by as she observed the various appliances being used by the elderly, particularly the canes, walkers, and wheelchairs. One day the mother found the little girl staring at a pair of false teeth soaking in a glass. As the mother braced herself for the possible barrage of questions, the little girl simply turned and whispered, "The tooth fairy will never believe this!"

My beloved spake, and said unto me, Rise up, my love, my fair one, and come away (Song of Solomon 2:10).

♦   In quoting Francis Bacon's statement, "The pencil of the Holy Ghost hath laboured more in describing the afflictions of Job than the felicities of Solomon," author Hebert Lockyer pointed out, that if Solomon had more afflictions than felicities, his career would have ended in triumph, rather than tragedy. (MP, pg. 249)

♦   What was truth in the Gospel is light in the Epistles; what was grace in the Gospels is love in the Epistles. Why is this? Because light in God, when brought to men, becomes truth; love in God, when brought to men, becomes grace. Truth and grace are here, light and love back there in God. That is why it is always possible for grace to be misused, truth mishandled.

-Watchman Nee
(WN, Oct. 31)

♦   There is scarcely anything so dull and meaningless as Bible doctrine taught for its own sake. Truth divorced from life is not truth in its biblical sense, but something else and something less. Theology is a set of facts concerning God, man, and the world. These facts may be and often are set forth as values in themselves; and there lies the snare both for the teacher and for the hearer.

-A. W. Tozer
(AG, Sept. 6)

♦   Jesus has such a vision of the spiritual unity of the body of Christ through all its members that He felt himself actually dependent upon the prayer of the churches. It is only when this sense of unity binds minister and people—binds all believers together—that the full power of the Holy Spirit can be expected to work.

-Andrew Murray

Endeavoring to keep the unity of the Spirit in the bond of peace (Ephesians 4:3).

♦ Fellowship with known and vital error is participation in sin.
-Charles Spurgeon

♦ Truth is revolutionary. It even revolutionizes its own definition.
-Richard Wurmbrand
(AWG, pg. 22)

♦ God's people can do nothing without the prompting, leading, and preparation of the Spirit upon their hearts, minds, and lips.
-RJK

♦ But there would never have been a Pentecost had there not been a Calvary.
-Hebert Lockyer
(MP, pg. 311)

♦ By contrast, the sin of this age has peculiar and definite characteristics. It is true that we still have the sins of all the other ages. But the dominant characteristic of the sin of our age is imitating the Holy Spirit; first, by attempting to impose an organized interpretation upon the gospel; second, by insisting that each individual's responsibility is based upon that interpretation; and third, by boasting about the infallible certainty of having the mind of God.
-Oswald Chambers
(DL, Dec. 29)

♦ One never knows what is going to happen when he puts a truth to soak in the juices of the mind.
-Charles E. Jefferson

♦ Definition of a man of truth: A man into all whose life the truth has been pressed till he is full of it, till he has been given to it, and it has been given to him, he being always the complete being whose unity is in that total moral, intellectual and spiritual life which makes what we call character.
-Phillips Brooks

And with all deceivableness of unrighteousness in them that perish; because they received not the love of the truth, that they might be saved (2 Thessalonians 2:10).

♦ It is foolish to pray for the fullness of the Spirit if we have not first placed ourselves under the full power of the Cross! Christ gave Himself up entirely to the cross. The cross demands this also from us; it would have our entire life.

-Andrew Murray
(AP, Oct. 7)

♦ Since He is the foundation of all our religious beliefs, it follows that if we err in our ideas of God, we will go astray on everything else.

-A. W. Tozer
(AG, Oct. 26)

******

God Has Spoken

There will not be any excuse for why people operate in unbelief towards God, for He has clearly spoken, first through His prophets, than in the last days through His Son. What He has said through these vessels has been clearly recorded in the Word of God.

In his article in *Zion's magazine*, Marvin Rosenthal writes about the significance of God speaking. He penned these words:

❑ Only because God has spoken is there an answer to man's question.
❑ Only because God has spoken is there a solution to man's problem.
❑ Only because God has spoken is there hope for man's end.

Rosenthal goes on to say, "God has spoken by His Son. In so doing He has given to man a completed and perfected revelation. That revelation is the truth concerning Himself found in the New Testament."

To me Rosenthal summarized this matter in this sentence, "God has spoken by His Son, who sat down, that we might stand up and become forever the sons and daughters of God."

Today, man is falling into the abyss of unbelief. He is being swallowed by the foolishness of illogical reasoning, drowned in an ocean of deception and heresy, and hung out to dry by a demonic philosophy of death.

The main reason for unbelief is because people do not believe the Word of God is infallible. Since they do not believe it, they often show contempt towards it rather than regard it in a sober, respectable way.

God, who at sundry times and in divers manners spake in time past unto the fathers by the prophets, Hath in these last days spoken unto us by his Son, whom he hath appointed heir of all things, by whom also he made the worlds (Hebrews 1:1-2).

A Matter of the Heart

~

The Ultimate Desire of the Heart

Have you ever met a person whose main desire was to die for Christ? No doubt such people make up the great cloud of witnesses. These individuals see beyond the present world into the glory of the next. They march to a different drumbeat that this present world cannot begin to understand. Sometimes such people's names remain unknown, but they are known around the throne of God. Sometimes their stories have been preserved. Although occasionally buried by the sands of time, their stories are uncovered and resurrected. There is a record of such a martyr. Her name was Eulalia. She lived in the fourth century in Merida, Spain during the "Great Persecution." The "Great Persecution" started when those subject to the Roman Empire were commanded to sacrifice to the gods or face execution.

Eulalia saw this as an opportunity to stand up for her Lord and Savior, knowing full well that it would mean her death. Those of her family realized her fervor to give her very life for Jesus. They managed to send her away, but she escaped that very night and appeared before the tribunal the next morning. Her question to those of the tribunal was, "Are you not ashamed to cast your own souls and those of others at once into eternal perdition by denying the only true God, the Father of us all, and the Creator of all Christians, that you may put them to death. Behold, here am I, an adversary of your satanical sacrifices. I confess with heart and mouth God alone.

The enraged tribunal judge not only demanded that she be executed but that she also would be tortured. Before the executioner began his work, the judge offered Eulalia freedom from the punishment facing her if she would sacrifice to an idol. However, she would not bend or concede to such a repulsive notion. She was immediately stripped and tortured with hooks and torches.

As Eulalia counted the gashes in her body, she exclaimed with great peace and happiness, "Behold, Lord Jesus Christ! Thy name is being written on my body; what great delight it affords me to reach these letters, because they are signs of thy victory! Behold, my purple blood confesses thy holy name." In her ecstasy, she did not seem to feel the pain as the blood flowed from her body.

After repeatedly piercing her body with hooks, the executioners applied burning lamps and torches to Eulalia's wounds in her sides and abdomen.

Their last phase of cruelty was to ignite her hair, and it was then that she finally succumbed to blessed death due to suffocation.

We have many stories of such martyrs that have become part of the cloud of witness in the journal of heaven, but what makes Eulalia unique is that she was only 13 years old.

-The Voice of the Martyrs Magazine

Keep thy heart with all diligence; for out of it are the issues of life (Proverbs 4:23).

♦ There are times when God allows us to face great difficulties and challenges, not to hurt us or make us feel hopeless, but to teach us to turn our heart to Him and cry out for His help.

-Anna Alden-Tirrill
(SP, Feb 9)

♦ The secret of Christian holiness is heart-occupation with Christ Himself. . .We do not become holy by looking into our own hearts. There we only find corruption. Instead we must look away from ourselves and "unto Jesus" contemplating His holiness, purity, love, compassion, and devotion to the Father's will.

-H. A. Ironside
(CBO, Oct. 6)

♦ I recently meditated on the empty pages of people's lives. There are many things we can fill our lives with, but how many activities have the power to write upon our hearts concerning the things of eternity that truly possess lasting substance and hope?

-RJK

♦ There is nothing that reveals what is in the human heart so clearly as what a man does with Christ.

-R. A. Torrey
(RA, pg. 59)

♦ Repentance, my brethren, in the first place, as to its nature, is the carnal and corrupt disposition of men being changed into a renewed and sanctified disposition. A man that has truly repented is truly regenerated: it is a different word for one and the same thing; the motley mixture of the beast and devil is gone; there is, as it were, a new creation worked in your hearts.

-George Whitefield
(GW, pg. 149)

♦ It is only the fully surrendered heart that can fully trust God for all he has promised.

-Andrew Murray
(AP, Dec. 9)

♦ Formalism in religion apart from true heart-exercise is an abomination in the sight of God.

-H. A. Ironside
(CBO, Jul 15)

He that descendeth is the same also that ascended up far above all heavens, that he might fill all things (Ephesians 4:10).

♦ If we are to be of use to God in his great purposes it is essential that we respond not merely with our head but with our heart when his Word comes to us in a present, personal way.

-Watchman Nee
(WN, Feb. 13)

♦ A half-hearted servant is neither hot nor cold—he is in-between. On the outside he or she looks like a vibrant, active Christian, but on the inside is a spiritual wreck.

-E. A. Johnston
(NTB, pg. 58)

♦ When we sanctify the Lord God in our hearts and give Him the place of supreme authority, all controversy is at an end, and the life is entirely under His control. This is the path of victory and blessing. No one can be successful in his Christian life who is endeavoring to have God and the world share his heart.

-H. A. Ironside

♦ Those whose hearts have not been circumcised by the sharpness of God's Word, purified and prepared by the fiery ovens of faith, and molded by obedience will fail to experience all of God's promises.

-RJK

Prayer: Oh God, under whom all hearts be open, and unto whom all will speaketh, and unto whom no privy thing is hid, I beseech Thee, so for to cleanse the intent of my heart with the unspeakable gift of Thy grace, that I may perfectly love Thee and worthily praise thee.

-Unknown

♦ What is the desire of your heart? God put those in you not to tease or frustrate you—He created them in you to give you direction! To put you on the right path—He bridles your passion! So stop and think about what you love to do, then look for signposts along the way that confirm you're on the right path to doing that—doors opening, people with your best interests at heart supporting what you're doing.

-Sarah Palin
Former Alaska Governor

♦ We cannot always withdraw to quiet hillsides to pray, but Christ will meet with us in the quiet places of our hearts.

-Sheila Walsh

♦ Men of the breaking hearts had a quality about them not known to nor understood by common men. They habitually spoke with spiritual authority. They had been in the presence of God and they reported what they saw there. They were prophets, not scribes, for the scribe tells us what he has read, and the prophet tells what he has seen. We are overrun today with orthodox scribes, but the prophets, where are they?

-A.W. Tozer
(AG, Jan. 31)

♦ Give me a hundred men who love God with all their hearts, and fear nothing but sin, and I will move the world.

John Wesley

My heart is fixed, O God, my heart is fixed; I will sing and give praise (Psalm 57:7).

******

♦ Bar the door of your heart against carnal policies and sinful shifts, which war against your own faith, and God's faithfulness, as much as any other enemy whatsoever.

-John Flavel
(RR, pg. 127)

♦ People who are half-hearted towards their spiritual inheritance are in danger of losing all of their future blessings and promises.

-RJK

Prayer: Lord, my heart is a dangerous place unless You have given me a new heart. However, with a new heart I need to make sure it remains cleansed from hypocrisy, purged of wrong influences, and separated from wrong thinking. Turn the searchlight on it, and keep it on because I can be easily deceived by the wishful thinking that comes from high opinions of myself. Amen.

♦ The great cause of neglecting the Scriptures is not want of time, but want of heart, some idol taking the place of Christ.

-Robert Chapman
(RC, pg. 166)

♦ Forms and ceremonies, no matter how impressive; doctrines and traditions, no matter how venerable, are all to be refused if contrary to the mind of the Lord as set forth in the Bible. The supreme test is "What says the Scripture?" Where the Word speaks, it should be ours to obey. Where Scripture is silent, we may well be silent too. But a merely mental acceptance of Bible doctrines will not do for God. There must be heart subjection to His truth.

-H. A. Ironside
(CBO, Nov. 19)

♦ Prayer in secret will be followed by the secret working of God in my heart.

-Andrew Murray
(AP Jan. 50

♦ Tribulation is God's plow to keep the ground of the heart broken up and ready for His truth.

-Oswald Chambers
(DL, Aug. 17)

For thus saith the LORD to the men of Judah and Jerusalem, Break up your fallow ground, and sow not among thorns. Circumcise yourselves to the LORD, and take away the foreskins of your heart, ye men of Judah and inhabitants of Jerusalem: lest my fury come forth like fire, and burn that none can quench it, because of the evil of your doings (Jeremiah 4:3-4).

♦ In solitude you learn to nourish in your heart the lively longing for God.

-Unknown

♦ Gratitude is the memory of the heart.

-French Proverb

♦ Praise is the spontaneous outcome of a grateful heart that has experienced the saving grace of God and recognizes His providential dealings and Fatherly care day by day.

-H. A. Ironside
(CBO, Apr. 4)

♦ Silence of the heart can prove to be a time of rest, silence of the soul a time of peace, and silence in our activities a test. If silence is not properly appropriated, it will cause one's heart to become anxious, the soul to become irritable, and the mind to faint.

-RJK

And Jesus answered and said unto her, Martha, Martha, thou art careful and troubled about many things: But one thing is needful: and Mary hath chosen that good part, which shall not be taken away from her (Luke 10:41-42).

♦ ...the natural heart is always a false heart; it is only regeneration that gives the heart a right temper and frame; all the duties and labours in the world can never keep that heart right in its course, which is not first set right for God by a principle of renovation.

-John Flavel
(RR, pg. 222)

♦ Our careless, thoughtless, unstudied words reveal what we are at heart. Our studied speeches do not reveal what we are, but what we would like to be; but our idle words, that we drop accidentally, they are the best revelation of what there is in our hearts.

-R. A. Torrey
(RA, pg. 57)

******

Tender Heart

One of my concerns as a Christian is that I become unresponsive towards the things of God. I always want my heart to remain tender before Him. I want to have the assurance that when the Holy Spirit's presence comes into my midst, that my heart is very tender and can be easily melted by His gentleness as I consider the salvation and promises of God and what it cost Him to secure both for me.

The truth is I never want to become so familiar with the Lord that I fail to realize how great His character and salvation is. I want to always be brought to a point of awe so that I can be raised up in an attitude of thankfulness as I begin to soar in the sweetness of praise and worship.

There are times when I have felt the sweet presence of the Lord and I have been so overwhelmed by the sense of His love, power, and holiness that I felt the wells of my heart begin to swell to overflowing as tears began to ever so-slightly emerge from the corners of my eyes. No matter what I tried I could not stop the tears or the brokenness in my voice. It is not a matter of sentiment, but one of an overwhelming sense of something that reaches beyond words. However, in each matter I had no intention of letting such a time pass. Its tenderness made my heart feel as if a faucet of warm water was bathing my soul with cleansing and renewing.

Prayer: Lord, deliver me from the curse of a dry-eyed Christianity!

-William MacDonald
(ODT, Aug. 6)

♦ Blessed are the single-hearted, for they shall enjoy much peace. If you refuse to be hurried and pressed, if you stay your soul on God, nothing can keep you from that clearness of spirit which is life and peace. In that stillness you will know what His will is.

-Amy Carmichael

♦ Jesus has succeeded in making every human soul an appendage of His own.

-Napoleon

♦ Do not lose yourself in your activities. Lose yourself in God. Let your innermost heart be centered on Him. Live in His presence and abide in Him. Then your work will follow you into eternity, and you will reap a rich harvest.

-Basilea Schlink

♦ Due to sin and death, everyone begins as a barren wasteland. However, God knows how to bring forth the deep fountains and cultivate the ground of man's heart to once again make his life productive and beautiful.

-RJK

A new heart also will I give you, and a new spirit will I put within you: and I will take away the stony heart out of your flesh, and I will give you an heart of flesh (Ezekiel 36:26).

♦ To be a half-hearted Christian can only insure a miserable existence. To be out and out for Him is the surest way of enjoying His best.

-William MacDonald
(TD, pg. 95)

♦ Genuine praise is a matter of humility and sincere devotion to the Lord from within. It originates from a surrendered heart.

-Anna Alden-Tirrill
(SP, Feb. 26)

♦ Suffering according to the will of God is Christ-like. To "be in the will of God" is a state of heart, not an intellectual discernment.

-Oswald Chambers
(DL, Mar. 24)

♦ Life on this earth has many hassles. God reminded me that He will give us lands and homes, but they are temporary. To keep us sojourners in heart, the hassles of life must be present. And, our desire for perfection in our worlds will always elude us, always pointing us to our real ultimate hope, Jesus Christ.

-RJK

To whom God would make known what is the riches of the glory of this mystery among the Gentiles; which is Christ in you, the hope of glory (Colossians 1:27).

♦ An Israelite, pointing to the tabernacle could say, God is there. A Christian with his hand on his heart, can say, God is in here!

-Hebert Lockyer
(MP, pg. 353)

♦ The love that keeps His commandments is the only way to remain in His love. In our whole relationship to Christ, love is everything. Christ's love to us and our love to Him is proved in our love to each other.

-Andrew Murray
(AP, Sept. 6)

♦ In order to walk with God it is not necessary to flee from the world to some monastic cell or to a convent's gloomy shelter. Whatever we may be called to do, however heavy the burden that may rest upon our shoulder, it is possible to walk with God and to enjoy His blessed companionship. All that is needed is a yielded will, and subjection of heart to Him who has saved us by His grace.

-H. A. Ironside
(CBO, Jan. 3)

Prayer: Lord Jesus, I take hands off as far as my life is concerned, I put Thee on the throne of my heart.

-Borden of Yale

♦ The gods of Greece and Rome may be worshipped well enough with classical music, but Jehovah can only be adored with the heart, and that music is the best for His service which gives the heart most play.

-Herbert Lockyer Sr.
(DP, pg. 269)

♦ It does not matter what kind of mosaic or patchwork humanity presents, for if the ground of men's hearts has not been plowed up by truth, their souls have not been cultivated by the seeds of the Gospel, and their lives producing eternal fruits, they will prove to be useless fields in light of the great judgment that is coming.

-RJK

I will praise the name of God with a song, and will magnify him with thanksgiving. This also shall please the LORD better than an ox or bullock that hath horns and hoofs. The humble shall see this, and be glad: and your heart shall live that seek God (Psalm 69:30-32).

******

Examining the Pose of
My Heart

I constantly struggle with the demands of my flesh and the emotional fickleness of my heart. All too often in my struggles I come face to face with my inability to keep my flesh on the cross and my heart steadfast towards the Lord. It is at such times that I realize how weak the flesh is and how unpredictable the heart can become when it is being overwhelmed by the depth of fleshly emotions.

Clearly, the heart can be quite deceptive. The attitude of the heart determines the flexibility of my "neck muscles" when it comes to the matters of God. In considering my personal take on matters, I realize that the truth is I cannot be sure of what is going on in my world until I take the time to honestly exercise my "neck muscles" in regard to the matters of God. I must also use every point of reflection to make sure I am correctly seeing those obscure areas to discern the attitude of my heart.

So many times my neck is stiff towards maintaining my particular take on reality that I often miss that which has the potential of destroying me. It is for this reason that the Lord condemns those who prove to be stiff-necked. Such individuals are unreceptive towards His instructions and warnings.

To be able to exercise my "neck muscles" correctly, I must get rid of the obstinate arrogance of demanding my own way by ignoring unpleasant reality. This is the only way I can avoid being slammed by the waves of destruction and judgment that can quickly come upon me. It is only by being shut in the Ark of God's truth, Jesus Christ, that I can be ready to face the tidal waves that are rushing toward the shores of my life.

Prayer: Lord, my neck will either be broken by judgment or bowed in an attitude of worship towards You. I choose to bow my neck under the circumcision of Your Spirit and Word. Make my heart tender before You so that my neck will naturally bow in awe and worship of You. Amen.

A Matter of Prayer and Worship

~

A Spiritual Mystery

Andrew Murray wrote about how prayer is a deep spiritual mystery. The fact that God, in His holiness and sovereignty, hears our prayers is indeed a mystery. He does not have to hear our prayers or respond to them. However, it is His heart to hear them and meet with us in sweet fellowship.

The question is what assures that He hears us? There are criteria that ensure a right environment of prayer. The first reason God will choose to hear our prayers is when we back them up with authority and power. This requires us to pray in light of the authority of His Son as we allow His Spirit to pray through us with power and proper intent. Clearly, the Godhead must be present to ensure the integrity of our prayers. It will remind us that all answered prayers are a matter of the grace and workings of God on our behalf.

Another criterion is that in prayer our goal should be to seek His will. If we do not pray in line with the character of His Son, while being inspired by the Spirit for the sole purpose of realizing His will in a situation, He will have no reason to hear us. So many times our prayers are powerless because we are praying amiss. They are based on selfishness instead of seeking out the will of God.

Another important criterion that is missing is silence. We are busy telling God what we perceive we have need of, but we fail to take the time to listen to Him. Prayer is to be a two-way conversation. However, most people do not expect to hear the Lord answer their prayers.

This brings us to a very important principle: that of expectation. Prayer stands on hope but it can only rise to the throne of God on the wings of expectation. Many people stand on wishful thinking because real hope eludes them since there is no real expectation. These people lack the assurance that God will answer. They may put out their wings but it is in a half-hearted attempt. They may stand at the abyss of fickleness, while they somehow pray that hope will swoop them up in spite of their unbelief.

When you study those who sought God out to realize His will, they approach to believe Him. They were not simply wishful in their attitude because they knew God was true to His Word. As long as they were in line with the purpose and reality of the Godhead, they could be assured that He would answer them.

It is true unbelief can often undergird us, but such skepticism exists because we know that we do not deserve God's consideration. We want to be able to control how He answers our prayers, but if we had such a formula, the mystery of the *why* and *what for* in our prayer life would cease. We would not have to approach a matter to believe and we would not have to be concern about the rock that we stand on, nor would we have to put our wings out, while trusting Him to work out the details. In essence, we would not have to humble ourselves and seek Him out.

Prayer is a privilege, as well as an opportunity to get a hold of God.

And this is the confidence that we have in him, that, if we ask any thing according to his will, he heareth us (1 John 5:14).

♦ Forsaking all for Christ saves us from hypocrisy in prayer.
-William MacDonald

♦ Do believers know what it means to have a costly answer to prayer? If we want God to answer our prayers, we must be willing to receive His answers under any circumstances. A costly answer to prayer is one that involves us in the process.
-Extreme Devotion
(ED, pg. 37)

♦ God wants worshipers before workers; indeed the only acceptable workers are those who have learned the lost art of worship...Gifts and power for service the spirit surely desires to impart; but holiness and spiritual worship come first.
-A. W. Tozer
(AG, Aug. 4)

♦ Worship is lowered as we become occupied with the externals even of Christianity. It reaches its highest point as our spirits are absorbed in contemplation of the matchless perfections of the eternal God, in the light of the cross and the empty tomb.
-H. A. Ironside
(CBO, Aug. 6)

♦ As God's own, we are called to praise Him in calamities and sufferings as well as in prosperity and happenings. For many of us, it is easy to praise Him from the heights of His love, but it is not so easy, but just as important, to worship Him from the depths of His love—both on the exhilarating mountaintops and in the excruciating valleys below.

-Anna Alden-Tirrill
(SP, Jul. 5)

Prayer: Lord, I have travailed in prayer, rejoiced in it, soared because of it, and used it as a torch of hope to help me through the dark times of the soul. In it all I knew that You were the platform that held me up, the wind that caused me to rise up, and the light that guided my steps. Thank You for being the One who hears and catches my prayers. Amen.

♦ Those who persevered before God are those who have had the greatest power in prayer.

-Andrew Murray
(AP, Jan. 18)

******

He (Jesus) prayed alone, for all of His own,
In the shadow of Calvary:
When Jesus went out to the mountaintop,
And prayed, alone, for **me.**

-F. Ellsworth Powell
(KG, pg. 34)

♦ Prayer that remains steadfast in uncertain times reveals that our faith is still present and active regardless of the darkness of the circumstances.

-RJK

♦ In relationship to us being clay vessels, Anna Alden-Tirrill made this statement, "Surrender daily. Keep your clay moist through prayer in accordance with His will." (SP, Mar. 9)

♦ The children of God today are taken up with far too many small things whereas their prayer is intended for the release of heaven's mighty acts.

-Watchman Nee
(WN, Feb. 13)

******

Speak, Lord, in the stillness
While I wait on Thee,
Hushed my heart
To listen in expectancy.
Speak, Thy servant heareth!
Be not silent, Lord,

Waits my soul upon Thee
For the quickening word!

-Unknown

♦ When considering your faults and inclined to dejection concerning them, don't talk with yourself—don't keep company. Talk with the Lord.

-William Hake
(RC, pg. 130)

♦ Prayer is not any particular action confined to times, or words, or places. It is the work of the whole being which continually stands in fullness of faith, in purity of love, in absolute willingness to do and be what pleases God. This is the spirit of prayer and is the highest union with God in this life.

-Andrew Murray

♦ None of God's children, as one observes, comes into the world stillborn; prayer is the very breath of the new creature: and therefore, if we are prayerless, we are Christless; if we never had the spirit of supplication, it is a sad sight that we never had the spirit of grace in our souls; and you may be assured you never did pray, unless you have felt yourselves sinners and seen the want of Jesus to be your Savior.

-George Whitefield
(GW, pg. 211)

Praying always with all prayer and supplication in the Spirit, and watching thereunto with all perseverance and supplication for all saints (Ephesians 6:18).

♦ We don't pray to be better Christians, but that we may be the only kind of Christians God means us to be; Christlike Christians, that is, Christians who will bear willingly the cross for God's glory.

-Underground Church in Romania
(ED, pg. 98)

♦ The truth is I cannot freely enter into a place of prayer and communion with the Lord unless I am being constantly converted to the ways of His righteousness. I cannot enter the place of fellowship with God if my conscience is disturbed by my attitude towards Him and my actions towards others. I must come to the Lord clean in conscience, pure in heart, and with clean hands.

-RJK

♦ The proud and lofty man or woman cannot worship God any more acceptably than can the proud devil himself. There must be humility in the heart of the person who would worship God in spirit and in truth.

-A. W. Tozer
(AG, Dec. 4)

♦ An unthankful child of God is a strange anomaly. . .We would worry less if we praised more. Thanksgiving is the enemy of discontent and dissatisfaction.

-H. A. Ironside
(CBO, Oct. 24)

******

The Wings of Revival

Have you ever heard the name of Marianne Adlard? Most likely you have not, but God was very aware of her. She was part of the harvesting of four hundred souls who professed faith during one of Moody's meetings held in London. What was her part in the successful harvesting? She prayed daily that Moody would come to her church and preach while in London. Marianne was bedridden but was aware of the power of prayer. It was during that time of harvesting Moody caught a new vision of what God could do through him in Great Britain. (PCK, pg. 189)

And he spake a parable unto them to this end, that men ought always to pray, and not to faint (Luke 18:1).

******

♦ We must partake of God's goodness, experience His abiding faithfulness, know His honorable intentions, and walk in His ways to develop a desire for more of Him. Once we begin to taste His goodness, witness His glory, and experience His grace, we will not settle for trickles from heaven, rather, we will beseech the throne of heaven to reveal more of our Lord to us. Each revelation will cause the Lord to become more precious to us, while His life in us makes us more precious to His kingdom.

-RJK

♦ You know the value of prayer; it is precious beyond all prices. Never, never neglect it.

-Sir Thomas Buxton

♦ When we worship the holiness of our own convictions instead of our holy Lord, there is an element in human nature that makes us all possible popes and intolerant upholders of our personal views.

-Oswald Chambers
(DL, Feb. 9)

♦ Worship God in His holiness until every thought of God in His glory and grace is connected with the deep conviction that the blessed God wills my holiness.

-Andrew Murray
(AP, Sept 25)

♦ The best prayer comes from a strong inward necessity...Someone has said that "the arrow that is to enter heaven must be launched from a bow fully bent." A sense of urgency, of helplessness, of conscious need is the womb from which the best prayers are born.

-William MacDonald
(TD, pg. 53)

♦ The mighty prayers of both Elijah and Emmanuel teach us that more things are wrought by prayer than this world dreams of.

-Hebert Lockyer

Elias was a man subject to like passions as we are, and he prayed earnestly that it might not rain: and it rained not on the earth by the space of three years and six months. And he prayed again, and the heaven gave rain, and the earth brought forth her fruit (James 5:17-18).

♦ If your day is hemmed with prayer, it is less likely to become unraveled.

-Unknown

******

A Silver Lining After All

We never know how God is going to answer our prayers. In the past I have often speculated about how He was going to meet me in my need. I learned early that all the speculation would prove to be just that. God often works in practical ways that will sometimes surprise us. He seems to not only find a silver lining of opportunity to prove Himself in a matter, but sometimes it might even prove to be a bit humorous. I can think of such times.

This is best illustrated by an amusing story. There was a little old lady who expressed her confidence in the Lord by stepping out on her porch every day. She would then raise her arms to the sky and yell, "Praise the Lord."

However, she met with a bit of opposition when an atheist moved next door. When she went out to acknowledge the Lord in her usual way, he would yell back, "There is no Lord."

In spite of the atheist's opposition, she would continue to honor the Lord in her zealous fashion. One cold, wintry day her zeal was put to the test. She could not get to the store. However, she still went out on her porch and raised her hands up to the sky and said, "Help me Lord, I have no more money, it's cold and I have no more food."

The next morning she was greeted by bags of food on her porch, enough to last her a week. "Praise the Lord," she yelled.

The Atheist stepped out from the bushes and said, "There is no Lord, ha ha ha, I brought those groceries!"

The little old lady raised her arms to the sky and said, "Praise the Lord, You sent me groceries and you made the Devil pay for them!"

I will therefore that men pray every where, lifting up holy hands, without wrath and doubting (1 Timothy 2:8).

♦ Those who do not seek after God become practical atheists.

-Herbert Lockyer

♦ It is because of who He is we worship Him. Such worship comes from a thankful heart, it expresses itself through our lives as our hands reach up in surrender, and our knees reach down in humility as they bow before Him, while the soul comes into a place of awe and adoration before Him.

-RJK

♦ The highest exercise of which the human spirit is capable, once touched by divine grace and regenerated by omnipotent power, is worship, which involves adoration, praise, and implicit devotion.

-H. A. Ironside
(CBO, Aug. 12)

♦ Thanksgiving and praise come from a heart full of a love for God and is not dependent on outward circumstances...Our thanksgiving fuels our praise, and our praise leads to worship, when we praise Him for Who He is and His wonderful qualities.

-Anna Alden-Tirrill
(SP, Jan. 7)

******

The Bible points to the fact that spiritual soil has to do with our heart condition. Our heart condition will determine what way we will be receptive. Alicia Williamson Garcia uses the word "soil" to describe worship.

Sacrifice—without sacrifice, there's no worship.
Obedience—incomplete obedience is disobedience.
Immediate—delayed obedience is disobedience.
Loving—without love we're nothing.

Saying with a loud voice, Fear God, and give glory to him; for the hour of his judgment is come: and worship him that made heaven, and earth, and the sea, and the fountains of water (Revelation 14:7).

♦ Our thought habits are those of the scientist, not those of the worshipper. We are more likely to explain than to adore.

-A. W. Tozer
(AG, Oct. 24)

♦ We thank the Lord for his gifts, but we praise him for his worth. Christ on the Cross calls forth from us our amazed thanksgiving; Christ on the throne our praise. We behold what he has done and we are profoundly grateful; we behold who he is and we adore.

-Watchman Nee
(WN, Dec. 7)

♦ We cannot be strong leaders of intercession unless we have a deep and growing acquaintance with the secret ways of the soul.

-John Henry Jowett

♦ Definition of worship: to quicken the conscience by the holiness of God, to feed the mind with the truth of God, to urge the imagination by the beauty of God, to open up the heart to the love of God, to devote the will to the purpose of God.

-William Temple

♦ If you cannot worship the Lord in the midst of your responsibilities on Monday, it is not very likely that you were worshipping on Sunday.

-A. W. Tozer
(AG, Nov. 2)

*****

Life Song

Our soul is drawn down memory's path,
Through the misty corridors of time,
    Haunting and enchantment intertwined
Emotions rising from secret chambers of suppressed memories,
    Notes of joy and sorrow,
Melancholy chords mingled together
    In memory's song-
Descending tones of somber
    Contemplation, blurred images
    of that which was lost,
    Never to return, to be grasped-
Music in a minor key,
    Dark and deep, overshadowing
Heaviness,
    Spurned opportunities,
Open doors unexplored, sour notes,
    Despair balances on the edge,
The Abyss of hopelessness beckons.
    Then, swiftly, as an eagle rising,
Our life song soars upward,
    Heavenly orchestration compels
Towards the Light Eternal—Jesus,
    Echoes of joy, visions of beauty,
Pure and serene,
    The holy angels, gloriously sing-
Our life song—and peace reigns.

-Jeannette Haley

♦   Meditation, the nurse of prayer.

-Gersom

♦   Meditation to the soul is the same as digestion to the body...For meditation is a kind of silent prayer, whereby the soul is frequently, as if were carried out of itself to God, and in a degree made like unto those blessed spirits who, by a kind of immediate intuition, always behold the face of our heavenly Father.

-George Whitefield
(GW, pg. 7)

♦   Meditation is like oil to the lamp; the lamp of prayer would soon go out unless meditation cherish and support it. Meditation and Prayer are like two turtles, if you separate one the other dies; a cunning angler observes the time and season when the fish bite best, and then he throws in the angle, when the heart is warmed by meditation, now is the best season to throw in the angle of prayer, and fish for mercy.

-Sir Thomas Watson

♦ Meditation is prayer in bullion (gold), prayer is the ore, soon melted and run into holy desires.

-William Gurnall

♦ Pray earnestly for the sanctification of all your troubles to your eternal good; an unsanctified comfort never did any man good, and a sanctified trouble never did any man hurt.

-John Flavel

♦ Sacrifice is the only basis of true worship and prayer.

-Herbert Lockyer

♦ How we need to learn to listen to the voice of God, but we cannot learn His voice until we learn how to listen for Him.

-RJK

******

Size of a Prayer

I have often wondered if you could put some type of size on prayers. We know that long flowery prayers or repetitious prayers do not impress the Lord because they lack the right spirit and heart. We also know all prayers in line with His will are important, but I have occasionally wondered if prayers for certain matters produce different affects. As I have regarded the impact prayers need to make, I started to put a size on them, not to indicate their importance to God; rather, to show what we learn about God in such prayers. In some ways the small prayers are gigantic because of their simplicity, while the big prayers are so because they require endurance to ensure the excellence of a matter. The medium prayers require us to keep them in perspective with God's purpose and will in a mind. Clearly, with such prayers we must walk a fine line of discretion and balance.

Even though there would be those who would disagree with my measuring stick as far as prayers, we need to remember that prayers are not only to make an impact on heaven, but on those who pray them.

Simple (Small-Beginning) Prayers (Childlike faith to trust Him as our Provider and Protector): Comprised of concerns in relationship to hindrances and daily needs—see God's faithfulness in action.

Focus (intermediate) Prayers (Effectual prayer—faith towards God will be confirmed by His intervention): There is a touch of simplicity that is mixed with intensity about a matter in these prayers. Comprised of obtaining or witnessing the impossible in a situation—a greater reliance on God is being developed.

Enduring (Big) Prayers (Persevering prayer—By faith in His Word, we align ourselves with what is important to God): Comprised of seeing God's will being done—ends in communion with God.

Be careful for nothing; but in every thing by prayer and supplication with thanksgiving let your requests be made known unto God (Philippians 4:6).

♦ When a Christian shuns fellowship with other Christians, the devil smiles. When he or she stops studying the Bible, the devil laughs. When he or she stops praying, the devil shouts for joy.

-Corrie Ten Boom

♦ Prayer should be simple, believing, and unquestioning. It is all too possible to become absorbed with the theological problems connected with prayer.

-William MacDonald
(TD, pg. 54)

♦ Prayer is not overcoming God's reluctance. It is laying hold of His willingness.

12th Century Woman

♦ If we do not watch and pray, we will let the cares of this life and the lust of other things harden our hearts until we will be in no condition after a time, to hear what God says.

-Oswald Chambers
(DL, Aug. 16)

♦ I see that prayerlessness is one of my great sins of omission. I am too short, ask too little, ask with too much want of forethought. Then, *too little meditation upon Scripture."*

-Andrew Bonar

♦ God is not wanting great men. He is wanting men who will dare to prove the greatness of their God. Prayer!

-Unknown

♦ When you consider prayer, it is actually a privilege wrought by Jesus on the cross. But, few know how to use this privilege in the right way. For those who religiously pray, it is not treated as a privilege, but a duty. In some cases, this duty can be very repetitious, proving to be lifeless. When it comes to those who selfishly pray, these people pray amiss for they ask for things to heap upon their flesh. For those who treat prayer as an option, they only pray in times of crises, and often become angry when God fails to perform according to their wishes.

-RJK

Ye lust, and have not: ye kill, and desire to have, and cannot obtain: ye fight and war, yet ye have not, because ye ask not. Ye ask, and receive not, because ye ask amiss, that ye may consume it upon your lusts (James 4:2-3).

♦ We only pray the way we live.

-Andrew Murray
(AP, Mar. 14)

♦ Labor that does not spring out of worship is futile and can only be wood, hay and stubble in the day that shall try every man's work.

-A. W. Tozer
(AG, Nov. 24)

♦ It is my conviction that true worship is the greatest need in our churches today.

-Warren W. Wiersbe

♦ The primary burden of our prayers should be the interests of the Lord.

-William MacDonald
(TD, pg. 56)

♦ We need to be as much before God when the world patronizes us as when it openly disapproves. It is never safe to forget to pray.

-H. A. Ironside

♦ Though my natural instinct is to wish for a life free from pain, trouble, and adversity, I am learning to welcome anything that makes me conscious of my need for Him. If prayer is birthed out of desperation, then anything that makes me desperate for God is a blessing.

-Nancy Leigh DeMoss

Pray without ceasing (1 Thessalonians 5:17).

♦ I know that praise is like the wings that are spread out to catch the blessed currents of the Spirit of God. As praise reaches up to embrace the beauty of heaven, the wind of the Holy Spirit is able to lift up the soul in great expectation.

-RJK

And one cried unto another and said, Holy, holy, holy, is the LORD of hosts: the whole earth is full of his glory (Isaiah 6:3).

♦ When the day comes for me, as it came for Hannah, that my Samuel, in whom all my hopes are centered, passes out of my hands into God's, then I shall know what it really means to worship him. For worship follows in the wake of the Cross, where God is All and in all. When our hands are emptied of all we hold dear and the focus shifts from ourselves to God, that is worship.

-Watchman Nee
(WN, Dec. 28)

******

Thou art coming to a King,
Large petitions with thee bring,
For His love and power are such
Thou canst never ask too much.

-John Newton

♦ True speech is prayer not complaint. The danger is that bitter waters make us bitter.

-Hebert Lockyer
(MP, pg. 292)

♦ Prayer is not only wishing or asking, but believing and accepting.

-Andrew Murray
(AP, Jun. 3)

♦ I say that the greatest tragedy in the world today is that God has made man in His image and made him to worship Him, made him to play the harp of worship before the face of God day and night, but he has failed God and dropped the harp. It lies voiceless at his feet.

-A. W. Tozer
(AG, Dec. 4)

But the hour cometh, and now is, when the true worshippers shall worship the Father in spirit and in truth: for the Father seeketh such to worship him (John 4:23).

♦ I would rather be able to pray than to be a great preacher. Jesus Christ never taught his disciples how to preach, but only how to pray.

-Dwight Moody

♦ Half a dozen men on their knees for 60 minutes waiting upon the Lord with the absolute conviction that they have no answer, that their human ideas and programs are ineffective and bankrupt – they will accomplish more than 50 men around a table discussing problems for a whole year.

-Alan Redpath

♦ Prayer is an interesting point of discovering God's will. It is one of the greatest privileges that God's people possess, but how many of us truly take advantage of it. When riding high on the wave of self-sufficiency, we do not see any real need for God. When in shame, we seek to hide from Him. When in despair, we feel too weak to look up. When in desperation, we simply flounder in our own tears, while pleading with some unseen entity that according to our attitude appears to come across as being deaf or indifferent.

-RJK

♦ Learn to expect nothing from ourselves. Expect everything from God. These two thoughts lie at the root of all true prayer.

-Andrew Murray
(AP, Aug. 19)

******

The Difference

I got up early one morning
And rushed right into the day.
I had so much to accomplish
That I didn't take time to pray.

Problems just tumbled about me
And heavier came the task;
Why doesn't God help me, I wondered
He answered: You didn't <u>ask</u>.

I wanted to see joy and beauty
But the day toiled on gray and bleak.
I wondered why God didn't seek me,
Only to be reminded that I must first <u>seek</u> Him.

I tried to come into God's presence
I used all my keys at the lock;
God gently and lovingly chided
My child you didn't <u>knock</u>.

I woke up early this morning
And paused before entering the day;
I had so much to accomplish
That I had to take time to pray.

-Unknown
Church's Newsletter

And I say unto you, Ask, and it shall be given you; seek, and ye shall find;
knock, and it shall be opened unto you. For everyone that asketh receiveth;
and he that seeketh findeth; and to him that knocketh it shall be opened (Luke
11: 9-10).

♦ It is delightful to worship God, but it is also a humbling thing. The man
who has not been humbled in the presence of God will never be a
worshiper of God at all.

-A. W. Tozer
(AP, Dec. 6)

♦ Devotion must be the child of reflection; it may rise on wings, but they
must be the wings of thought. . .It should aim at the marriage of qualities
which are commonly supposed to be antagonistic—the insight of the
thinker and the fervor of the worshiper. . .Religious sentiment, if it is worth
anything, must be preceded by religious perception.

-George Matheson

♦ Clearly, if we are going to survive the spiritual season that is now upon
us, we must recognize what period of time it is and begin to prayerfully,
soberly, and wisely prepare for it. Otherwise, it will come upon us as a
thief in the night that will possibly rob us of our resolve to stand, kill any
faith in us, and destroy any future hope of glory that might be awaiting us.

-RJK

♦ Prayer is a supernatural weapon to bring down the strongholds that try to
enslave us and others. Prayer is meant to be filled with holy audacity and
bold and courageous confidence in God's Word and His promises.

-Anna Alden-Tirrill
(SP, Apr. 26)

♦ If we don't acknowledge who He is, prayer is not prayer at all. Instead, the recitation of our worries is simply an attempt to worry God.

-Andrew Murray
(AP, Oct. 2)

*****

Lord, what a change within us one short hour
Spent in Thy presence will prevail to make;
What heavy burdens from our bosoms take,
What parched grounds refresh, as with a shower!
We kneel, and all around us seems to lower,
We rise, and all the distant and the near
Stands forth in sunny outline, brave and clear;
We kneel, how weak! We rise, how full of power!
Why, therefore, should we do ourselves this wrong,
Or others, that we are not always strong,
That we are ever overborne with care,
That we should ever weak or heartless be,
Anxious or troubled, when with us is prayer,
And joy, and strength, and courage are with Thee?

-Richard C. Trench
(1807-1886)

♦ The simple truth is that worship is elementary until it begins to take on the quality of admiration. Just as long as the worshiper is engrossed with himself and his good fortune, he is a babe. We begin to grow up when our worship passes from thanksgiving to admiration.

-A. W. Tozer

God is a Spirit: and they that worship him must worship him in spirit and in truth (John 4:24).

♦ A man is what he is on his knees before God—and nothing more.
-Robert McCheyne

♦ Weak children of God pray only for themselves, but persons growing in Christ understand how to consul with God over what must take place in the kingdom.

-Andrew Murray
(AP, Oct. 4)

♦ Preaching is a rare gift; prayer is a rarer one. Preaching, like a sword, is a weapon to use at close quarters; those far off cannot be reached by it.

Prayer, like a breechloader, has longer range, and under some circumstances is even more effective.

-Wenham

♦ The whole concept of ineffable worship has been lost to this generation of Christians. Our level of life is so low that no one expects to know the deep things of the soul until the Lord returns. So we are content to wait, and while we wait we are *wont to cheer our hearts sometimes by breaking into song.

-A. W. Tozer
(AG, Dec. 21)

♦ It is a great lesson to learn that to be silent before God is the secret of true adoration. It is only as the soul bows itself before Him in honor and reverence that the heart will be opened to receive the divine impression of the nearness of God and of the working of His power.

-Andrew Murray
(AP, Dec. 5)

♦ Prayer never causes me an effort. When I pray, I know I am addressing the Deity, but when I preach, the Devil may be among the congregation.

-George Matheson

♦ Worship in spirit and in truth is what God requires; and the very absence of pomp and fleshly dignity will conduce to lowliness of heart and self-abasement, and will at least help towards reality as drawing nigh to God.

-Hebert Lockyer
(MP, pg. 378)

♦ In true thankfulness and worship, the soul will boast of God's greatness. The will of a person will be in awe of His beauty, the intelligence will begin to exalt Him in His majesty, and the emotions will soar as all affections are directed heavenward to the One who deserves to receive all glory.

-RJK

But ye are a chosen generation, a royal priesthood, an holy nation, a peculiar people; that ye should shew forth the praises of him who hath called you out of darkness into his marvellous light (1 Peter 2:9).

♦ I can safely say, on the authority of all that is revealed in the Word of God, that any man or woman on this earth who is bored and turned off by worship is not ready for heaven.

-A. W. Tozer
(AG, Nov. 27)

♦ Alone with God—that is the secret of true power in prayer. There is no true holiness, no clothing with the Holy Spirit and with power, without being alone daily with God.

-Andrew Murray
(AP, Dec. 8)

♦ If men are unmoved by our prayers, they are not likely to be profoundly stirred by our preaching.

-John Henry Jowett

♦ Isn't there a difference between worship and entertainment? The church that can't worship must be entertained.

-A. W. Tozer
(AG, Nov. 17)

♦ The mystics wrote to cultivate the inner, and certainly this is a neglected activity in our churches today. We have more Marthas than Marys! But, in the long run, the ideal Christian will not be one or the other: he will be a balance of both. Worship and work will not compete; they will cooperate.

-Warren W. Wiersbe
(PCK, pg, 358)

♦ Prayer that costs nothing is worth nothing; it is simply a by-product of a cheap Christianity.

-William MacDonald
(TD, pg. 55)

♦ Intercessory prayer is brutal warfare.

-Anna Alden-Tirrill
(SP, Apr. 28)

♦ The essence of spiritual worship is to love supremely, to trust confidently, to pray without ceasing and to seek to be Christlike and holy and to do all the good we can for Christ's sake.

-A. W. Tozer
(AG, Oct. 2)

******

A Place of Agreement

When it comes to prayer, one must be in agreement with heaven, and when it comes to worship, one must have agreement in the Spirit to ensure purity. This was brought out in a story about soldiers who broke into a church during one of its meetings and begin shouting at the members who were cowering in their pews.

The order that came from one of the soldiers was clear, "Those who are faithful to God, move to the right side of the church." They were also informed that those who complied would be shot; therefore, they had to choose to die at that moment. However, those who wished to go home and keep their lives were to stand on the left side.

True to the word of the soldier, those on the left were released. Although some were sad about the fate of those on the right side, and a bit sheepish about their fickle faith, they exited out of the church.

Once it was evident that all of those who chose the present world had gone on their way, the soldiers put down their weapons. "We, too, are Christians," they said, "but we wish to worship without hypocrites." (ED, pg. 46)

In America it has been easy to believe that we have the character to face any real challenge to our faith, but the truth is, until it has been tested, we do not know what choice we would make in such a defining moment. It is for this reason that I have often challenged Christians in America to realize that the choice we must make is not to die for Jesus, but to live for Him in an exemplary way. It is in living for Him that we will be prepared to stand for Him, and if necessary make the right decision to die for Him.

It is also true that to be able to worship without hypocrisy we must know who we worship. We must possess the Spirit of God and love the Lord in order to truly honor Him in personal worship.

Saying with a loud voice, Worthy is the Lamb that was slain to receive power, and riches, and wisdom, and strength, and honour, and glory, and blessing...And the four beasts said, Amen. And the four and twenty elders fell down and worshipped him that liveth for ever and ever (Revelation 5:12, 14).

A Matter of Grace and Faith

~

The Eyes of Faith

Faith serves as those eyes that can see afar off in light of eternal hope. It is the muscle that allows us to walk in expectation of seeing the fulfillment of glorious promises. It is the eternal virtue of optimism that causes us to be a stranger and a pilgrim in this world, while being an ardent citizen of the world to come.

Oh, to have faith like Abraham, confidence like Moses, assurance like David, and boldness like Paul. Oh! That we would know the liberty that faith brings to each step of our Christian walk, ever allowing us to advance in this present, dark world towards our final destination.

For we walk by faith, not by sight (2 Corinthians 5:7).

******

♦ Personally, I have lived enough years to know that any point of reliance and confidence outside of God is going to end in utter disappointment and disillusionment. In the past, I have been immature and foolish enough to put my confidence in things other than God. I have also hit dead ends and immovable walls, as well as fallen into ditches of despair and pits of depression. To trust God is a choice and to walk in such confidence serves as an antidote against fearing that which is temporary and powerless to destroy that which is heavenly.

-RJK

♦ The Christian Faith begins not with a big DO but with a big DONE.

-Watchman Nee
(WN, Jan. 26)

♦ But it is not faith that does the work. It is but the means which God uses to unloose His unlimited power. Faith is the hand which lays hold of omnipotence.

-H. A. Ironside
(CBO, Jul. 19)

♦ Faith isn't believing God can, it's knowing God will.

-Unknown

105

♦ Putting our faith into action is all about taking the first step on an uncertain journey. . .It is "going without knowing". . .There are no maps on a journey of faith. We navigate by the starlight of God's provision.

-Extreme Devotion
(ED, pg. 20)

♦ If there was a person who exhibited the steps of faith during his grave trial of temptation, it was Job. Job revealed that there are six steps to faith before one can come to rest in the Lord. These steps include: the assurance of faith, the hope of faith, the expectation of faith, the reality of faith, the declaration of faith, and the fruit of faith.

-RJK

♦ Our journey of faith is filled with seeming contradictions and paradoxes. One of them is that it is only when we are weak that we can be made strong. Only when we are emptied of self can we be filled with His power.

-Anna Alden-Tirrill
(SP, Aug. 15)

♦ To abandon all, to strip one's self of all, in order to seek and follow Jesus Christ to Bethlehem where He was born, to the hall where He was scourged, to Calvary where He died on the cross, is so great a mercy toward us, that the blessing of salvation and redemption is given but through faith in the Son of God.

-John Wesley

♦ Faith towards God is what makes God precious to us. The more precious He becomes to us, the more of His preciousness people will be able to taste Him in our lives.

-RJK

But without faith it is impossible to please him: for he that cometh to God must believe that he is, and that he is a rewarder of them that diligently seek him (Hebrews 11:6).

♦ Too many disciples have faith in their faith, or in their joy in the Lord; and when a spiritual storm comes, they have neither faith nor joy. Only one thing can endure, and that is the love for God.

-Oswald Chambers
(DL, Mar. 8)

♦ As the eye is the organ by which we see, so faith is the power by which we see the light of God and walk in it.

-Andrew Murray
(AP, Dec. 7)

♦ Believe not your eyes if they contradict your ears, provided it be God that speaks.

-William Hake

♦ Wherever faith has been original, wherever it has proved itself to be real, it has invariably had upon it a sense of the present God.

-A. W. Tozer
(AG, Feb. 4)

Prayer: Lord, You have allowed Your people to experience the ways of faith so that they could encourage us to not give up in the storms of life. Thank You for Your examples. Amen.

******

The Ultimate Example

We are told about a great cloud of witness in *Hebrews 12:1*. This cloud was made up of saints whose lives spoke of faith that would obtain the heights of a better resurrection and left an example that the world could not fathom. They live the lives of heaven in the midst of the workings of devils. They never lost their focus as to how righteousness would express itself in the virtuous ways of love and compassion.

This was brought out in the life of a Christian by the name of Mrs. Rathenau. Her husband was the finance minister of Germany when Hitler took over. He was killed by a Nazi. His only crime was that he was Jewish. True to her Christian testimony, Mrs. Rathenau found an incredible opportunity to bless the man who had killed her husband when he was in prison. She cared for him and even defended him. This man later became a leader of the Gestapo in Marseilles. He returned good for the evil he had committed by helping multitudes of Jews escape. In the end he was hung.

Mrs. Rathenau's Christianity was sincere and true to her Master's instructions and examples towards her enemies. Because of her example, her life produced incredible fruits through the life of her former enemy. (AWG, pg. 42)

Wherefore seeing we also are compassed about with so great a cloud of witnesses, let us lay aside every weight, and the sin which doth so easily beset us, and let us run with patience the race that is set before us (Hebrews 12:1).

Favor shown to the poor we call pity.
Favor shown to the suffering we call compassion.
Favor shown to the obstinate we call patience.
Favor shown to the unworthy we call grace.

-Hebert Lockyer
(MP. Pg. 419)

♦ In regard to the relationship between mercy and truth, and righteousness and peace in *Psalm 85:10*, a man by the name of George Horne added this insight, "These four divine attributes parted at the fall of Adam, and met again at the birth of Christ. *Mercy* was ever inclined to save man, and *Peace* could not be his enemy; but *Truth* exacted the promise of God's threat—'The soul that sinneth, it shall die'; and *Righteousness* could not but give to every one his due, Jehovah was to be true in all his ways, and righteous in all his works. Through *grace*, union has been restored between the four attributes." (DP, pg. 284)

Mercy and truth are met together; righteousness and peace have kissed each other (Psalm 85:10).

♦ Truth will always make demands, and grace will always be there to meet them.

-Watchman Nee

♦ For God has received more glory through the finished work of Christ than He lost through the sin of Adam. "He lost creatures through sin, He gained sons through grace."

-William MacDonald

♦ When a person repents, he or she becomes an illustration of God's grace and glory. True repentance is life changing, where God transforms us from the inside out. Works are not a part of saving faith, but the evidence of saving faith. True repentance WILL show up in new ways of doing things. And these new ways will be ways of love.

-Anna Alden-Tirrill
(SP, Jun. 3)

♦ Holiness is likewise a gift of grace, given to a surrendered soul by God. It comes whenever a justified person willingly gives up the right to oneself and presents one's body "a living sacrifice"...acceptable unto God.

-Oswald Chambers
(DL, Feb. 15)

♦ Faith is not necessarily a testimony about how God works, but about How He is! He is faithful.

-RJK

♦ Friendship with Jesus is costly. Faith alone saves, but saving faith is never alone. It is always accompanied by great sacrifices for Christ's sake.

-Richard Wurmbrand

♦ Faith is not even worthy of the name until it erupts into actions.

-Catherine Marshall

Even so faith, if it hath not works, is dead, being alone (James 2:17).

♦ To know what you believe, look at what you do.

-Unknown

♦ In her book, *The Secret Place,* author Anna Alden-Tirrill gives a vivid picture of the grace of God: <u>G</u>od's <u>R</u>iches <u>A</u>t <u>C</u>hrist's <u>E</u>xpense. (Jan. 5)

♦ Genuine faith will always produce the response of obedience. Without such obedience, Christianity ceases to be a life and becomes another religion that simply stands on lifeless theology.

-RJK

******

The Test of Faith

Waiting is a test. The key to waiting is coming to rest on the Person and character of God. It is about having faith, and allowing it to be enlarged in the waiting period. Most people hate to wait, and they always get into trouble by intruding into God's plans and timing. Some become complacent, rather than watchful and prepared when God does open the right door. Some bolt out of the ranks and get ahead of God. Such people are set up to fall into temptation. Some people become restless and take matters into their own hands. Like the Israelites they simply end up erecting a golden calf that will serve their purpose, calm their anxiety, and quiet their religious conscience.

Waiting is hard, but necessary. We must bring our spirit and soul to a quiet place so that we can be led by the Spirit in obedience and submission to God's will. After all, it is only in God's will that we discover the best He has for us.

For as many as are led by the Spirit of God, they are the sons of God (Romans 8:14).

◆ Praise is a "gate-pass" of faith that brings us into the Presence and Power of God!

-Anna Alden-Tirrill
(SP, Apr. 5)

◆ The life of faith is a life of obedience. As Christ lived in obedience to the Father, so we need to live in loving obedience to God.

-Andrew Murray

◆ Faith is never passive. It demands a response. It asks for a mission. It demonstrates the indwelling presence and power of the Holy Spirit.

-Richard Wurmbrand

◆ God ever delights to honor faith.

-H. A. Ironside
(CBO, Feb. 7)

◆ We are told in the Word that unless we mix faith to the truth and ways of God, it will not profit us. Without the pure intent of knowing and pleasing God that is found in the inspiration of blessed assurance in our Lord, we will never profit from the wisdom of heaven. We may intellectually know a matter is true, but if we do not walk in it, we will never experience the reality of truth where we actually come to a place of abiding in our Lord. The place of abiding entails that blessed anchor of quiet confidence and joy in the Holy Ghost.

-RJK

For unto us was the gospel preached, as well as unto them: but the word preached did not profit them, not being mixed with faith in them that heard it (Hebrews 4:2).

◆ Obedience is the fruit of faith, patience, the bloom on the fruit.

-Christina Rossetti

♦ People say that Christianity is blind faith; not a bit of it. Christianity is a rational faith that comes from honest, candid, close thought.

-R. A. Torrey
(RA, pg. 84)

♦ Faith must not violate evidence and reason or it would be irrational. Faith takes a step beyond reason but only in the direction that reason and evidence have pointed.

-Dave Hunt

******

Childlike Faith

In the Bible we read about childlike faith. Children have a way of cutting through the maze that is often created by intellectual speculation and logic. It is because they operate on the uncomplicated level of simply believing what they are told by those they trust that Jesus used them as an example of faith that is active and powerful in its attitude and responses.

Sometimes the trap that rational adults fall into is that truth is too simple and pure. They believe there must be something more to a matter and will automatically complicate it by presuming there are yet hidden meanings to be discovered. In their attempts to find such hidden meanings, they become confused and are rendered ineffective.

There was a story about Sunday School children learning to memorize Psalm 23. They were given a month to learn it before they were to recite it before the congregation.

There was a boy by the name of Bobby who was quite excited to learn the psalm but had a problem remembering it. After much practice, he barely got past the first line. The day came when the children were to recite it. When Bobby's turn came, he was quite nervous. However, he stepped up to the microphone and said with pride, "The Lord is my shepherd...and that's all I need to know!"

Bobby may have not been able to quote the text, but he clearly understood the intent of it. This is true for us as believers, but we cannot understand the pure intent of something unless we have a childlike faith to believe it is so and embrace it as such.

And said, Verily I say unto you, Except ye be converted, and become as little children, ye shall not enter into the kingdom of heaven (Matthew 18:3).

♦ Childlike faith silences logic, puts reason on hold, and allows us to securely land on the work and promises of God.

-RJK

Prayer: Lord, as Your people we read about faith, hear about faith, and see the examples of it, but we need to live and experience its incredible qualities. Lord, give me the measure or gift of faith that will enable me to go the way of Your Spirit to possess all of Your promises. Amen.

♦ All of God's promises are FACTS through faith. When God proclaims a fact, faith accepts and acts upon it. When God makes a promise, we comply with its conditions, claim its fulfillment by faith, and receive the promise. The function of the prayer of faith is to turn God's promises into facts of experience.

-Anna Alden-Tirrill
(SP, Jul. 31)

♦ Faith enables our spiritual sense to function. Where faith is defective the result will be inward insensibility and numbness toward spiritual things.

-A. W. Tozer
(AG, Feb. 1)

♦ Jesus teaches us that a life of faith requires both prayer and fasting. Prayer grasps the power of heaven, fasting loosens the hold on earthly pleasure.

-Andrew Murray

******

The Power of Faith

There is a story about the Indian Christian mystic by the name Sadhu Sundar Singh, which reveals the power of faith. On one of his adventures, he found himself in the Himalayas. He entered a cave to rest, and as he lay down he observed the glimmering eyes of a tiger. Singh cried out to God to save him and walked softly out of the cave. His prayer had been answered because the tiger had not moved towards him, but when he was outside, remorse filled him.

He realized as a child of God he should have not walked out. Instead, the tiger should have yielded to him. So he prayed for the tiger to leave the cave. This time the tiger walked out leaving Sadhu to enter the cave without any opposition. (AWG, pgs. 77-78)

As believers we have been allotted much, but we can only possess it when we walk by faith in regard to the matters of heaven. It is only the walk of faith that will advance us towards all that awaits us.

And Jesus said unto them, Because of your unbelief: for verily I say unto you, If ye have faith as a grain of mustard seed, ye shall say unto this mountain, Remove hence to yonder place; and it shall remove; and nothing shall be impossible unto you (Matthew 17:20).

******

♦ Sometimes, it is a straight, narrow path that faith will lead you on. On one side of the path is the abyss of doubt and torment. On the other side is the mountain of impossibility. The path can be slow going as it curves and winds around obstacles of uncertainty and blind curves of anxiety. Subsequently, one almost feels as if he or she is moving like a snail towards an unknown destination.

-RJK

♦ It is in mercy that He afflicts. Faith recognizes this, and so we can bow the head before Him and exclaim, "It is the Lord. Let Him do what seems good to Him" (1 Samuel 3:18).

-Unknown

♦ I have found that the man who believes in the Bible always comes out ahead in the long run, and that the man who is too wise and too advanced to believe the Word of God comes out behind in the long run, every time.

-R. A. Torrey
(RA, pg. 68)

♦ ...unless you get a faith of the heart, a faith working by love, you shall never sit with Abraham, Isaac, Jacob, or Jesus Christ, in the kingdom of heaven.

-George Whitefield
(GW, pg. 25)

♦ Faith is true faith only when it engages truth. When it rests on falsehood, it leads to eternal tragedy. It is not enough that we believe. We must believe the right thing about the right One.

-Anna Alden-Tirrill
(SP, Aug. 19)

Examine yourselves, whether ye be in the faith; prove your own selves. Know ye not your own selves, how that Jesus Christ is in you, except ye be reprobates (2 Corinthians 13:5)?

♦ True faith brooks no delay. One who reckons God faithful to his word declares this not merely by doing his will, but by doing it instantly.

-Watchman Nee
(WN, Feb. 20)

♦ So many people believe in their beliefs, have faith in their faith, and are confident in their confidence. All of this is of no avail. It is our confidence in *God* that abides, faith in *God* that remains, and belief in *God* that lasts.

-Oswald Chambers
(DL, Feb. 12)

******

Servant of Christ, stand fast amid the scorn
Of men who little know or love thy Lord;
Turn not aside from toil; case not to warn,
Comfort and teach. Trust Him for thy reward:
A few more moments; suffering, and then
Cometh sweet rest from all thy heart's deep pain.

For grace pray much, for much thou needest grace;
If men thy work deride,--what can they more?
Christ's weary foot thy path on earth doth trace;
If thorns wound thee, they pierced Him before:
Press on, look up, though clouds may gather round'
Thy place of service He makes hallowed ground.

-J. J. P.

♦ Often God places His children in positions of profound difficulty, leading them into a wedge from which there is no escape. It seems perplexing and very serious, but it is perfectly right. It is a platform for the display of His almighty grace and power.

-Unknown

♦ A believer can go through intense fiery trials without having his or her faith destroyed. Instead, his or her trial becomes food for faith to feed on. And a strong, unwavering faith not only brings glory to God. It becomes a blessing to others as well.

-Micca Campbell

♦ We indeed need mercy and grace from God. For Him to turn our way is mercy and for Him to regard us is grace. Clearly, because of both of these virtues, He is faithful to do the impossible on our behalf.

-RJK

◆ Confidence in an unfaithful man in time of trouble is like a "broken tooth."
Herbert Lockyer
(MP, pg. 506)

******

Grace Formed An Ark

To walk with God as did Enoch and to find grace as did Noah points to being consumed by the Lord's everlasting faithfulness, while being translated into His eternal kingdom. We must remember that our days are numbered in which we can learn to walk with God and grow in the knowledge of His bountiful grace.

I must keep this in mind as I consider the age in which I now live. There are countless things of this present world that can produce the ice of indifference, causing the love of God to grow cold in the heart. However, there is the revelation of the Son of God and His grace that will once again thaw the coldness of a heart.

In following the Lord, I have learned that His grace will form an ark in which I will find refuge from the coldness that is abounding. I know this ark to be Jesus. The ark reminds me that I do not have to be consumed by sin that abounds around me, and that I can truly find rest from the weariness that the battles of the world have brought my way.

Obviously, it is vital that I do not let this world cause me to faint in my mind as the veneer of indifference grips my heart with a stiff but fragile resolve to somehow survive this present world. It is the warmth of the Son of God that reminds me that I have an ark I can hide in. I do not have to face the rampant darkness of this world with the cold indifference of a stiff upper lip and a cold heart. In Christ, I will be able to endure to the end of the long cold winter of my spiritual life.

For ye are dead, and your life is hid with Christ in God (Colossians 3:3).

◆ Unfathomable oceans of grace are in Christ for you. Dive and dive again—you will never come to the bottom of these depths.
-Robert McCheyne

◆ No one can know the true grace of God who has not first known the fear of God.
-A. W. Tozer
(AG, Apr. 16)

Prayer: Lord, thank You for Your grace. As the timeless song declares, we will be singing about Your grace for ages to come. Amen.

♦ It has been said that the holiness of God is the union of God's infinite distance from sinful man with God's infinite nearness in His redeeming grace. Faith must always seek to realize both the distance and the nearness.

-Andrew Murray
(AP, Apr. 21)

♦ The Lord can bless a wrong decision made in faith from a pure heart more than He can bless indecision.

-Anna Alden-Tirrill
(SP, Nov. 26)

♦ Instead of fixing your problems, God may be wanting to use your problems to teach you to trust and obey Him.

-Nancy Leigh DeMoss

♦ Faith does not control circumstances, but it can inspire excellent attitudes and responses in their midst.

-RJK

♦ God has ordained to move into our lives with fullness through faith. The pathway that the Spirit cuts through the jungle of our anxieties into the clearing of joy is the pathway of faith.

-Unknown

♦ It is easy to believe the mighty power of God in a calm, but not so easy to resign ourselves to it, and securely rest upon it in a storm of adversity: but oh what peace and rest would our faith procure us by the free use and exercise of it this way!

-John Flavel
(RR, pg. 78)

Holding faith, and a good conscience; which some having put away concerning faith have made shipwreck (1 Timothy 1:19).

♦ If we equate pursuing faith with activities we deem spiritual and miss the moment by moment choices of yielding, we miss the whole picture of this life of Grace. Pursuing faith is much more than a quiet time in the morning or prayer time at noon. It has feet that obey, hands that serve, eyes that have hope, and a heart that surrenders. It's following the ONE Who does understand, and finding all we need for life and godliness IN CHRIST.

-Dina Martin

♦ Nothing strengthens us so much as isolation and transplantation . . . under the wholesome demand his soul will put forth all her native vigor . . . it may not be necessary for us to withdraw from home and friends; but we shall have to withdraw our heart's deepest dependence from all earthly props and supports, if ever we are to learn what it is to trust simply and absolutely on the eternal God.

-F. B. Meyer

******

Understanding Mercy

Occasionally, I have pondered God's mercy. I have assumed much about this virtue. I always thought it was available for the sinner. However, this is not true. A sinner who loves sin does not seek mercy. He or she sees no need for it. Therefore, who seeks mercy?

The humble seek mercy. They recognize they have need of it. They know their plight and will seek the Lord to intervene on their behalf.

The broken in spirit will seek mercy. They realize they must be made whole and restored if they are to continue forward in their lives. After all, they have no enduring spirit in them to seek anything that can revive the inner man from the pit of despair and hopelessness.

The righteous will seek mercy. These individuals understand that without God, there is no hope. They need God every day. They know that they must continually seek mercy before they can obtain God's grace or favor in a matter.

I know I have need of God's mercy. I am poor and needy when it comes to life. Without His intervention, I am a sitting duck ready to be struck down on the rotating, grinding belt of the world.

Prayer: Lord, thank You for Your mercy. I need it everyday to wade through the endless maze of my flesh, the cesspool of my selfishness, the foolishness of the world, and the traps of Satan. Thank You for providing it, blotting out my sins, enabling me in my weakness, and helping me overcome in my despair. Amen.

******

♦ Grace is not something that covers us in our sin. In fact, it only abounds after sin is properly dealt with. Grace is the act of God, where He actually shows favor towards undeserving man. In the case of salvation, His favor towards man translates into eternal life. Therefore, grace is not a means to cover the bondage of sin, but is the means that gives us liberty to enjoy the life God has for us. It is important that believers realize that grace gives us the liberty to do what is right before the Lord and not cover a sinful matter with wishful thinking that somehow grace will cover it.

-RJK

♦ True humility proves its integrity by not seeking for anything but simply trusting His grace. And so it is the strength of a great faith. Don't let your littleness hinder you for a moment.

-Andrew Murray
(AP, Jun 24)

♦ God never gives us grace in advance.

-Hebert Lockyer
(MP, pg. 303)

For by grace are ye saved through faith; and that not of yourselves: it is the gift of God: Not of works, lest any man should boast (Ephesians 2:8, 9).

******

Jesus, I will trust Thee,
Trust Thee with my soul;
Guilty, lost, and helpless,
Thou hast made me whole:
There is none in heaven
Or on earth like Thee;
Thou hast died for sinners,
Therefore, Lord, for me!

-Frances Ridley Havergal
(1836-1879)

♦ Holiness by faith lays hold on God and accepts from Him His righteousness. Hundreds fail by striving to give up things to God, striving to become holy by their acts and deeds; this is the righteousness of the law, not the righteousness by faith.

-Oswald Chambers
(DL, May 18)

- Fear knocked at the door. Faith answered. There was no one there.

  -Unknown

- Faith is not acting so much as believing.

  -E. A. Johnston
  (NTB, pg. 74)

- Faith towards God is the choice of the will, trust is the preference of the wisdom of the intellect, and assurance is the place where all undisciplined emotions have landed on the pathway of righteousness.

  -RJK

- Abraham was justified by faith when he believed God, who spoke of the coming Seed, our Lord Jesus Christ. He was justified by works, when in obedience to the voice of God he offered up his son Isaac upon the altar. Therefore faith shaped his works and by works faith was made perfect. So it must be with us.

  -H. A. Ironside
  (CBO, Dec. 7)

- Trained faith is a triumphant gladness in having nothing but God—no rest, no foothold—nothing but Himself. A triumphant gladness in swinging out into the abyss, a rejoicing in every fresh emergency that is going to prove Him true—*the Lord Alone*—that is trained faith.

  Lilias Trotter

That ye be not slothful, but followers of them who through faith and patience inherit the promises (Hebrews 6:12).

- The will of God will never lead you where the grace of God cannot keep you.

  -On a bookmark

******

With joy we meditate the grace
Of God's High Priest above;
His heart is filled with tenderness,
His very name is Love.

Touched with a sympathy within,
He knows our feeble frame;

He knows what sorest trials mean,
For He has felt the same.

-Isaac Watts
(1674-1748)

♦ It is always good to have mountains to the right and left, and enemy behind and the sea in front, for then faith has its opportunity. One great hindrance to faith is lack of need. If God blesses you with need he will bless you with faith, and faith works best in really desperate need. Faith, we are told, can remove a mountain. Nothing is said about anthills!

-Watchman Nee
(WN, May 13)

♦ God's promises are promissory notes or bonds. He is looking for those with childlike faith, who will endorse them and make them their own.

-Anna Alden-Tirrill
(SP, Aug. 4)

♦ In our instant society we do not know what it means to endure, not until the issues of life begin to remain unresolved. Then, we are told to trust God. Our flesh rages against such a challenge, our pride resents it, and all of our religion proves to fail. At this point, we must choose to believe God in spite of the opposition.

-RJK

♦ I do not take any stock in any faith that does not lead to an open confession of Christ before the world, and I do not take any stock in the Christianity of your professed Christians unless it leads you to go out into the world and witness for the One who saved you.

-R. A. Torrey
(RA, pg. 141)

♦ The Law required *works*—do and thou shalt live! The gospel requires *faith*—believe and then behave. It is far easier to live and do as the Gospel says, than to do and live as the Law demanded.

-Hebert Lockyer
(MP, pg. 316)

Wherefore also we pray always for you, that our God would count you worthy of this calling, and fulfil all the good pleasure of his goodness, and the work of faith with power (2 Thessalonians 1:11).

♦ When I examine my spiritual life, I cannot help but examine my faith. Every mountain I climb requires me to exercise the sturdy cords of my belief. Every challenging wave that I encounter on the ocean of life tests the steadfastness of my confidence towards my Creator. Every storm I have had to endure exposes the source of my faith. Every time I encounter calm waters, the sharpness of my faith is tried.

-RJK

♦ The Christian faith engages a spiritual kingdom where quality of being is everything.

-A. W. Tozer
(AG, Nov. 19)

♦ The daily enjoyment of the leading of God's spirit is indispensable for a joyous life of faith.

-Andrew Murray

♦ No one will disagree that it is hard waiting for God to move. However, it is in the waiting that you must choose faith over doubts, confidence in Christ over uncertainty, and rest in His promises over torment.

-RJK

Prayer: Lord, thank You for the measure and gift of faith. There is no way we could walk or survive this present world without faith towards You. Your mercy made faith available to us, Your grace provided it, and Your love inspires and sustains it in our lives. Amen.

♦ I have had but one passion, and I have lived for it—the absorbingly *arduous yet glorious work of proclaiming the grace and love of our Lord and Savior Jesus Christ.

-John Henry Jowett

♦ The more you can trust God, the more you secure yourselves from danger; he that can live by faith, shall never die by fear.

-John Flavel
(RR, pg. 212)

These things I have spoken unto you, that in me ye might have peace. In the world ye shall have tribulation: but be good cheer; I have overcome the world (John 16:33).

♦ Courage is the bridge that carries us from a nominal existence on earth to an inexplicable longing for a heavenly future.

-Extreme Devotion
(ED, pg. 27)

◆ God will certainly embrace the trembling faith that clings to Him and will not let Him go. A weak faith in an almighty Christ will become the great faith that can remove mountains.

-Andrew Murray
(AP, Sept. 24)

◆ There is little sense in believing if at the same time you provide yourself with an alternative way out! Faith works most convincingly when there is none.

-Watchman Nee
(WN, May 13)

◆ To stand for the truth is simply a test of faith, and to wait on God is the exercise of faith.

-RJK

◆ Where faith is defective the result will be inward insensibility and numbness toward spiritual things.

-A. W. Tozer
(AG, Feb. 11)

Prayer: Lord, my flesh rages against being disciplined by Your timing. My pride cries foul at having to wait, and my logic would want me to think that waiting is a sick game, but I choose to believe in Your very character and know that Your ways are perfect. Therefore, I say away with the foolishness of the flesh, the arrogance of pride, and the conceit of my logic. Amen.

◆ Anything but 'the grace of Christ' is 'another gospel' and under *anathema.

-Herbert Lockyer
(MP, pg. 465)

◆ The work of Grace is more glorious than the work of Creation.

-Adolph Saphir

◆ It is easy to abandon ship when one perceives that all is lost, but faith allows God to change the probabilities and outcome of a matter.

-RJK

And when Abram was ninety years old and nine, the LORD appeared to Abram, and said unto him, I am the Almighty God; walk before me, and be thou perfect. And I will make my covenant between me and thee, and will multiply thee exceedingly (Genesis 17:1-2).

♦ Before the birth of Isaac, God sought to strengthen Abraham's faith. Step by step, God led him until his faith was perfected for full obedience in the sacrifice of Isaac.

-Andrew Murray
(AP, Aug. 26)

♦ Many people are quite pleased with their take on faith, but the real test in the end is will it please God?

-RJK

♦ In relationship to Galatians 2:20, Andrew Murray wrote, "Faith was the power that possessed and permeated Paul's whole being and his every action. Here we have the simple but full statement what the secret of the true Christian life is. It is not faith only in certain promises of God or in certain blessings that we receive from Christ. It is a faith that has a vision of how entirely Christ gives Himself to us."

♦ Faith is your acceptance of God's fact. Had you thought of this? True faith always has its roots in the past. What relates to the future is hope rather than faith, though of course the two are closely interlinked... The Christian life is lived progressively, as it is entered initially, by faith in divine fact.

-Watchman Nee
(WN, May 28)

Prayer: Lord, unbelief will nip at our heels unless we stop trying to dodge the bullets of uncertainty and face the darkness of its deception. We must choose to step over it and declare what we know about You. Thank You for giving me the measure of faith to overcome unbelief. Amen.

♦ Faith enters when there is no supporting evidence to corroborate God's word of promise and we must put our confidence blindly in the character of the One who made the promise.

-A. W. Tozer
(AG, Sept. 20)

♦ Faith towards God is the propelling motion that keeps us moving forward, even when we are being invaded by the noxious weed of fear, overwhelmed by the formidable appearance of the terrain, and scared stiff by the enemy.

-RJK

♦ Faith does not operate in the realm of the possible. There is no glory for God in that which is humanly possible. Faith begins where man's power ends.

-William MacDonald
(ODT, Apr. 29)

♦ False security is based on nothing more than an unrealistic emotional expectation that has nowhere to go but downward into disappointment and disillusionment.

-RJK

For our gospel came not unto you in word only, but also in power, and in the Holy Ghost, and in much assurance; as ye know what manner of men we were among you for your sake (1 Thessalonians 1:5).

♦ Thank God, to every doubt there is a divine assurance. "The word of the Lord came to Abram." As to his fears? God would be to him a protecting shield. As to the future? He offered *himself*, no less as Abram's superlative reward.

-Watchman Nee
(WN, Sept. 20)

♦ The province of faith begins where probabilities cease and where sight and sense fail.

-George Muller

♦ Faith is simply the bringing of our minds into accord with the truth. It is adjusting our expectations to the promises of God in complete assurance that the God of the whole earth cannot lie.

-A. W. Tozer
(AG, Sept 20)

****

Doubt sees the obstacle,
Faith sees the way!
Doubt sees the darkest night,
Faith sees the day!
Doubt dreads to take a step,
Faith soars on high;
Doubt questions, "Who believes?"
Faith answers, "I."

-Unknown

Prayer: Lord, You have reminded me You are the only, abiding solution to all matters. Help me to quit treating You like an option and cause me to fling myself on You as the only eternal Rock that will never be moved by the world's ever changing tides of false promises and unceasing foolishness. Amen.

♦ Active faith is located between the point of self-denial and the place of obedience. We deny self because of faith, and apply or obey what is right to express our confidence and reliance in God. This is the route that is counted by God as righteousness.

-RJK

For if Abraham were justified by works, he hath whereof to glory; but not before God. For what saith the scripture? Abraham believed God, and it was counted unto him for righteousness (Romans 4:2-3).

♦ Let all your actions spring from the love of Jesus; let him be the Alpha and Omega of all your actions;...but if this principle be wanting, our most pompous services avail nothing; we are only spiritual idolaters; we sacrifice to our own net, and make an idol of ourselves, by making ourselves, and not Christ, the spring of our actions; and therefore, my brethren, such actions are so far from being, accepted by God, that according to the language of one of the articles of our church, "We doubt not but that they have the nature of sin, because they spring not from an experimental faith in, and knowledge of, Jesus Christ."
-George Whitefield
(GW, pg. 289)

♦ Faith only operates freely within the province of the will of God. Outside of that will we may cry, believe, act in faith, and a great deal more, without perceptible result; God is not backing us. Trying to believe along some line of our own, we shall only prove that mountains of faith cannot remove a single mustard seed of difficulty!
-Watchman Nee
(WN, Oct. 4)

♦ In the judgment of faith, God is the grand answer to every question—the grand solution of every difficulty.
-C. H. Mackintosh

♦ The dark night of the soul affords the opportunity to exercise genuine faith.
-RJK

- Pseudo-faith always arranges a way out to serve in case God fails it...For true faith, it is either God or total collapse.

  -A. W. Tozer
  (AG, Oct. 1)

- It seems that when conditions are easy, faith is difficult; when they are more difficult faith becomes easier; and when once they are downright impossible, the faith of stark desperation, having God alone to cling to, at least give promise of that eventual laugh of amazement.

  -Watchman Nee
  (WN, Nov. 1)

- We must be established in our faith. This requires testing and adversity. It will always end in God pruning us back for the purpose of bringing forth fruit that will honor Him.

  -RJK

******

The Opposite of Grace

It has always been my desire to learn the lessons around me that would produce spiritual growth. Jesus used ordinary, everyday matters to teach those following Him the basic principles that should govern their lives.

One of the subjects that fascinates me is that of grace. I greatly appreciate the fact that I was saved by grace through faith. To ensure salvation both virtues must be present. God provides both, but to believe is a choice on my part and grace is what I will receive once I choose the way of faith.

As I think about the order of these two pillars, I realize that grace must come first, because without it faith would never have been made available. Faith is a gift that is given in measure according to the gift of grace that will be received. Jesus stated that you only need a mustard seed of faith to move a mountain, but the truth is without even a speck of faith from above, nothing will change. Therefore, grace offers faith so that the recipient can freely receive what is being offered by God as a precious gift.

However, there is more to grace than being a point of giving undeserved merit to those who are void of any value. Grace must flow like a river. One act of grace will simply flow into another act of grace. If the supply of grace ceased, all promises would dry up and all the gifts would be no more. Obviously, grace is a 24/7 exercise on God's part. Every moment, minute, day, month, and year speaks of grace penetrating every area of our lives.

Every blessing reveals that grace is present to sustain, and its consistent flow brings us that which is necessary for us to live every moment of the day.

The flow of grace into our lives was brought to the forefront by a very special creature. Her name was Angel. She was a Chihuahua, Shih Tzu mix. On November 10, of 2012, she turned 16. She had disc problems in her back, could not see well, and had problems with her teeth. However, she still loved life, but at times it was difficult for her to function.

This put added responsibility on us. Sometimes I had to get up at three or five a.m. to take her outside. No matter how much I tried, she still remained prone to accidents. At times my frustration levels hit their peak. My attitude and reactions made me realize that regardless of what I thought of myself, I am short on patience.

I was not happy when my attitude towards Angel turned foul. She was a special gift from God. For years she made my life joyful, but then when she was in need of great care, she was no longer able to interact with me as before. She was always faithful to us, but I have to admit, on my part it appeared to be one-sided. I was not willing to be faithful to see her through her ordeal when she needed me the most.

Clearly, I did not know where she was physically. She could not communicate with me. My initial action was to try to stay on top of her, but I soon discovered that I tried to fit her into a routine, instead of accepting where she was at the moment. Needless to say, I learned I had to adjust to her for she was the one who was truly at my mercy; therefore, I must always be ready to be an avenue of grace.

As I struggled to make peace with coming to a place of acceptance with where she was, I realized that my attempt to do right by her had miserably failed. Instead of being beneficial to her in her plight and merciful towards her challenges, at times I had displayed impatience and responded in a cruel manner. It was then that I realized the opposite of grace was impatience and that mercy without grace is indeed cruel and bitter.

Admittedly, I had to face the inevitable about my own character. My impatience was a product of utter selfishness. Angel was not fitting into my mode of convenience. She needed more of my attention. As a result, my selfishness was taking center stage. I had convinced myself that everything I was doing was for her, when in reality everything I was trying to do was to maintain my comfort zones. I did not want to be bothered when it was not convenient and I did not want to take the time to understand when my frustration was escalating.

As I considered my impatience, I knew the core of the problem was the matter of "love." We all can be "loving people" when things are going our way. When we feel on top of a matter, we can feel good about our so-called "piousness", but let a matter go against our bow and we will find out just what kind of character we really possess. The revelation will often cause us to display anger at the very source that is being used to reveal the truth about our inner character.

The Lord was using my dog to reveal to me that my selfish bent was still very present. Granted, I stepped over my selfishness in the past, but it can rear its ugly head at any time. I also had to remember that in my humanness I also have my limitations that I needed to recognize. When I am sliding towards frustration because of feeling overwhelmed, I simply need to step back and take time out to get perspective to avoid reacting in an unbecoming way. However, once I stepped over the frustration and gained a proper outlook, I needed to again avail myself to become a conduit in which God's grace could once again flow.

I am thankful that God uses precious gifts in my life to teach me how His many gifts work. Each gift has taught me that I cannot receive any of them unless it is at the point of humility. I have always been aware that Angel depended on me for everything and in turn was completely faithful in her loyalty towards me. Through the years I reminded God that I was not worthy of such trust from her, and that only He could truly oversee her well-being. Clearly, He has used her to remind me how small and inadequate I am even in the smallest matters.

The truth is Angel's trust towards me became an example of the type of confidence I need towards God. However, her reliance on me in her last year has taken on greater dimension, teaching me that the face of grace can only be extended and properly received at the point of great dependency and mercy.

We said goodbye to our sweet Angel on February 8, 2013. I am thankful for the many lessons He has taught me through her about unfeigned faith and, about His perpetual grace that flows from His abiding love.

(**Note:** As Angel's condition worsened, the difficult decision had to be made to take her to the vet to finally be put to rest from all of her suffering. It was a hard day, but also a wondrous day as to how faithful God is. Jeannette had asked the Lord to provide a box for her. A brother in Christ, John Wulff, volunteered to make such a box, but he made it in a coffin form and lined it with some blue, silky material. He also provided the burial place since we did not own our home. We may be Abrahams in this world, but God provides those much-needed places of blessings and rest until we reach our final destination.)

A righteous man regardeth the life of his beast: but the tender mercies of the wicked are cruel (Proverbs 12:10)....That as sin hath reign unto death, even so might grace reign through righteousness unto eternal life by Jesus Christ our Lord (Romans 5:21).

A Matter of the Deeper, Consecrated Life

~

The Tragedy of Modern Christianity

The Christianity of today has no prize that must be gained through loss, no depth in which to delve to discover treasures, no height in which to ascend to gain an heavenly perspective, no personal growth in which to aspire to, no challenge in which to forge character, and no battle in which one is seasoned to endure to the end.

The unrealistic presentation of Christianity is that it is a carefree life where one is going to be constantly blessed. There will be no sorrow brought on by loss. There will be no lamentation brought on by despair, no real challenge brought on by adversity, and no real battle to thwart any advancement in growth or accomplishment. Such a presentation is not only a fantasy, but it is unscriptural.

Confirming the souls of the disciples, and exhorting them to continue in the faith, and that we must through much tribulation enter into the kingdom of God (Acts 14:22).

♦ As Christians we must be willing to pay a price—even if we are never required to do so. This is the lesson of Abraham's life. . .Being willing to sacrifice for our commitment to Christ makes us strong. The idea of sacrifice clarifies our goals. Sacrifice solidifies our character.

-Extreme Devotion
(ED, pg. 13)

♦ We must learn to know God in secret if we would be courageous for Him in public.

-H. A. Ironside
(CBO, Dec. 10)

♦ Nothing less than unconditional surrender could ever be a fitting response to His sacrifice at Calvary. Love so amazing, so divine, could never be satisfied with less than our souls, our lives, our all.

-William MacDonald
(TD, pg.11)

♦ For some years past we have heard but little of a public persecution. Why? Because but little of the power of godliness has prevailed among all denominations.

-George Whitefield
(GW, pg. 205)

Prayer: My Master, lead me to Thy door: pierced this now willing ear once more. Thy bonds are freedom; let me stay with thee to toil, endure, obey.

-H.G.C. Moule

♦ Men take account only of the lily blooming in its weakness. God is concerned with the roots, that they shall be cedar-like in strength.

-Watchman Nee
(WN, Jan. 29)

♦ There are very few unqualified things in our lives, but I believe that the reverential fear of God mixed with love and fascination and astonishment and admiration and devotion is the most enjoyable state and the most purifying emotion the human soul can know.

-A. W. Tozer

♦ Christianity is the only profession in the world in which men remain disciples for life and never become independent workers.

-Richard Wurmbrand
(AWG, pg. 68)

♦ The Bible is a Book of preparation for the service of God. It is not a book simply for thrilling us with happy feelings and bringing us peace and joy; it is a Book of preparation for the service of God. We were saved that we might serve. We were sprinkled with the precious blood of Christ, but we were first bought with it, and we are bond-slaves of our Lord and Saviour Jesus Christ.

-Herbert Lockyer
(MP, pg. 392)

♦ The secret of a holy life is not struggling to live for God, but allowing God to live through us.

-Anna Alden-Tirrill
(SP, Jan. 25)

♦ Our problem is a hearing problem. Our problem is a seeing problem. Our problem is a doing problem. We do not wish to hear, to see, or to do if it entails a denying of self. We want the Saviour of the world to get us into heaven. But we shy away from the Lord of Life when it comes to counting the cost of discipleship.

-Unknown

♦ Ignatius lived during the reign of Emperor Trajan Antioch. He stated, "The life of man is a continual death, unless it be that Christ lives in him." Ignatius lived this reality, by living the consecrated life. After publicly reproving the emperor for worshiping idols, he was arrested and brought to Rome. He knew that true, lasting life, not death lay before him as he was being led away to the pit of lions. Before he was devoured by lions, he told the crowd. "I am the grain of God. I am ground by the teeth of the beast, that I may be found a pure bread of Christ, who is to me the Bread of Life."

Verily, verily, I say unto you, Except a corn of wheat fall into the ground and die, it abideth alone: but if it die, it bringeth forth much fruit (John 12:24).

♦ I believe in saints. I've met the comics; I've met the promoters; I've met the founder who puts his name on the front of the building so people will know he founded it. I've met converted cowboys not too well converted. I have met all kinds of weird Christians throughout the United States and Canada, but my heart is looking for saints. I want to meet the people who are like the Lord Jesus Christ...Actually, what we want and ought to have is the beauty of the Lord our God in human breasts. A winsome, magnetic saint is worth 500 promoters and gadgeteers and religious engineers.

-A. W. Tozer

♦ It costs to know God. We ask Him to bring us higher and He has to go deeper in us with a spade and shovel. We want to reach the mountain peak, but often we must first experience the canyon of uncertainty. We want to do great things for God, but He must first do deep things in us. We want to feel good about our Christian life, but we must first realize how far away from the mark we are before we can taste the real goodness of God to know the beauty of life. We must be broken before we can know fullness, humbled before we can experience His glory, and brought low before we can know the heights of His majesty.

-RJK

Prayer: Lord, I do not always appreciate the tribulation that comes my way, but Your Word assures me that out of such tribulation comes the patience to possess the life You have promised me. Amen.

♦ Labor hard, consume little, give much—and all to Christ.

-Anthony Norris Groves

♦ To receive and follow the gospel call is to reject all that can be seen with the eye and held in the hand in exchange for what cannot be seen. It is to reject personal autonomy and the right to self-government in order to enslave oneself to a Messiah who died two thousand years ago as an enemy of the state and a blasphemer. It is to reject the majority and its views in order to join oneself to a berated and seemingly insignificant minority called the church. It is to risk everything in this one and only life in the belief that this impaled prophet is the Son of God and the Savior of the world. To receive the gospel is not merely to pray a prayer asking Jesus to come into one's heart, but it is to put away the world and embrace the fullness of the claims of Christ.

-Paul Washer

♦ The Christian may lose his savor by laying up treasures on earth, by catering to his own comfort and pleasure, by trying to make a name for himself in the world, by prostituting his life and talents on the unworthy world.

-William MacDonald

♦ The finest jewels are most carefully cut and polished. The hottest fires try the most precious metal.

-Unknown

♦ I have desired the deep things of God, but how deep am I willing to let Him go in my life? I cannot understand the deep things of God until I have been prepared by the deep plows of God. Oh, how deep must He go in the soil of my soul before it is enlarged enough to receive the depths of His wisdom and truth?

-RJK

♦ Dietrich Bonhoeffer became a martyr because he stood for Scriptural truths and principles. He knew in the end that he could stand before the Almighty Judge and not be ashamed of the faith that he clearly displayed in his life towards God. In commenting on his stand, this statement was made in *Extreme Devotion* in regard to those who procrastinate as to when and what stand they will be taking: "Otherwise, we risk the danger of "falling for anything" while we are busy deciding whether or not to stand up for Christ." (ED, pg. 316)

Wherefore take unto you the whole armour of God, that ye may be able to withstand in the evil day, and having done all, to stand (Ephesians 6:13).

♦ This is our desire, but conforming to Christlikeness doesn't always come easy or feel good. However, when it hurts the most, God is actually doing some of His best work in us.

-Anna Alden-Tirrill
(SP, Jul. 17)

♦ For Christianity is not a matter of removing boulders, but of having deeper water!

-Watchman Nee
(WN, Jan. 4)

♦ We shall need to put away our phobias and our prejudices against the deeper life and seek again to be filled with the Holy Spirit.

-A. W. Tozer
(AG, Nov. 20)

♦ A man can love many things, but he can have a passion for only one. Results are achieved only if the man desires one thing exclusively and does not squander his energies simultaneously on a hundred other things...Our passion is the triumph of Christ, the establishment of His kingdom, which necessarily includes the overthrow of everything that opposes it.

-Richard Wurmbrand
(AWG, pg. 43)

******

Becoming A Mountain Climber

Much of the Christian life is learning to climb mountains. However, most of us would like to avoid such mountains. But, we must keep in mind that there is much to see and learn when it comes to mountain climbing. The way up may look long, but it does train our vision as to where we must be looking if we are going to reach the proper goal in our spiritual lives.

There is a precious story about the wife of the famous preacher, G. Campbell Morgan that illustrates this point. Before he became famous, he had been rejected by the Methodist ministry. As a result, there was hesitation on his part in asking his future wife Annie to marry him. He could not offer the life he felt she deserved. However, Annie knew God's hand was upon Morgan. She told him, "If I cannot start with you at the bottom of the ladder, I should be ashamed to meet you at the top." (PCK, pg. 275)

It is natural for people to want to be at the top of the mountain, without first climbing it. They want to sit in places of honor without first learning how to honor others. They want to be recognized by those around them without having to regard them as peers and possibly more worthy of consideration. Such people are always trying to figure out how to climb on top and over others to get to their desired place, without first getting rid of the folly that compels them in their arrogant attempts to reach such underserved heights of exaltation.

But when thou art bidden, go and sit down in the lowest room; that when he that bade thee cometh, he may say unto thee, Friend, go up higher: then shalt thou have worship in the presence of them that sit at meat with thee (Luke 14:10).

******

♦ Holiness is not merely a feeling, state of mind, or good intention. It involves practical separation from sin and real separation unto God.
-Paul Washer

♦ God never takes away anything that He doesn't replace with Himself.
-Jacquelyn K. Heasley

♦ Sanctification is a supreme desire not to want to have your own way.
-Unknown

♦ As Christians we are to hate sin in our own lives, be indifferent to its temptation, reject its cruel ways, show utter contempt towards its destructive ways, shun its prejudices, flee its arrogant attitude, resist its anger, and despise its murderous fruit. In essence, we must never have any part or agreement with the ways of wickedness. As the Bible instructs, we must come out and be separate.
-RJK

♦ Without the offering up of ourselves to God, redemption is a sterile, empty thing.
-Watchman Nee
(WN, Mar. 6)

******

The Struggle

Regardless of how we desire to live the Christian life, it becomes obvious that it is always being birthed in each of us in greater measure through adversity. It is a wrestling match, a battle, and a struggle to ensure that the Christian life becomes firmly establish in who we are becoming.

I recorded one such struggle in my diary. As I read it I realized how such struggles are not unusual. I recognize that this type of struggle is an unseen one that pulls every aspect of the soul into the conflict. No doubt many will relate to the following inner state of affairs that occurred in my life to ensure a greater life is brought forth. Consider the following entry and see if you can relate to the inner battle of the soul.

"The emotional pit I have been in has been dug with such tenacity, for not just months, but years. The spade of opposition has taken great chunks out my resolve, while the shovel of weariness has left me tasting the depths of despair.

"In order to run the race, I would jump out of each hole of despair, only to fall into a ravine of utter distress. I would climb out of the ravine in order to take up the torch to continue my journey, only to fall into a chasm of depression. I would crawl up out of the chasm of depression in an attempt to run the race, only to find myself tripping over the challenging rocks of problems. Each fall would cause me to roll down the slopes of defeat onto the canyon floors of hopelessness.

"It is so easy to be beset by the despair of it all. It is as if I must fling myself against the eternal Rock of heaven in order for my strength to be renewed like the eagle. I realize such strength rises out of the ashes of complete surrender and consecration in order to soar on the heights of blessed assurance."

Prayer: Lord, thank You for taking care of my disappointments, as well as meeting me in my despair. My ways may seem right, but the disappointments of life have taught me that Your ways and timing are perfect and sustaining. Amen.

******

♦ Noah, Daniel, and Job left a legacy of righteousness. Noah overcame the wicked world with faith, Daniel overcame fleshly paganism with an excellent spirit, and Job overcame the temptations of Satan with abiding resolve based on what he knew was true of his God.

-RJK

♦ Never forget that God tests his real friends more severely than his lukewarm ones.

-Kathryn Hulme

♦ There is no room for earthly pomp or worldly glory in the circle of Christ's followers. To seek personal advancement and to endeavor to lord it over one's brethren is thoroughly contrary to the spirit of Him who became a servant of all, though he created the universe.

-H. A. Ironside
(CBO, Nov. 22)

♦ Beloved, the deeper things of God are not lightly gained. We never behold the glories of Christ unless we are prepared to pay the price of entering the door which means for you and me absolute and entire surrender to Him—"The secret of the Lord is with them that fear Him."

-Herbert Lockyer
(MP, pg. 418)

The fear of the LORD is clean, enduring for ever: the judgments of the LORD are true and righteous altogether (Psalm 19:9).

♦ When a man is truly committed to Jesus Christ, it seems to be a matter of no importance to him whether he lives or dies. All that matters is that the Lord be glorified.

-William MacDonald
(TD, pg. 91)

♦ For how is it possible to know you have great faith, humility and love, unless God put you into great trials, that you may know whether you have them or not. I mention this because a great many of the children of God (I am sure it has been a temptation to me many times, when I have been under God's smarting rod), when they have great trials, think God is giving them over. If therefore you are God's children, if you are converted and become as little children, do not expect that God will be like a foolish parent; no, he is a jealous God; he loves his child too well to spare his rod.

-George Whitefield
(GW, pgs. 79, 80)

Prayer: Lord send us great trials.

-George Whitefield

♦ Failure is part of the preparation. We must be brought low in our personal strength and confidence to recognize our need for God.

-RJK

******

The Source of Passion

What does it mean to totally consecrate yourself to something? First, whatever you consecrate yourself to, must be bigger than you are. In fact, you must have a vision concerning it that is so compelling that you can do nothing less than pursue it, regardless of what it costs you. This vision must be inspired by heaven itself because it will take the impossible intervention of God to bring it about.

This type of vision was brought out in the life of a Jew by the name Eliezer Perlman, who was born in Russia in 1858. He was frail and had TB, but a fire was smoldering inside his being. There were those around him that spoke of revolution. He could agree with them to a point, but his idea of where the battle lines had to be drawn differed from those who were his contemporaries.

They were political for those around him, where his vision embraced something that was not only prophetical, but appeared to be impossible. Eliezar wanted the Jewish people to be restored back into their own land. However, he realized for it to happen, the Hebrew language had to be revived. To have a nation there must be a national language that will bind the people together.

Since he had TB, he felt his time was short, but he was willing to pay the necessary price to get the ball rolling. He sensed that he had to lead the way through example. Not only would he have to go to the land of Palestine, if he married he would insist that his wife and children would only speak Hebrew.

The first thing he did was drop the name of Perlman and adopt a Hebrew name. He would become known as Eliezer Ben-Yehuda. True to his vision, upon his marriage, he traveled to Palestine which was under the rule of the Turkish Ottoman. He even dropped his citizenship as a Russian and became a citizen of the land.

Since he had TB, he spent 17 to 19 hours a day to promote his cause. He used the power of the pen to present his vision. He wrote editorials that were put in various papers throughout Europe and later acquired a newspaper in Palestine to advance his vision. He introduced a Hebrew word in each edition to try to encourage the Jews who spoke variations of a mixture of Hebrew words intertwined with the language of the land that they had been raised in.

However, Ben-Yehuda was met with opposition from every side. For Hebrew to be spoken as an ordinary language was considered sacrilege by the religious group. He was labeled a heretic. Eliezer could not promote any Jewish nationalism without getting into trouble with the Turks. In fact, he spent time in a Turkish jail because of an article another person had written for his paper that had a very vague reference that could be taken out of context. His paper license was revoked and a big part of his voice silenced, until all the necessary bribes were made to once again be reinstated as a legitimate paper under his wife's name. He found himself constantly in the midst of conflict. In most cases he was presented as the "bad guy" and not the visionary. He even had to escape one night and migrate to America until the Ottoman power was subdued by Great Britain in 1917. When he returned, he was once again rejected by the people and accused of abandoning them and his cause during a difficult time.

Eliezer took whatever time he had to advance his other project: to prepare a Hebrew dictionary. This frail man spent hours in the different libraries of Europe hunting down Hebrew words to ensure the integrity of the Hebrew language. However, when he encountered the challenge of creating a word for the latest invention, he strove to keep true to the concept of the words already established.

Ben-Yehuda not only was affronted from every side on religious and political fronts, but on a personal front. He lost his first wife and three of their five children. Although, he later married his wife's younger sister who shared his vision, he would lose two other children.

Eliezer proved to be a vehicle of change. Against great odds, a whole new generation was speaking the Hebrew language within a decade. After the Balfour Declaration of 1917, many scrambled to learn the language. After forty years of working towards the Hebrew language becoming the official language of the land, the High Commissioner of Palestine, Sir Herbert Samuel, who was appointed by Great Britain, announced that henceforth there would be three official languages recognized in Palestine: English, Arabic, and Hebrew.

This visionary also had written five volumes of the Hebrew alphabet to compile a Hebrew Dictionary. He had enough material collected to complete the remaining volumes which would end up comprising eleven volumes altogether.

Ben-Yehuda did not appear to be a hero. He was often considered a traitor by those who did not understand his compelling fire. He frequently tried to be a voice of reason, only to find that his words fell on deaf ears.

In 1922, the pen of Eliezer wrote its last ten lines just before his death. The man with a compelling fire could not cause his pen to advance past the ten lines. He knew then he had come to the end of his journey.

Eliezer once stated, "The living are persecuted, but the dead are sanctified!" This proved to be true for him. In his death he was finally recognized as a great man. Upon the announcement of his demise, Palestine was ordered to observe three days of national mourning. Its people wept, knowing a man had died who had all the qualifications of greatness. In a British magazine, a writer wrote this about Ben-Yehuda, "His was one of the rare cases of a life's dream fulfilled; long before he died he saw the ideal for which he had lived, labored, and suffered transformed into a solid reality, a reality which could not be disputed."

Ben-Yehuda's life shows us that consecration is the fire that compels one to focus on the ultimate goal with such singleness that the impossible is brought forth as a sanctified offering that continues on long after one's body has returned to dust.

Where there is no vision, the people perish: but he that keepeth the law, happy is he (Proverbs 29:18).

♦ Change usually comes when it hurts so much that you have to change, when you learn so much that you want to change, and when you receive so much that you welcome change.

-Unknown

♦ Let me be very frank with you. You cannot serve God from a distance. Only by learning to draw near to him can you know what it really is to serve him.

-Watchman Nee
(WN, Dec. 29)

♦ The most deeply taught Christians are generally those who have been brought into the searching fires of deep soul-anguish. If you have been praying to know more of Christ, do not be surprised if He takes you aside into a desert place, or leads you into a furnace of pain.

-Unknown

♦ The problem with people is that they will not move from what is comfortable and what is known. They will not go forward, let alone, go toward or upward to reach beyond what they know. Yet, the Christian life is unknown until it is explored. It is meant to challenge anyone who dares to climb the heights of its promises, explore the length of its incredible hope, and strive to discover the depth of its great wisdom. It is an adventure that is not for the weak in heart, or those who insist on being timid about it. After all, it is a life. It is meant to be explored, discovered, experienced, and possessed.

-RJK

******

The Call to Holiness

God calls every believer to a life that separates him or her from the world. Jerry Bridges writes of this subject in a very eloquent way. He maintains that there are no exceptions to this call. It is not just for those who are in leadership roles or positions in the kingdom of God. This call has gone out to every nation and every believer in every walk of life. Like the cross, it is the great equalizer that is to bring into focus the excellent life we are each being called to walk in and walk out.

The call of holiness is based on the fact that God Himself is holy. It is clear that we are to be holy in the same manner as God. Bridges put forth this statement, "Many Christians have what we call a 'cultural holiness.' They adapt to the character and behavior pattern of Christians around them. As the Christian culture around them is more or less holy, so these Christians are more or less holy. But God has not called us to be like those around us. He has called us to be like Himself. Holiness is nothing less than conformity to the character of God."

But as he which hath called you is holy, so be ye holy in all manner of conversation (1 Peter 1:15).

♦ This (painful thing) happens to me with the permission of God, according to His providence. All tribulation that He sends me He wills only one single thing: my sanctification.

-Woman from 12th Century

♦ Humility is not an ideal: it is the unconscious result of living in right relationship to God, centered in Him.

-Oswald Chambers
(DL, Aug. 8)

♦ Every attempt of man to reach God, every step higher is only a further discovery of the nakedness of the flesh. Every outward amendment as a plea for the mercy of God, is a fresh exposure of the uncleanness and evil of the heart.

-Hebert Lockyer
(MP, pg. 379)

Prayer: Lord, Christianity is not for the fainthearted. Give me a strong heart towards You and a sound mind to clearly see the way set before me by Your Spirit, Word, and examples. Amen.

♦ Today what the altar signifies is not *doing* for God, but *being* for God. He desires not our work but ourselves.

-Watchman Nee
(WN, Apr. 14)

♦ Unless the clay be well pounded, no pitcher can be made.

-Latin Proverb

♦ We must be willing to let go of our own lives and lose all sense of ownership. Only then can we find our true life and accept God's full will for our lives.

-Extreme Devotion
(ED, pg. 304)

I beseech you therefore, brethren, by the mercies of God, that ye present your bodies a living sacrifice, holy, acceptable unto God, which is your reasonable service (Romans 12:1).

♦ Choosing a master will give us a semblance of peace for a season, but choosing the right master will assure us of peace forever.

-RJK

♦ We are partakers of the divine nature, and nothing less than oneness with the Creator can satisfy us.

-Richard Wurmbrand
(AWG, pg. 47)

♦ We need to learn to live life, not from the premise of the goodness of others and how they make us feel about ourselves, but because the goodness of God is reigning in us and we feel satisfied with the life that is present in us.

-RJK

Prayer: Heavenly Father, open the eyes of Your children to the vision that even as Your Son was perfected for evermore, so You are willing to do that same work in each of us. May your equipping work bring glory to Yourself. Amen.

-Andrew Murray

♦ There must be full surrender before there can be full blessedness.
-Frances Ridley Havergal

******

A Matter of Devotion

Consecration entails unfeigned devotion. However, there are four types of devotion displayed by religious people.

The slider: This group is comprised of the people who have an outward show of devotion. However, they eventually become lukewarm when the newness or excitement wears off. Behind the lukewarm show of devotion is someone who is simply trying to slide into heaven. He or she does not really want to run the race.

Religious: There is also a religious devotion. This is where people have a passion for being right. This passion is all wrapped up in their theology. The most devotion these people show is in the criticism of others who do not agree or live up to their religious notions.

Self-serving: There is a self-serving devotion. This is where a person is devoted to his or her personal causes. It is all about how such devotion makes him or her feel about self. These individuals must be recognized, exalted, and honored for them to continue in their loyalty. It is mainly a pride trip. Ultimately, the type of devotion of these individuals must make them feel good about themselves before they can continue on with the same intensity.

Godly devotion: This type of devotion is where the person is truly devoted to God. His or her main desire is to know, love, serve, and please God. These individuals' love for God is enduring, their commitment is to His heart, and they have one cause—Christ crucified. Their whole life and heart is caught up with the reality of the one true God of heaven. This is truly an example of unfeigned consecration towards the Lord.

For I determined not to know any thing among you, save Jesus Christ, and him crucified (1 Corinthians 2:2).

♦ The measure of our devotion to Christ is the measure of our separation from the world.

-C. Stacey Woods

♦ The depths of our spiritual lives remind us that our life in Christ is not meant to be lived out on the rigid, religious plateaus of stagnation and familiarity.

-RJK

******

Nothing between, Lord, nothing between;
Let not earth's din and noise
Stifle Thy still small voice;
In it let me rejoice—
   Nothing between.

Nothing between, Lord, nothing between,
Nothing of earthly care,
Nothing of tear or prayer,
No robe that self may wear—
   Nothing between.

Nothing between, Lord, nothing between;
Till Thine eternal light,
Rising on earth's dark night,
Bursts on my open sight—
   Nothing between.

-Evan Hopkins
(1801-1900)

♦ I caught a glimpse of a wider, larger life, in which mere denominationalism could have no place, and in which there was but one standard by which to measure men, namely their devotion to, and knowledge of, the Son of God.

-F. B. Meyer

♦ This old world of ours has yet to witness how holy the Spirit of God can make a person and what he can do through such a man or woman who is willing to pay the price of utter abandonment to His influences and power...let us hold up our little lives to Him, for if we can't hold much we can overflow a great deal. What He wants is not merely receptacles that only hold His supply, but channels that convey His inexhaustible fullness to others.

-Hebert Lockyer
(MP, pg. 390)

♦ To grow up in Christ means to be consumed in His life and by His life. Our function, walk, and purpose in this present age must be about Jesus, for Him, and because of Him.

-RJK

Prayer: Lord, we thank You that You are our all in all, but we must grow from, grow in line with, and grow up in You if we are going to experience Your complete life. Amen.

♦ Please bear with me when I say that spiritual work is God's work, and when God works, man does not need to expend so much effort that he perspires over it.

-Watchman Nee
(WN, Nov. 3)

♦ The average Christian has a very different standard regarding a life of service to God than that which Scripture gives us. We think about our personal safety—grace to pardon our sin and to secure our entrance into heaven. The Bible's standard is that we surrender ourselves, our time, our thoughts, and our love to God.

-Andrew Murray
(AP, Nov. 15)

♦ It is the mark of deepest and truest humility to see ourselves condemned without cause and to be silent under it. To be silent under insult and wrong is a very noble imitation of our Lord.

-Unknown

♦ Sometimes the greatest darkness of the soul can cause one to become enlightened to the powerful life-changing truths of heaven.

-RJK

******

Desire Great Things?

W. P. Nicholson had a profound experience that brought forth the reality about being dead to the world's different forms of recognition. It happened when he came under the *tutelage of a Salvation Army officer. One day the officer told him, "If you mean business for God, wear this sign-board for a few hours in the center of town." On the board were the words, "DEAD TO PUBLIC OPINION."

And seekest thou great things for thyself? Seek them not... (Jeremiah 45:5).

♦ Our lack of consecration has held back God's blessing from the world. He was ready to save, but we were not willing for the sacrifice of a whole-hearted devotion to Christ and His service.

-Andrew Murray
(AP, Nov. 22)

♦ For something to be sanctified means, that it will not only belong to God, but it will bring Him glory. It will uphold Him in His holiness, speak of His majesty, and manifest His power, love, and commitment.

-RJK

♦ God wants us to be broken in accepting and obeying His will.

-William MacDonald

♦ The Lord is bringing us forth through His Spirit. We are being sanctified unto obedience. We have been begotten unto a living hope by His resurrection. Our faith is clearly alive. Our future has been already set before us. Our hope is sure as it rests upon the One who could not be held back from fulfilling the plan of salvation, even by the grip of death and the silent hopelessness of a grave.

-RJK

♦ Oh that God would give me the thing which I long for! That before I go hence and am no more seen, I may see a people wholly devoted to God, crucified to the world, and the world crucified to them. A people truly given up to God in body, soul and substance! How cheerfully would I then say, "Now lettest Thou Thy servant depart in peace."

-John Wesley

♦ Consecration requires us to offer our complete lives on the altar to ensure we become a sacrifice that will cease to live for self and live unto God.

-RJK

And the very God of peace sanctify you wholly; and I pray God your whole spirit and soul and body be preserved blameless unto the coming of our Lord Jesus Christ (1 Thessalonians 5:23).

Pondering Time

(**Notation:** I noticed in one of my journals a space where I had skipped a couple of pages. I decided to write my thoughts on the blank pages. I called it, *Pondering Time*. Following are my thoughts about blank pages.)

Blank pages are unacceptable. They must be filled with some nuggets or bits of wisdom. After all, God's precious Word has filled pages with eternal treasures from heaven. There is always so much to say about God and His glorious works.

At this time deliverance continues to be my heart's cry, but why? What do I really want to be delivered from: My circumstance, myself, or my process? In many cases I want to be delivered from the process of the fiery tests of faith, the ovens of adversity, and the refining fires of redemption.

The process is God's instrument in my life. How can I dictate to the Sculptor how to use His chisel, direct the hands of the Potter on the wheel, or guide the brush of the great Artist who designed creation? God is the greatest artist of all. No one can improve on His creation, and the truth is most imitations of it fail to capture the real majesty of His creation. Therefore, how could any of us presume to tell our Lord how to define, refine, and purify our lives? Granted, the flesh hates the process and pride mocks and resents it, yet one must submit if he or she is ever going to be conformed to the image of Christ.

In fact, the clay vessel (me) must be broken because of sin, pride, fear, rebellion etc. Upon brokenness the Lord can construct a new vessel, resurrect a blank canvas, and begin to form the very life of Christ in me. It is true without the work of the great Artist, I stand defiled, but the blood of Jesus cleanses me from all unrighteousness, making me a pure canvas and my heart, an untouched altar.

I in them, and thou in me, that they may be made perfect in one; and that the world may know that thou hast sent me, and hast loved them, as thou has loved me (John 17:23).

A Matter of Godly Wisdom And Obedience

~

The Truth About Temptation

Godly wisdom understands the difference in the matter of temptation. God never tempts us to do evil; rather, His temptation comes along the line of obedience that can be counted as righteous because the response must come out of sincere faith. Such a temptation is a test for believers to take the higher road of excellence to ensure the integrity of their faith and testimony, while the other form of temptation justifies taking the base road of the flesh, always justifying some form of rebellion. Clearly, the two types of temptation result in different forms of sin. The temptation that involves evil can lead to the sin of commission where God will be offended, while the sin of disobedience in the testing of our faith is a sin of omission where righteousness was omitted due to unbelief.

Let no man say when he is tempted, I am tempted of God: for God cannot be tempted with evil, neither tempteth he any man (James 1:13).

♦ It is obvious we have much lifeless and dangerous knowledge floating around, but there is only life in revelation inspired by the Spirit that parts our limited understanding with a heavenly reality that will forever change our perspective about God.

-RJK

♦ "Right or wrong" is the principle of the Gentiles and tax gatherers. Not that, but conformity to him, must govern my life.

-Watchman Nee
(WN, Mar. 22)

♦ We have learned that suffering is not the worst thing in the world— disobedience to God is the worst.

-Vietnamese Christian Pastor
Imprisoned for His faith

Prayer: Lord, we know that contrary winds will come our way if we are obeying You, but help us to be resolved to trust You instead of looking at the waves of circumstances that are coming at us. Amen.

♦ The Dead Sea justly earned its name by constant input without corresponding outflow. In our lives, information without application leads to stagnation.

-William MacDonald

♦ Some Christians sit, soak, and sour.

-Pastor Rob Greenslade

♦ Where God and man are in relationship, this must be the ideal. God must be the communicator, and man must be in the listening, obeying attitude.

-A.W. Tozer
(AG, Feb. 10)

♦ Even a rock is smarter than an atheist or an evolutionist according to Luke 19:40.

-Jeannette Haley

And he answered and said unto them, I tell you that, if these should hold their peace, the stones would immediately cry out (Luke 19:40).

♦ We never receive a complete knowledge through mere research, with our minds. Knowledge of God comes through our hearts—the windows of our soul.

-Oswald Chambers
(DL, Feb. 12)

♦ Heavenly wisdom and active faith finds their springboard in the fear of the Lord.

-RJK

♦ Passion does not compensate for ignorance.

-Warren W. Wiersbe
(PCK, pg. 249)

Prayer: Lord, You have given me many opportunities to learn from the teacher of hindsight in order to show discretion in relationship to foresight. This is the way of Your wisdom. Lord, help me to embrace the lessons of the past, to change the terrain of the present in order to wisely face the future. Amen.

♦ It is better for things to go in one ear and out the other than to go in one ear, get all mixed up and slip out the mouth.

-Church Newsletter

♦ The supreme difference between the teaching of the Bible and the teaching of modern thought is this—the teaching of the Bible is an infinite God and an infinitesimal man, except as God's goodness makes him great. The teaching of modern literature and modern thought is—an infinite man and an infinitesimal god. We live in a day that has a very great man and a very small god.

-R. A. Torrey
(RA, pg. 12)

♦ The lesson is clear. People have a tendency to obey the Lord only as long as it suits them. When it no longer suits them, they can always think up excuses for doing whatever they want.

-William MacDonald
(ODT, Sept. 14)

♦ God's curriculum for all who sincerely want to know Him and do His will always includes lessons we wish we could skip. With intimate understanding of our deepest needs and individual capacities, He chooses our curriculum.

-Elisabeth Elliot

******

It Is Not A Mystery
After All

How many of us desire the wisdom from above? In our limited understanding, we think that God's wisdom is too great to grasp. It is true that some matters surrounding God are hidden, but what we need to know has been recorded in black and white. It can be found in the Word of God. Even though His Word can seem overwhelming to us, and those who know it can impress us with insights, the reality is we can possess such wisdom if we care to open and dig into God's treasure chest.

The Bible contains simple truths and all the answers to life's questions and problems. Granted, it contains profound insight, but such insight can be grasped by a child. The problem is that we complicate or even confuse ourselves with what the Bible says because we approach it from an intellectual stance as a means to come out "intelligent" about it. In some cases, we want to develop formulas and methods that work the same in each unpredictable situation so we do not have to walk by faith. Or, we are looking for something spiritual in that which is practical.

This was brought out by humorous story. There was a Sunday School teacher who needed some supplies from the cupboard which was seldom used, but clearly secured with a combination lock. The teacher did not know the combination, but the clergyman offered to give it a try. He placed his fingers on the lock's dial and raised his eyes heavenward for a moment. Then he confidently spun the dial and opened the lock. Seeing how impressed she was with this demonstration of faith, he smiled and confided, "The numbers are written on the ceiling."

The moral of the story for believers is that the answers of the ages are written in the Bible.

That the God of our Lord Jesus Christ, the Father of glory, may give unto you the spirit of wisdom and revelation in the knowledge of him: The eyes of your understanding being enlightened; that ye may know what is the hope of his calling, and what the riches of the glory of his inheritance in the saints (Ephesians 1:17-18).

♦ The wisdom of this world is utterly opposed to the wisdom of Heaven which is presented in all perfection in the Lord Jesus Christ. Human philosophies center in self. The wisdom that comes from above centers in God as revealed in His Son.

-H. A. Ironside
(CBO, Dec. 8)

♦ Knowledge without the right Spirit is lifeless, knowledge that is never tested will lack authority and credibility, and knowledge that is not walked out will be void of wisdom, ultimately proving to be foolish and useless.

-RJK

♦ The world is full of people who hate to think, and because they hate to think they go into things blindfolded, and come out with blighted hope and broken hearts and blasted lives.

-R. A. Torrey
(RA, pg. 145)

♦ Our Lord's first obedience was to the will of His Father, not to the needs of men; the saving of men was the natural outcome of His obedience to the Father.

-Oswald Chambers

♦ If God is to move among His people, man must not be an observer, but a humble participant in His work.

-RJK

♦ The path of obedience is the path of blessing . . . Disobedience always results in sorrow and disappointment.

-H. A. Ironside
(CBO, Mar. 16)

♦ Unquestioning obedience is essential if we would know God's will and God's ways. Is our faith the cheap, easy kind that pays no price? Or are we prepared to have it founded on the truth of God, however great to us the cost of coming by that truth?

-Watchman Nee
(WN, May 16)

♦ Wisdom may ensure that you make sound judgments, but righteousness ensures that you keep on the right path.

-RJK

Prayer: Dear Lord, there is success in Your ways, victory in Your strength, and confidence in Your wisdom. Thank You for being our all in all. Amen.

♦ The journey of a thousand miles begins with a first step.

-Lao-tze

******

Think it not strange, then, pilgrim,
    neither faint,
Much less indulge in murmuring and
    complaint,
If what you meet with in your heavenly
    road
Is hard to bear; since all is planned by
    God,
His child to train in wisdom's holy ways,
And form a chosen vessel for His praise.
Now we are slow those ways to
    understand;
But let us bow beneath His mighty hand,
Sure that His wisdom over all presides,
His power controls and love unerring
    guides.

-J. G. Deck
(1802-1884)

♦ Nowadays, common sense is an endangered species.

Sydney Hunnington
Alaska Native leader

Prayer: Lord, I do desire the understanding of heaven. After all, it will serve as my light as I walk through this world. Amen.

♦ No other class of people will drive the Christian closer to God than the stupid. They will tax every bit of patience and endurance you have. These dear people always pretend to want to do something for God. Yet they are "ever learning and never able to come to a knowledge of the truth." Why? Because they do not wish to obey the Word of God they have heard!

-Oswald Chambers
(DL, Oct. 17)

♦ Heavenly wisdom may be ancient, but it will never become obsolete, useless, or outdated.

-RJK

******

Higher Criticism

Christians in every age and generation must contend with attacks from the counterfeits that are erected by the god of this world: Satan. Counterfeits are just repackaged lies of Satan that are designed to appeal to that particular generation. A good example of such attacks is "higher criticism." Higher criticism became an effective affront against scriptural truths in the 1800s. One of the preachers who took it head on was C. H. Spurgeon. He preached strongly against it and as a result he became a hot potato in the hands of other Christian leaders who did not see the dangers of mixing this heretical philosophy with the true faith that was first delivered to the saints.

The question is what is higher criticism? This is the definition that author Robert L. Peterson gave of it, "Higher criticism is the philosophy that starts from the following assumptions: The Bible is not the inspired Word of God, but a collection of stories designed to illustrate certain truths; many Biblical characters never existed; and many events described in the Bible never happened."

Today higher criticism is alive and well. It is no longer a hidden, cancerous seed that was subtly taking minds captive during the days of Spurgeon, but it is the reality that is being advocated by many who stand behind the pulpit. Clearly, the authority and power of the Word of God has been systematically stripped in the minds of many churchgoers by this intellectual quagmire of speculation, false accusations, and lies.

153

As a result of higher criticism, many religious people's conception is that we have a tolerant God, an ineffective Bible, a weak gospel, and we must adopt a worldly, political correct religious presentation of spiritual matters. To these deluded souls, there is no real truth and everything has become relative where the Bible is concerned. Today the call from many pulpits is not in regards to genuine faith towards the one, true God of the Bible; rather, it is a call to take up the mantle of social justice to ensure the false promise of collective salvation.

Robert Chapman constructed this allegory in relationship to higher criticism to show its inferior, dangerous side to the real faith that was clearly outlined in the Word of God. "One day, while walking in the noon-day light of a mid-summer sun, beneath a cloudless sky, I was accosted by a person wholly a stranger to me, who, with kind, condescending air, made offer to show me the way. I saw in his hand a lantern, and in it a lighted (penny) candle. Pity checked my rising laughter; so as gravely as I could, I declined his offer, and went on my way. I was afterwards told that his name was Higher Criticism." (RC, pg. 167)

Beloved, when I gave all diligence to write unto you of the common salvation, it was needful for me to write unto you, and exhort you that ye should earnestly contend for the faith which was once delivered unto the saints (Jude 3).

♦ How much richer we would be if we would refuse the books of the hour and discover again the books of the ages.

-Warren W. Wiersbe
(PCK, pg. 84)

♦ The Cross of Jesus Christ calls us to pattern our lives after the example of Jesus. There is no sanctified life that is not crucified, or dead, to the lure of this present age. We are not saved and sanctified to see our Lord glorified in our way of thinking, but for God to take us victoriously along the pathway of obedience with Him. The characteristic of the sanctified life is obedience.

-Oswald Chambers
(DL, Apr. 1)

♦ If human edicts be positively opposed to the expressed will of God, the Christian is to obey God rather than man.

-H. A. Ironside
(CBO, Jul. 9)

Then Peter and the other apostles answered and said, We ought to obey God rather than men (Acts 5:29).

♦ We clean up our spiritual lives through repentance and confession. We make sure that everything is in order through obedience. We are assured of being pleased with the outcome because of humility, and we will always be ready to meet with the Lord as long as we submit to Him in meekness.

-RJK

♦ If we are trying through systematic theology to know God, we are absolutely on the wrong road.

-Watchman Nee
(WN, Aug. 22)

Prayer: Lord, we must be a doer of Your Word, not just one who admires it or quotes it. Lord, give me a fervent love for Your Word that will compel me to assimilate it through obedience. Amen.

♦ Our enemy is more aware than we are of the spiritual possibilities that depend upon obedience.

-Amy Carmichael

♦ An holy obedience to God's will, which is treading in Christ's steps, will be attended with sufferings; and the more you and I labor to live near the Lord Jesus, the more desperate will Satan, sin, death, the world, our old man, and hypocrites be against us continually.

-John Rusk

♦ God will not reveal more truth to us or more of His will until we obey the truth He has already given us.

-Anna Alden-Tirrill
(SP, Mar. 9)

♦ We want to benefit from the deep things of God without first launching out into the deep where such treasures can be located and brought forth through faith and obedience.

-RJK

******

Dealing with the Clutter

So many people's lives are cluttered with things. The more things a person surrounds oneself with, the more confusing life can become. Obviously, excess clutter is not just a problem in the physical realm; it can also be a spiritual problem.

Our lives can become cluttered with besetting sins, irritating ways, unhealthy attitudes, and unbecoming ways. Once in awhile, we need to clear the air with God. Taking care of the spiritual clutter in our lives is a point of godly wisdom. It is obvious that worldly and fleshly clutter gets between the Lord and us. Whether it is sins, demands from the world, the enticement of the world, or just self-centeredness, it proves to be unbecoming. Ultimately, we lose sight of what is important: we lose sight of God. As a result, I need to schedule house cleaning in my spiritual life. I need to make sure those unacceptable spiritual hindrances are humbly dealt with.

The question is how do we, as Christians, clear the air between God and us? Repentance is the main wind that must blow out the various spiritual wastes in our lives. However, repentance involves coming to a place of humility that enables the person to humble self. The place of humility entails submitting to God's ways, in order to draw near to Him about a matter.

It is His perspective about our ways and actions that will break us, not our guilt or frustration about it. After our focus has been changed by repentance that is born out of true brokenness before the Lord, then our direction will change as well. This is when much of the clutter of our lives will either be put off or left behind.

I tell you, Nay: but, except ye repent, ye shall all likewise perish (Luke 13:3).

******

♦ The wisdom of God gloriously displays itself, in causing the designs of the wicked, like a surcharged gun, to recoil upon and destroy themselves. It often falls out with the undermining enemies of the church, as it sometimes doth with them that dig deep mines in the earth, who are destroyed and buried in their own work.

-John Flavel
(RR, pg. 96)

♦ Ignorance is the only platform in which arrogance can operate in delusion.

-RJK

♦ Peace is the deliberate adjustment of my life to the will of God.

-Unknown

♦ The reader of God's Word often encounters examples of gross stupidity. Note that *stupidity* is not the same as *ignorance:* A stupid act is anything done without reason or judgment, while an ignorant act is something done without knowledge.

-Oswald Chambers
(DL, Oct. 15)

And the times of this ignorance God winked at; but now commandeth all men every where to repent (Acts 17:30).

♦ How many of you are guiding your life based on principles, commands, and laws, and statements of wisdom that Jesus has given? How many Christians do you actually know that are living that way? "Depart from Me, those of you who said, 'Lord Lord,' and considered yourselves to be My disciples, but you lived as though I never gave you a law to obey." [Matt. 7:23]

-Paul Washer

♦ The wisdom from above will always remind me of my need for God's constant intervention. I need to know that His wise hand is upon all situations. My prayer is that I will feel its firmness when I start to go my own way, know its gentleness when I need comfort, its pressure when I need to move, its restraint when I need to stop, and its protection when the darkness enfolds me.

-RJK

♦ But God demands both inward and outward purity. To have the outer without the inner is spiritual death, but to have the inner without the outer is only spiritualized life.

-Watchman Nee
(WN, Dec. 2)

♦ Abiding in loving obedience is the gateway through which we receive God's gifts and blessings. God's gifts are wrapped and sealed until opened by obedience. There is no end to the possibilities that open to us through obedience.

-Anna Alden-Tirrill
(SP, Mar. 5)

157

♦ It has been well said that we may have revival in any place, at any time, when willing to pay the price. There will always be blessing when the people of God return to obedience to the written Word. It is appalling how far the professing Church has drifted in many instances from that which God has revealed as His holy will, in the Bible.

-H. A. Ironside
(CBO, Mar. 18)

♦ Christianity is a life that must be established in holiness, maintained in righteousness, and manifested in godliness. It is a life that must be worked in us through childlike faith and worked out by us in daily obedience to His Word and practice of His ways.

-RJK

Prayer: Lord, so many times You are waiting outside of the profane camps of the world and self. We need to come outside of it all to experience Your presence. Amen.

The Valley of Decision

People often stand between two opinions *(1 Kings 18:21)*. They often perceive that the middle ground is the safest place there is, when in reality it is the most dangerous ground. Such thinking will always prove to be foolishness. The reason people refuse to choose is because their preference is for the irrational ways of destruction.

It is in the state of indecisiveness that the Lord will spit a person out because he or she is spiritually lukewarm towards Him *(Revelation 3:14-19)*. Instead of displaying godly wisdom, such people are displaying worldly logic. Such individuals have failed to recognize no decision is a decision.

The people of Elijah's day had an altar for God, but it was neglected and lay in ruin. Their attitude clearly revealed that they were choosing and preferring their idols to Jehovah God. They were prostituting themselves with these silent, powerless, and lifeless idols while giving some sick semblance of maintaining their identification with their Creator and Maker.

Elijah asked the people how long would they insist on their ridiculous front. They needed to choose. The main reason people avoid choosing is because they know they will have to pay some type of price. If they choose the God of heaven and earth, they will have to pay the price of their association with the world, but if they choose the world, they will have to pay the price of their soul *(Matthew 16:26)*. The prophet Joel best described this place as the valley of decision *(Joel 3:14)*.

What do my decisions say about my life in Christ?

Prayer: Lord, every soul will prove to be a test to my virtue, and every soul will be tested with the truth. You are always bringing us to the valley of decision to decide what we are going to do with You and Your Word. We will either believe or we will go the way of unbelief. I choose to believe. Amen.

A Matter of Sacrifice
And Suffering

~

The Way of Sacrifice

Jesus left us an example of suffering that we are to follow. Suffering points to some type of loss, wounding, or sacrifice. In the case of Jesus He suffered from the five wounds that can happen to the body. They are penetration, laceration, cutting, puncture, and piercing. When they put the crown of thorns on His head, they penetrated the skin, causing a head wound. When they used the cat-of-nine-tails on Him, they lacerated His skin, as well as cut deep into His body. When they put the nails through His hands and feet, they punctured His flesh. And, when the soldier thrust his spear into Jesus' side, He was pierced. The Bible is clear that Jesus was wounded for our transgressions and bruised for our iniquities.

Jesus also suffered emotionally. He felt the bitterness of betrayal, the despair of rejection, the fear of failure, and the hopelessness of injustice. He felt it all, tasted it all, and experienced the depths and death of it. However, He knew that on the other side of the lifeless grave the power of resurrection would lift Him into newness of life.

In the Apostle Paul's second epistle to Timothy, he made this statement, "Yea, and all that will live godly in Christ Jesus shall suffer persecution." I have stated that there are three fires that will purge Christians. The first one is the Word, the second is the Holy Spirit, and the third is persecution.

Jesus told His church that persecution would come, but rejoice for it is a point of identification and a tool of becoming a living martyr for His sake. As Jesus proclaimed, persecution has earmarked the church, refining and purifying it.

In a Zion magazine article in the September/October issue of 2012 by David Ettinger, he summarized the persecution the Church has received for the last 2000 years. Under the Roman Empire, Christians suffered persecution for 129 years, but did experience some peace such as between A.D. 64 and 313. It was estimated that those martyred under Roman control is estimated to be from 25,000 to 100,000. However, 72 million Christians have been martyred for their faith since the birth of Christ. Shocking enough, 48 million or 67 percent, have been offered on the different altars of the world since 1900. From the middle of 2008 to the middle of 2009, about 179,000

Christians were martyred. This averages out to 482 deaths per day—one every three minutes.

We are entering a time when it has been prophesied that many believers will experience persecution and death. Therefore, the first two decades of the 21st century may prove to be more devastating than the whole of the 20th century.

Surely he hath borne our griefs, and carried our sorrows: yet we did esteem him stricken, smitten of God, and afflicted (Isaiah 53:4).

♦ This was the supreme reason why Christ was continually teaching His own about the Cross. By principle, and by precept and by parable, Christ taught the Cross. Somebody has said, "God often touches our best comforts that we may live loose to them."

-L. E. Maxwell

♦ Persecution is often the final battleground in the fight between natural instinct and spiritual conviction.

-Extreme Devotion
(ED, pg. 39)

♦ Men do not die for what they know is a lie.

-Paul Little

♦ If we are not prepared to suffer for Christ—perhaps even unto death, if necessary—in that coming day, we are not ready to live for Christ triumphantly today.

-Marvin Rosenthal

♦ Jesus said that we should go. He never said we would come back.

-Unknown

♦ Calvary was a place of no esteem. The cross has no attractiveness for the eye and He who hung on it had "no beauty that we should desire him."

-Hebert Lockyer

As many were astonied at thee; his visage was so marred more than any man, and his form more than the sons of men (Isaiah 52:14).

♦ Our redemption was not by muscle, but by love. It was not wrought by vengeance, but by forgiveness. It was not by sword, but by sacrifice.

-A. W. Tozer
(AG, Aug. 23)

♦ I must wrestle with each challenge, confront each hindrance, endure each test, seek the right passageway around each obstacle, climb up the trail of each mountain, and finish the course that is before me. However, in the process of the struggle, my soul can become marred and weary, my spirit can experience a wounding that comes from the hopeless blanket of despair, my heart can be broken by failure, and my body riddled with weakness and uncertainty as my strength ebbs from me. At this point, I must choose to remember my solution. The Lord is the only One who can guide and heal me.

-RJK

♦ In the midst of suffering, the word sounds with deeper, truer significance: "if any man will come after me, let him deny himself, and take up his cross, and follow me" (*Matt. 16:24*). The true disciple learns the meaning of "follow me" in the hour when the dilemma perplexes him, the billows overwhelm him, and the noise of God's water spouts deafen him.

-Oswald Chambers
(DL, Aug. 14)

♦ The witness of Scripture and of experience testified that no one who lives sacrificially for Christ will ever suffer want. When a man obeys God, the Lord takes care of him.

-William MacDonald

♦ I am afraid that all the grace I have got out of my comfortable and easy times and happy hours might almost lie on a penny. But the good I have received from sorrows and pains and griefs is altogether incalculable. What do I not owe to the hammer and the file? Affliction is the best bit of furniture in my house.

-Charles Spurgeon

The Spirit itself beareth witness with our spirit, that we are the children of God: And if children, then heirs; heirs of God, and joint-heirs with Christ; if so be that we suffer with him, that we may be also glorified together (Romans 8:16-17).

♦ Those who suffer for Christ must have the ability to see the bigger picture.
-Extreme Devotion
(ED, pg. 300)

♦ Suffering will be found to be the best preferment, when we are called to give an account of our ministry at the great day.
-George Whitefield
(GW, pg. 212)

♦ There is so much adversity, but if you find God's will in a matter, the warmth of His love and the gentleness of His Spirit will reach into the very depth of your soul. The glorious revelation of His warmth and caring ways in the midst of temptation and uncertainty can warm the heart, still the spirit, and calm the soul.

-RJK

Prayer: Lord, there are always troublemakers, but through the years You have used them to make my faith more precious and my love for You more sure. I never thought I would say this, but thank You for the troubled waters stirred up by the troublemakers. Amen.

******

There must be thorns amid life's flowers, you know,
And you and I, wherever we may go,
Can find no bliss that is not mixed with pain,
No path without a cloud. It would be vain
For me to wish that not a single tear
Might dim the gladness that you hold so dear.
I am not wise enough to understand
All that is best for you. The Master hand
Must sometimes touch life's saddest chords to reach
Its sweetest music, and His child to teach
To trust His love, till the long, weeping night
Is all forgotten in the morning light.
Trust, trust Him, then, and thus shall good or ill
Your trustful soul with present blessing fill.
Each loss is truest gain if, day by day,
He fills the place of all He takes away.

-Message, Ballarat

♦ Are there sorrows that sorely test your heart? Be assured your Father intends each to be a road for you to Christ, so that you may reach Him and know Him in some character of His love and power, that otherwise your soul had not known.

-Unknown

♦ A message that sees in the cross simply a martyr's death is not the gospel.

-H. A. Ironside
(CBO, Oct. 3)

♦ A martyr is, he who has become the instrument of God, who has lost his will in the will of God, not lost it but found it, for he has found freedom in submission to God. The martyr no longer desires anything for himself, not even the glory of martyrdom.

-T. S. Elliot

♦ The way of the transgressor is hard. However, it always amazes me that in our foolishness we shy away from, flee, or reject the hard, narrow way of the cross. Granted, the way of the cross is not pleasant to the flesh. It serves as repudiation to all selfishness, and is a complete affront against our pride, but it rids us of those things that make life hard for us in relationship with our Lord and Savior.

-RJK

******

Those Who Have Gone Before Us

Hebrews 6:12 tells us, *"That ye be not slothful, but followers of them who through faith and patience inherit the promises."* As Christians we have a great cloud of witnesses who have traveled the narrow way before us. The fact that they finished the course in spite of the various obstacles they encountered along the way proves we can also finish the course. They have indeed left us an example of what active faith enables us to do in regard to the kingdom of God.

In the devotional book, *Extreme Devotion,* there are many stories of those martyrs that have gone before us, some which are being summarized in this writing. Even though there are names we are acquainted with, the book gives details or legends that have followed these individuals' martyrdom. In the devotion, it is pointed out that the word, "martyr" means "confessor." To be a martyr signifies being a "witness" of one's faith. A martyr's weapon of choice is his or her confession of his or her faith. The idea of martyrdom also points to those who are the walking dead. In other words, they are always walking towards their demise.

We know that many believers entered through the door of death through grave persecution. Those who led the way were the first disciples. We know that Peter was crucified upside down for his faith. He was seventy years old. However, you might not be aware that he was urged by fellow believers to flee Rome before his demise. As he approached the gate, he saw a vision of Jesus. The Lord was walking into the city. Peter fell to his knees to worship Him. He then asked Jesus where He was going.

The Lord's answer was, "I have come again to be crucified. Follow me." Peter followed the Lord to his own personal cross, his own martyrdom.

We know that the Apostle John was the only disciple of Jesus to die of old age, but he suffered much. Before he received "Revelation" historical sources say that he had been put into a pot of boiling oil.. During his whole ordeal, he preached. When they could not kill him by boiling him to death, they poisoned him, but that did not affect him. It is hard to say why some people are delivered from persecution and others are delivered through it by way of the door of physical death, but the Lord knows what He is doing. As George Whitefield declared, "we are immortal until our work for the Lord is finished."

Before James was beheaded for his faith by King Herod's soldier, he had witnessed to the guard. It is said that before he knelt to be thrust into glory by the guard he had witnessed to, as the guard lifted the sword up to bring it down, it shook with uncertainty. The guard then hurled it to the ground beside James, and declared he could not carry out the execution. That day James and the guard both kneeled before the sword so they could together receive their crown of righteousness.

Andrew embraced his cross with great joy. He declared that if he had feared the death of the cross, he would have never preached the majesty and glory of the cross of Christ. His proclamation as he looked upon it was, "O beloved cross! I rejoice to see you erected here. I come to you with a peaceful conscience and with cheerfulness, desiring that I, who am a disciple of him who hung in the cross, may be crucified. The nearer I come to the cross, the nearer I come to God."

Andrew used the cross to preach the timeless message of redemption and hope. The old rugged instrument served as his blessed pulpit for three days before he gave up his spirit to receive his crown.

Bartholomew angered the king of Armenian, the capital of Albania, when he refused to sacrifice to false gods. He had already made an impact with the message of the cross in the area. He was accused of perverting the people, but he declared that he had converted them to the truth. The king ordered Bartholomew to be beaten with rods and tortured. However, the disciple of Jesus would not recant, while urging others to hold to the truth. He was then hung upside down on a cross and flayed alive with knives. However, he would not budge from his stand. Finally, his head was cut off, but his witness and example remained alive for others to follow.

We know that at the age of 64, the Apostle Paul was beheaded by the order of Emperor Nero, but I did not know that Timothy who followed in his footsteps was stoned to death around A.D. 98.

There were other noted Christians of the early Church that left a powerful witness that remains today as a token, a beacon of light to those who follow. It was during the reign of Roman emperor Marcus Aurelius Antoninus (A. D.

161-170) that Christians kept records of their sufferings to encourage other believers. Their records included the events that surrounded a believer named Blandina.

She was hung on a post but her example encouraged others. She was then put into the arena with lions, but it only served to encourage a fifteen-year-old believer to stand fast in the face of death. In fact, she was thrown before starving lions twice, but they did not touch her. Eventually, she was torn by lions, put into a net and tossed about by a wild bull, and placed naked into a red-hot metal chair, yet she lived to encourage others. Finally, she was killed with a sword after her torturers could not make her deny her faith.

It was the year A.D. 165. A believer name Carpus was nailed to the stake. He praised the Lord for allowing him to be a martyr as the flames consumed his body, serving as an incredible witness to those in the crowd.

His example reached one such woman by the name of Agathonica. As Carpus had prayed, she saw the glory of God roll out before him. The heavens had literally opened up to reveal the glorious table of the wedding feast of the Lamb of God. She recognized the call to come to the wedding feast. She jumped to her feet and declared that she too must receive the meal of glory. She threw off her outer robe and jubilantly allowed herself to be nailed to the stake. In the flames, she cried, "Lord, Lord, Lord, help me, for I flee unto thee." She gave up her soul and joined her Lord in glory.

Yea, and all that will live godly in Christ Jesus shall suffer persecution (2 Timothy 3:12).

♦ To conclude, manage all your sufferings for Christ which Christian meekness. As righteousness must bring you into them, so meekness must carry you through them. If you avenge yourselves you take the cause out of God's hand into your own; but the meek Christian leaves it to the Lord, and shall never have cause to repent of his so doing.

-John Flavel
(RR, pg. 225)

♦ If you in heart are after the Lord Jesus, you must expect losses and crosses all your days.

-John Rusk

♦ I've come to believe that God , in his wisdom allows martyrdom in every generation in part because, without them, the reality of Christ's death for us becomes increasingly blurry....As we look at (the martyrs), the mist that sometimes enshrouds first-century Golgotha is burned away, and we see....the Lord nailed to the cross.

-Mark Galli

♦ Afflictions and adversity are meant to, not only *prove us*, but also to *improve us*.

-Anna Alden-Tirrill
(SP, pg. 296)

******

God writes in characters too grand
For our short sight to understand;
We catch but broken strokes, and try
To fathom all the mystery
Of withered hopes, of death, of life,
The endless war, the useless strife,
But there, with larger, clearer sight,
We shall see this—His way was right.

-John Oxenham
(1852-1941)

♦ The persecution of Christians is not about human rights, it is a rite of passage.

-Steve Cleary

♦ Sacrifice and suffering will come with the Christian life. The narrow way will cause opposition and murmuring, suffering will cause many to slip into the shadows of obscurity, persecution will cause some to flee the battle, and harsh elements will cause others to turn back to the comforts of their former life.

-RJK

Prayer: Lord, I choose to glory in Your cross and embrace my personal cross. It may represent the hard way, but in the end it will prove to be the liberating way. Amen.

♦ Just as His own Cross was the supreme expression of his own perfect obedience, tried to the utmost, so must Jesus bring each disciple, through an awful process of inner crucifixion, to the end of his own self-will, and bring him to the will of God. As we have said before, Christ did not come to straighten out the natural, but "cross" it out.

-E. A Johnston
(NTB, pg. 25)

For ye know the grace of our lord Jesus Christ, that though he was rich, yet for your sakes he became poor, that ye through his poverty might be rich (2 Corinthians 8:9).

♦ Christ became poor. His poverty began at the incarnation and ended at the cross whereby we are made rich. The sacrifice of this poor man becomes the poor man's sacrifice.

-Herbert Lockyer

♦ If [following Jesus Christ] doesn't cost you anything, it's because you've bought into "American Christianity."

-Paul Washer

******

The Principle

It is hard to believe that justice will eventually come when it seems like the wicked get away with unspeakable atrocities when it comes to the righteous, the poor, and the oppressed. However, the Bible is clear that people reap what they sow. It may not be obvious up front, but history eventually tells the real story of what happens to such individuals. The wicked not only are judged in like manner, but they often fall into the very pits they have dug for others and begin to reap the consequences. There is one such story that brings out this principle.

The officer was now asking Sister Wong to pray for his sister for she was very ill. This was the same man who had confiscated hundreds of Bibles and Christian books, as well as questioned and abused her days earlier. It was when he was questioning Sister Wong that he received a phone call that his mother had been hit by a car. When he admitted to his mother what he had been doing at the time of her accident, she told him his actions brought on her accident. However, he chalked up such a conclusion to superstition.

The next day he resumed questioning Sister Wong. This time he received word his brother had been injured in an accident. This accident was also blamed on the officer's attacks on Christians. It was when his sister became sick that he had to concede that his actions towards Christians were resulting in consequences.

He now humbly asked Sister Wong to pray for his sister. Not only did Sister Wong testify to her persecutor, but her fervent prayer for his sister resulted in her healing. The officer's heart was changed and he returned all the Bibles that were confiscated, but he also started supporting the church. (ED, pg. 5)

When we consider the divine judgment upon the Roman Emperors with others in high places who zealously and bitterly persecuted the early Christians, they also should serve as a warning and indictment to leaders today who are foolish enough to think they can get away with cruel and indifferent wickedness directed at the righteous and the less fortunate. Consider their fate: One became blind, one ended up deranged, while one was slain by his own son, another drowned, the eyes of one started out of his head, one was strangled, one died in a miserable captivity, one fell dead in a manner that will not bear recital, one died of a disease that several of his physicians were put to death because they could not abide the stench that filled the room, two committed suicide, a third attempted it, but had to call for help to finish the work, five were assassinated by their own people or servants, five others died the most miserable and excruciating deaths, several of them having an untold complication of diseases, eight were killed in battle, or after being taken prisoner. (DP, pg. 19-20)

History also shows that nine months after the death of the queen Marie Antoinette by the guillotine, every one who was part of her untimely end from her accusers to the judges, the jury, the prosecutors, and witnesses perished by the same instrument. (DP, pg. 38)

In the 1700's there was much persecution going on against the preachers during the great revival. There was one incident where a writer presented the great preacher, George Whitefield in a despicable way in a publication called *The Minor*. A few years after his article, the writer was charged with a great crime, of which he was not guilty of, and died a broken-hearted and beggared man. Eventually we do reap what we sow. (PGR, pgs. 125, 126)

People do reap according to their judgments and actions against others, and as the great, just Judge, God is able to wield vengeance in such a way that it will address and meet the wicked deeds. I perceive that Psalm 9:20 addresses the wicked attitude of despots in a most proper way, "Put them in fear, O LORD; that the nations may know themselves *to be but men*. Shelah." (Emphasis added.)

Be not deceived; God is not mocked: for whatsoever a man soweth, that shall he also reap (Galatians 6:7).

♦ Jesus offered for free, as a gift, a sacrifice that was infinite in worth and eternal in duration, providing for man what he could not provide for himself.

-Marvin Rosenthal

♦ We often wonder why God allows us to go through the deep valleys, but *2 Corinthians 1* tells us why. It is so we can be a consolation to those who find themselves in similar valleys of sorrow and despair.

-RJK

******

Songs Born in the Night

So many songs were born in the night of sorrow and despair. For Elizabeth Prentiss the loss of her two children was overwhelming. Although she had experienced great pain and loss when she also lost the used of her legs, the sorrow of losing her children was consuming. However her faith in Christ had always kept her smiling, which encouraged others in their spiritual pilgrimage.

Subsequently, it was in the depth of great loss that she asked the Lord to minister to her broken spirit. God answered her prayer and the result is the inspiring hymn, "More Love to Thee, O Christ."

When the deep things of God are born in the deepest part of the night, it is hard to believe that the results can become points of victory for those who are facing the dark night as well. For example, when the late Communist leader, Kim II Sun discovered 30 Christians living underground, he brought them out to make them a public example. As they were ready be offered up on his despotic altar, the last words they proclaimed were actually sung as they faced their death. They sang the words of Elizabeth Prentiss' song, "More Love to Thee, O Christ." (ED, pg. 243)

The truth is when you study many of the hymns and even some present songs that have had such an impact on our souls, some were raised out of the dust of utter despair. Like a phoenix rising up out of the ashes of great loss, illness, anguish, and hopelessness, these songs were lifted up out of the valleys of desolation by the currents of God's abiding comfort. Their consolation often brings such hope and victory to those who must face the grave darkness of their own journey.

I have learned this truth in greater measure while studying the history attached to the different Psalms. Many of these were born in the deepest of nights, and through the centuries they have been quoted or sung as martyrs faced their martyrdom, armies their enemies, and those on their sick and death beds their plight.

It is true that what has been born in the dark in regard to the kingdom of God does become a beacon of light to those who are facing their own dark night of the soul. It is also true the Lord will never leave us comfortless. He not only provided His Spirit who is able to comfort, but the testimony in song of those who have experienced such matters in a personal way and came out triumphant.

Who comforteth us in all our tribulation, that we may be able to comfort them which are in any trouble, by the comfort wherewith we ourselves are comforted of God. For as the sufferings of Christ abound in us, so our consolation also aboundeth by Christ (2 Corinthians 1:4-5).

******

♦ The meaning of the altar is the offering of our lives to God to be ever consumed, yet ever living; to be ever living, yet ever consumed.
-Watchman Nee
(WN, Apr. 14)

♦ A shepherd cannot shine. He cannot cut a figure. His work must be done in obscurity...His work calls for continuous self-effacement. It is a form of service which eats up a man's life. It makes a man old before his time. Every good shepherd lays down his life for the sheep.
-Charles E. Jefferson

******

Come ill, come well, the cross, the crown,
The rainbow and the thunder;
I fling my soul and body down
For God to plow them under.

-Unknown

♦ I suppose that God's crosses are often made of most unexpected and strange material.
-Frances Ridley Havergal

♦ The unchangeable God hath secured his loving kindness to his people by promise under all the trials and smarting rods of affliction with which he chastens them in this world: he hath reserved to himself the liberty of afflicting them, but found himself by promise never to remove his favour from them.
-John Flavel
(RR, pg. 142)

♦ Adversity must come or people do not see any need to deal in reality. Challenges must come for people to see their inabilities to change reality. Sorrow must come for us to lose our grip on the things of the present world that are void of life and meaning. Despair must come so we will become a sojourner in this age. Death must come so that we, as believers, can enter into the abundance of the life that is yet to be realized.

-RJK

******

Which Cross is Mine?

The Bible tells us we must deny our right to a self life and pick up our cross and follow Jesus. We like to choose our cross, but we will not be allowed to choose the size or makeup. Others outside of us will choose the cross we must bear. And, there are also times we will not just be required to carry the cross, but we will find ourselves embracing the work it must do in us.

This is best illustrated by Ibaragi Kun's story, which took place in November of 1596. After being urged to recant his faith in Christ, Kun looked at the official and asked him which cross was his. The perplexed official looked at him and pointed to the smallest of the twenty-six crosses. Kun ran to the cross, knelt before it, and embraced it. When the nails went into his hands and feet, he did not cry in pain; rather he courageously accepted the path God has laid out for him.

Over the next 70 years, as many as one million Japanese Christians would follow Kun's example and embrace their crosses as well. The unique thing about Kun's story is that the reason the smallest cross was chosen for him is because he was only 12 years old. (ED, pg. 32)

But God forbid that I should glory, save in the cross of our Lord Jesus Christ, by whom the world is crucified unto me, and I unto the world (Galatians 6:14).

♦ Suffering always follows when love seeks to save the object of its love. It is only by suffering that love can gain its end and so attain the highest happiness.

-Andrew Murray

♦ Sacrifice; after all that is the great test of love. People tell you that they love you, but you cannot tell whether they really love you till the opportunity comes for them to make a sacrifice for you.

-R. A. Torrey
(RA, pg. 25)

******

He was better to me than all my hopes,
He was better than all my fears;
He made a bridge of my broken works,

172

And a rainbow of my tears.
The billows that guarded my sea-girt path
But carried my Lord on their crest;
When I dwell on the days of my wilderness march
I can lean on His love for the rest.

-Anna Shipton
(1815-1901)

♦ Though we despise suffering, it educates us, transforms us, allows us to share in the inheritance of Christ, and gives us a ministry of compassion for others who suffer.

-Micca Campbell

♦ God does not desire a sacrifice or offering that has no real humility behind it. He will not require a burnt offering unless there is first submission to Him, or a sin offering unless there is first confession and repentance.

-RJK

♦ Any sacrifices we make are no sacrifices at all, when seen in the light of Calvary. Besides all this, we only give to the Lord what we cannot keep anyway and what we have ceased to love.

-William MacDonald

******

The Strength of Humility

The Apostle Paul spoke of the reality that, for a good man, few would venture to become a sacrifice on his behalf, yet Christ died for sinners. What does it take to become a sacrifice that will leave an indelible memory or mark with those who witness it?

There was a man by the name of Richard who left such a mark on those around him. In fact, his example was so great, he was given the title of "Saint Richard." We know that "saint" means holy person or a person set apart. St. Richard not only displayed the attitude of a saint but the conduct of one. However, the secret to the caliber of his life was humility. To become a sacrifice, one must humble self beneath the burden, yoke, chains, or cross in order to be offered up on the altar.

St. Richard was a peasant during a time of great persecution. Due to his faith, he was ordered to be imprisoned. When the arresting officer mounted his horse after apprehending him, the animal went crazy, throwing the official, fatally injuring him. The prosecution not only had a case against him because of his faith, but it charged him with the murder of the constable. It reasoned that if he had not been a believer, the official would not have died.

173

Richard was sent to the gallows, but the hangman had difficulty fixing the noose of the rope. Richard, being the kind, compassionate man he was could not stand quietly by as the hangman struggled with the rope. Since he was skilled in such matters, Richard volunteered to fix the noose. After he had fixed it, Richard graciously thanked the hangman for giving his kind permission to secure it. After that he passed from this world to the next. But, the strength he displayed in humility secured for him the title of "St. Richard." (AWG, pg. 64)

It is only in humility that we can choose how we can live and at times choose in what manner we will be offered up as a sacrifice. Although our life may cease on the altar, our example will become the smoke or fragrance that continues long after our exit from this life.

Humble yourselves therefore under the mighty hand of God, that he may exalt you in due time (1 Peter 5:6).

♦ Brokenness is a prerequisite for serving the Lord. The broken vessel pours forth the wine of the Spirit. The broken chord produces the most beautiful music.

-Catherine Jackson

♦ And the more God favors you with His presence the greater will your trials and sufferings be; for none feel themselves so weak as those do that enjoy a good share of His presence.

-John Rusk

******

What a sacrifice! All was burnt
    Upon Calvary's altar.
He left all as His Incarnation,
He gave all at His Death.
He got all at His Ascension.

Herbert Lockyer

♦ When the Christian is strongest in the Lord he is often most conscious of inability; when he is most courageous he may be profoundly aware of fear within; and when he is most joyful a sense of distress readily breaks upon him again. It is only "the exceeding greatness of power: that lifts him on high."

-Watchman Nee
(WN, Mar. 24)

♦ If you are going to walk with Jesus Christ, you are going to be opposed by everything in the world and by the great majority of evangelicals. You're going to be opposed.

-Paul Washer

♦ The school of suffering graduates rare scholars.

-Unknown

Though he were a son, yet learned he obedience by the things which he suffered; And being made perfect, he became the author of eternal salvation unto all them that obey him (Hebrews 5:8-9).

♦ Let the best man be without afflictions, and he will quickly grow dull in the way of duty.

-John Flavel
(RR, pg. 146)

♦ We have all of these so-called "sacrifices," but God would prefer the morsel offered out of a state of spiritual poverty than all the heartless sacrifices that have no meaning or purpose to them.

-RJK

♦ Although it costs nothing to become a Christian, it costs plenty to be a consistent believer walking in a path of sacrifice, separation and suffering for Christ's sake. It is one thing to begin the Christian race well, but it is quite another thing to slug it out, day after day, through fair weather and foul, through prosperity and adversity, through joy and through grief.

-William MacDonald

♦ Self-emptying and self-sacrifice, obedience to God's will, and love to men, even unto the death of the Cross—this was the character of Christ for which God so highly exalted Him. It is the character of Christ that we are to imitate. He was made in the likeness of men, so we could be conformed into the likeness of God.

-Andrew Murray

♦ All the calls of the gospel are calls to hardship, to sacrifice, to battle. Christ would have no man follow him under the delusion that he was going to have an easy time of it.

-J. D. Jones

Behold, I send you forth as sheep in the midst of wolves: be ye therefore wise as serpents, and harmless as doves (Matthew 10:16).

♦ A life can only yield its treasures when it is smitten.

-Hebert Lockyer
(MP, pg. 311)

♦ Pain is pain and sorrow is sorrow. It hurts. It limits. It impoverishes. It isolates. It restrains. It works devastation deep within the personality. There is nothing good about it. But the gifts God can give with it are the richest the human spirit can know.

-Margaret Clarkson

♦ The reality of personal growth comes down to death. Personal strength must be offered up, our present life must be sacrificed, future hopes must give way to eternal purposes, and personal expectations must be replaced by total confidence in an unseen God.

-RJK

♦ If thou be in Christ, thy greatest afflictions shall prove thy best friends and benefactors.

-John Flavel
(RR, pg. 199)

*****

The cross on which our Lord expired
Has won the crown for us!
In thankful fellowship with Him
We bear our daily cross.

Set free in grace—He vanquished him
Who held us in his chains—
But more than this, He shares with us
The fruit of all His pains.

-W. Trotter
(1818-1865)

♦ When Christ prayed "Abba, Father" in Gethsemane, He surrendered to death so that the will of God in redemption of sinners might be accomplished. He was ready for any sacrifices.

-Andrew Murray

♦ The trials confronting us on the way to full enjoyment of our inheritance in Christ may be quite as gigantic as were some of the Canaanites, but God intends to use them for our increase. Faith sees them as its food. If we but knew it, we thrive and grow on difficulties. But the reverse is also true.

-Watchman Nee
(WN, Nov. 18)

That the trial of your faith being much more precious than of gold that perisheth, though it be tried with fire, might be found unto praise and honour and glory at the appearing of Jesus Christ (1 Peter 1:7).

♦ I have learned that affliction and trials transform lives, either for good or for bad. They will make you or break you. God speaks to us through our pain. He can use it to make us more aware of Him.

-Jan Markell

♦ First of all, perfect surrender to God, and then sacrifice for man. Christ's surrender was the basis of His sacrifice.

-Herbert Lockyer

♦ The way of the cross reminds us that we must be willing to forsake all for the sake of gaining the excellence of our Lord. We must be willing to lose it all for the sake of knowing Him. If required or necessary, we must be willing to walk away from all that we know in this present world for His sake, to gain the fullness of His life.

-RJK

♦ I have learned to love the darkness of sorrow; there you see the brightness of His face.

-Woman of the 15th Century

♦ Many a man is sacrificing conscience, sacrificing honour, sacrificing obedience to God, to gain money.

-R. A. Torrey
(RA, pg. 35)

♦ Suffering times are resigning times...Resignation to God necessarily implies our renunciation and disclaiming of all other refuges.

-John Flavel
(RR, pg. 213)

******

A Face in the Midst of the Masses

Have you ever heard of a lady by the name of Nellie Conroy? Her name most likely has no significance. It seems common; therefore, we can conclude it must have belonged to a common woman. However, Nellie was not insignificant or common to one man.

This man had been a millionaire in New York City. Instead of living the high life, he turned from his lavish lifestyle to a life of abandonment for the cause of the Gospel. His goal was to reach into the masses and pull out those who were perishing from the very jaws of hell.

One night as he walked down the street he encountered one of those perishing souls. She had just come out of an underground den of infamy and groaned as he passed. The servant of God stepped up to her and told her of the love of God. He was met with unbelief, but he eventually persuaded this poor soul that God loved her.

He gave her a shelter. However, the woman did not live long, only about two years, before she died. But before she died this woman stood up before a great audience in the Cooper Institute. Imagine, a woman of the street, a face among the masses speaking before a crowd. She told those in attendance how God had saved her. At the end of her story, tears were streaming down the faces of all who heard this woman. Nellie Conroy would not leave an impression on this world, but the impression heaven left on her heart also impacted the hearts of those who heard her testimony.

As she lay dying she called out to the man who had counted the world as dung in order to gain heaven for himself, alone with others. Nellie so loved her mentor and she told him, "I will soon see, in a few hours, little Florence, and I will see Jesus."

Nellie Conroy's name may not mean anything to those who do not know her story, but the one thing she was assured of on her deathbed is that her name was known in heaven; in fact, it was written in the Book of Life. (RA, pgs. 20, 21)

...and at that time thy people shall be delivered, every one that shall be found written in the book. And many of them that sleep in the dust of the earth shall awake, some to everlasting life, and some to shame and everlasting contempt. And they that be wise shall shine as the brightness of the firmament; and they that turn many to righteousness as the stars for ever and ever (Daniel 12:1c-3).

A Matter of Life, Character, and Godliness

~

Where Are You Looking for Life?

Many people are looking for something to make sense out of life. They seek after things, only to find that they burden them down. They look to relationships, only to be greatly disappointed. They look towards man's religion, only to find there is much vanity in it. They try to fill their lives with good things and good deeds, only to find emptiness at the end of such activities.

To understand what we are looking for, we must understand why we are here. Are we here to live unto ourselves, to heap the things of the world upon ourselves without any regard to the harsh reality that such things fail to add any real substance to our lives? In the end, we might well discover that all that we have established was some type of lifestyle, but we cannot find any real life or substance in any of it.

Why are we here? Until we honestly answer that question, we cannot begin to understand what we are looking for. After all, we do not know what we are looking for unless we become aware of our purpose for being alive.

It has taken me years to understand that I can only find life in Christ. Although I have been a Christian for over forty years, the initial years of my Christianity found me replacing a relationship with God with religious pursuits. I often tacked Jesus on to my fleshly activities to validate them and clothed my worldly attitude with self-righteousness. I took on a religious pose to adjust my Christian life to my barren lifestyle. In the end, I came up empty as I found that the life of Christ was missing from all of my pursuits and activities.

I have realized that I possess the life of Christ. It is up to me to live this life. The more I live the life of Christ by faith, the more I will become like Him in character. My outward life will cease to take on a mere pose of religion, but I will take on the mind of Christ as my disposition, attitude, conduct, and approach manifest His life.

It is time to quit looking for life in the insignificant and look for it in the eternal matters of heaven. Jesus came to save us. Salvation is marked by the presence of His eternal life in our very inner beings.

Let this mind be in you, which was also in Christ Jesus (Philippians 2:5).

♦ Life does contain moments of adventure, but these times are interspersed with long periods of plain, unvarnished hard work. The real things of life are attained at these monotonous level periods, so to speak, more than they are at the high peaks of excitement.

-Isobel Kuhn

♦ Every journey presents different challenges. Like most people I would love to be spared from such challenges, but they are part of the journey. In some cases, they are the reason for it. Life would prove to be non-essential without challenges. We bring some on ourselves, while circumstances bring others. The key is we must learn the purpose for each challenge.

-RJK

♦ The principles of gain through loss, of joy through sorrow, of getting by giving, of fulfillment by laying down, of life out of death is what the Book teaches. And the people who have believed it enough to live it out in simple, humble, day-by-day practice are people who have found the gain, the joy, the getting, the fulfillment, the life.

-Elisabeth Elliot

Prayer: Lord, we are so earthbound it is hard for us to look towards our high calling in You. Help us to realize that we must quit looking down and around, because our life in You cannot be found or discovered from such a perspective. Amen.

♦ Holy desires must lead to resolute action.

-Herbert Lockyer Sr.
(DP, pg. 103)

♦ What a man is must be shown to be more important than what he does. While the moral quality of any act is imparted by the condition of the heart, there may be a world of religious activity which arises not from within but from without and which would seem to have little or no moral content.

-A. W. Tozer

♦ Plant a word in the mind, you will reap an act. Plant the act, you will reap a habit. Plant a habit you will reap a character. Plant a character, you will reap a nature. Plant a nature, you will reap a destiny.

-Unknown

♦ God is more interested in your character than in your talents and abilities.

-Jeannette Haley

♦ It is not a matter of how much headway one makes in life; rather, it comes down to how much headway God has made in us.

-RJK

♦ In other words, the Lord is more interested in the production of character than He is in the provision of comfort. Comfort is nice, but character is better. Many times God will sacrifice your comfort in order to produce in you His character.

-Anna Alden-Tirrill
(SP, Sept. 11)

******

Through A Child's Eyes

Love is the one distinguishing mark of a Christian. The eyes in which love regards others reveal its simplicity to embrace without prejudice or without pre-conceived notions. There was a story about a Christian who was forced to work under the ground in the mines in the Soviet gulags because of his faith. His environment was void of any compassion or relief.

One day there was an accident where his back was greatly injured. The result is that he had a hunch back. Needless to say he was considered a spectacle at times. However, one day there was a little boy who would not stop staring at him. Finally, the little boy asked him what he had on his back. He told him he was a hunchback.

The child smiled warmly, "No," he said, "God is love. He gives no one deformities. That is not a hunchback you have; it is a box below your shoulders. Hiding inside the box are angels' wings. One day, the box will open and you will fly to heaven with your angel wings." (ED, pg. 65)

Godly love sees no deformities, just opportunities to see the beauty in God's ability to make all things stunning. Needless to say, this child's view of this man's injury was from a heavenly perspective. It managed to see beyond the obvious to embrace the heavenly.

God's love looks beyond this present world and will ultimately take hold of the unseen currents. It is in the currents that we are allowed to see the beauty of God's marvelous work, even in the midst of a marred, cruel, dying world.

Behold, what manner of love the Father hath bestowed upon us, that we should be called the sons of God: therefore the world knoweth us not, because it knew him not (1 John 3:1).

♦ Happy is that soul that finds such evidences of integrity in itself, when it is brought to the trial of it at the bar of the word, at the bar of conscience, at the bar of afflictions, and at the bar of strong temptations. The eyes of the Lord shall run to and fro through the whole earth, to shew himself strong in behalf of such whose hearts are thus perfect towards him.

-John Flavel
(RR, pg. 223)

♦ The tragedy of much of life today is the failure to appreciate our high calling. We are content to spend our years "hugging the subordinate," or "majoring in minors...They creep instead of fly. As someone has said, they rake around in a muck heap, not noticing the angel above them who is offering them a crown. Their time is spent making a living instead of making a life."

-William MacDonald
(ODT, Dec. 14)

♦ It's not how we fall that defines us as Christians. It's how we get up again.
-Karen Kingsbury
Christian Author

♦ It is hard to grow when we allow the sourness of ingratitude to take hold in our attitude, the bitterness of disappointment to define our present life, and the foul root of selfishness to entangle our perspective into an insipid reality of vanity.

-RJK

♦ When Christian principles are abandoned in our national life, the consequences are disastrous.

-Dr. Larry Spargimino

♦ Anyone who serves God's people is engaged in a work for eternity. The humblest servant of Christ has superior vision to the wisest men of the world. His work will last while theirs will go up in a mushroom cloud.

-William MacDonald

******

Finding Life

Everyone is trying to find life. They know that if they find life the secret to the whys would be cleared up. In other words, why are they here, why is life hard and illusive, and why does life leave a sense of mockery upon one's soul? The truth is nothing really makes sense for those who seek some type of semblance outside of that which is eternal, holy, good, and unchangeable.

A life that has substance must be marked by eternal qualities that serve as a living, ongoing testimony to others. It cannot be conquered by the world's temptation, consumed by fleshly lusts, outwitted by the clever foolishness of the wisdom of the world, nor silenced by the skepticism of this present age.

There are testimonies of those who willingly offered it all to secure a better life. They counted the riches of the present age as being dung, its flattery as being a farce, and its ways as being vain and destructive.

As I learn more about the martyrs that left such testimonies, I discover that many are now referred to as "saints." All believers are considered saints, but to live as saints requires the ways of excellence and to die as saints requires a blessed assurance in the God who can and will preserve His people even through the fires of persecution.

One such saint is St. Christopher. He was branded with red-hot irons, roasted over a fire, and cooked in boiling old, but miraculously did not suffer any pain and was not bothered by his treatment. As a result, those observing his plight, which was numbered to be almost 50,000 people, were converted. It was even said that a drop of his blood healed someone who was accidentally injured while watching the saint's execution. Today this man's testimony lives on as a witness of God's sustaining power.

St. Lawrence was another man who had an incredible testimony of God serving as that abiding, eternal refuge. It was said of him that he engaged in pleasantries while being roasted on a gridiron. These saints died in the Lord, only to awake in His presence.

The reality of the life that waits us in the next world is what allows us to count the cost of our present lifestyle. In light of our future glory there is nothing this world can offer by comparison. It takes the eyes of faith to see glimpses into this glory and it takes the sober reality that as saints of the Most High God, we are always walking towards our present demise, knowing that the promises of eternity wait on the other side in glory.

He was in the world, and the world was made by him, and the world knew him not. He came unto his own, and his own received him not (John 1:10-11).

♦ It is interesting to consider the ways of life. Everything in creation speaks of life. The trees speak of the beauty of life, the river the constant flow of life, the flowers the grace that sustains life, and the wildlife the order that maintains life. And, God created all to declare His majesty.

-RJK

♦ The thought of God is undoubtedly the greatest thought that can occupy the human mind. Great thoughts of God ennoble all of life. Small thoughts of God destroy those who hold them.

-William MacDonald
(ODT, Jun. 4)

Prayer: Lord, it is not about things but about life. Thank You for the gift of life. Life holds uncertainty in this world. It is often enfolded in adversity to establish and test one's character. However, it also presents goodness as an insight into Your goodness. Life contains indifference in such states as drudgery. But, in its indifferent stages, it allows for rest, time, and opportunity. There is nothing stagnant about life that is found in You, except to those who refuse to embrace every aspect of it. Lord, I choose to embrace it to learn its many lessons. Amen.

♦ God calls us to a lifestyle of thanksgiving and praise—of worship—so that we can enjoy a life filled with and enjoying His continual Presence. This is the key to intimacy with our Lord. It is a lifestyle of choice, even amidst the challenges of life, the dark days, the lonely chapters, the hard times, and the dry seasons.

-Anna Alden-Tirrill
(SP, Apr. 4)

♦ A defining moment is any situation involving a question of character...Ready or not we meet our real character face-to-face the moment we decide to take sides.

-Extreme Devotion
(ED, pg. 46)

♦ Problems are the price of progress. Don't bring me anything but problems. Good news weakens me.

-Charles Kettering

♦ When spiritual stagnation takes place it is always replaced with complacency, suspicion, contempt, and judgmental attitudes.

-RJK

♦ [A lot of people] think that Christianity is you doing all the righteous things you hate and avoiding all the wicked things you love in order to go to Heaven. No, that's a lost man with religion. A Christian is a person whose heart has been changed; they have new affections.

-Paul Washer

******

A Bit of Humor

In order to get through life it pays to have a sense of humor. There are times I have felt God smiling at something going on in my life. At such times I never felt that He was laughing at me; rather; that He wanted me to see the humorous side of life.

The need for humor is illustrated in the following story. Even though Al Ling and her late husband had been put in prison for their faith, she found much to smile about. Her honesty about matters often required her to do 50 push-ups. Even though she was 70 years old, she found that such push-ups were worth it because they often came on the tail-end of her making some comment about her love and faith towards Jesus.

Upon her release, the guards decided to interrogate her one last time. "Where does your husband work?" the young guard asked.

She answered, "Oh, he is doing underground work." The interested guard took out a notepad. Al Ling smiled, "He passed away years ago."

And these things write we unto you, that your joy may be full (1 John 1:4).

♦ Plead with God that His people may know that every believer is only to live for the interests of God and His kingdom. If this truth were preached and believed and practiced, it would bring dramatic changes in our mission work.

-Andrew Murray

♦ …character and courage are two things that are difficult to fake.

-Extreme Devotion
(ED, pg. 268)

♦ The best defense against the Devil is to live in unclouded fellowship with the Lord, covered by the protective gear of a holy character.

-William MacDonald
(ODT, May 10)

♦ It is only as you walk out godly virtue, or give way to a bad attitude that you decide what kind of person you become.

-RJK

♦ Forgiveness means letting yourself off the hook and getting released from the tyranny of vengeful thoughts. Forgiving others for their wrongs gives you a chance to shine for Christ like never before.

-Extreme Devotion
(ED, pg. 73)

For if ye forgive men their trespasses, your heavenly Father will also forgive you (Matthew 6:14).

♦ The gospel is not that God loves us with unmerited mercy and blots out our sins. The miraculous work that Jesus Christ came to do is the making of saints—stamped and sealed by Golgotha and Pentecost.

-Oswald Chambers
(DL, Jan 15)

♦ When we place Him first and foremost in our lives, worry drops away.

-E. A. Johnston
(NTB, pg. 50)

******

The Cycles of Life

Life clearly entails cycles and seasons. Its very pulse represents a current that ensures the rhythm of all creation. It never misses a beat. It is forever walking to a drumbeat that is governed by an unseen hand of Providence.

We know that the life that comes from God is the life of His Son. There are also seasons that govern His life in relationship to it being brought to full maturity in His people. However, the one thing we can be assured of is that His life is eternal, and that it is fresh in the springtime, refreshing in the heat of summer, fruitful in the fall, and enduring through the wintertime.

Verily, verily, I say unto you, He that heareth my word, and believeth on him that sent me, hath everlasting life, and shall not come into condemnation; but is passed from death unto life (John 5:24).

♦ We cannot live for ourselves alone. Our lives are connected by a thousand invisible threads, and along these sympathetic fibers, our actions run as causes and return to us as results.

-Herman Melville

♦ It is often the little things that betray us.

-Watchman Nee

♦ Whatever weakens your reasons, impairs the tenderness of your conscience, obscures your sense of God, or takes away the relish of spiritual things; whatever increases the authority of your body over your mind, that thing is sin.

-Suzanne Wesley

♦ People want God to deliver them from those things which cause distress to their flesh and lifestyle. The Lord has graciously shown me that such distress could and is part of our spiritual maturity. Do I really want to be delivered from the ovens of adversity or challenges before God is finished with me? No! Keep me in the fires Lord until I have become the vessel You desire.

-RJK

Prayer: Lord, life is uncertain. It is made up of so much of "wishful thinking" and "hope so" that it certainly can leave one in a wake of disillusionment. However, we must always remember that You never change. You are the only source that remains constant in an ever-changing, fickle world. Amen.

♦ It is impossible to keep our moral practices sound and our inward attitudes right while our idea of God is erroneous or inadequate.

-A. W. Tozer
(AG, Mar. 2)

♦ The distinctions that make Christianity unique are irreconcilable with any other religious belief, and any attempt at ecumenical unity is a denial of biblical Christianity.

-Dave Hunt

♦ We have too many high-sounding words, and too few actions that correspond to them.

Abigail Adams

For I say, through the grace given unto me, to every man that is among you, not to think of himself more highly than he ought to think; but to think soberly, according as God hath dealt to every man the measure of faith (Romans 12:3).

♦ Great leaders will inspire others to greatness.

-RJK

♦ I don't believe that God put us on earth to be ordinary.

-Lou Holtz

♦ Integrity means the unimpaired state of a thing.

-Oswald Chambers
(DL, Jun 8)

♦ We are to a large degree the sum of our loves and we will of moral necessity grow into the image of what we love most; for love is among other things a creative affinity; it changes and molds and shapes and transforms. It is without doubt the most powerful agent affecting human nature next to the direct action of the Holy Spirit of God within the soul.

-A. W. Tozer
(AG, Dec. 24)

******

The Confession

Amy Carmichael drew up a "Confession of Love" for the group of Indian girls who banded together to serve Christ. Consider what it says.

My Vow: Whatsoever Thou sayest unto me, by Thy grace I will do
My Constraint: thy love, O Christ, my Lord.
My Confidence: Thou art able to keep that which I have committed unto thee.
My Joy: To do Thy will, O God.
My Discipline: That which I would not choose, but which thy love appoints.
My Prayer: Conform my will to Thine.
My Motto: Love to live—live to love
My Portion: The Lord is the portion of mine inheritance.

And when he had found him, he brought him unto Antioch. And it came to pass, that a whole year they assembled themselves with the church, and taught much people. And the disciples were called Christians first in Antioch (Acts 11:26).

♦ It matters not what we may call ourselves, whether Churchmen, Dissenters, Baptists, Calvinists, etc., nothing will secure our standing, but our having the love of God shed abroad in our heart, which proves us to be the elect of God; and this will keep us from falling away, and nothing short of it.

-John Rusk

♦ As a believer, I must always look for the precious light of Christ in the darkness. However, I must realize that darkness is necessary for righteousness to be established. It was only in darkness that the lights of Noah, Job, and Daniel shined brightly, revealing the true ways of righteousness (Ezekiel 14:14).

-RJK

Prayer: Lord, when we hide in darkness, it is because we refuse to see Your light. We know it will reveal all of our wicked ways and deeds. Lord, shine Your light upon me for I desire all wickedness to be exposed in my life, rooted out by Your fire, and swept away by the winds of Your Spirit. Amen.

♦ (In reference to 2 Corinthians 5:14-15) Paul describes here a threefold life. First, the life of the Christian who lives according to his old nature: for himself alone. The second, the life of the true Christian, he lives wholly for Christ. Third, the life of Christ in heaven: He lives wholly for us.

-Andrew Murray.

♦ Holiness is the remaking of our inward and hidden desires and affections, when the Holy Spirit of God dwells in our mortal bodies.

-Oswald Chambers
(DL, Jan. 19)

♦ If Jesus Christ isn't strong enough to motivate you to live biblically, you don't know Him at all.

-Paul Washer

♦ The way to unity is through humility.

-William MacDonald

♦ Godliness is the spiritual discipline and exercise of the soul.

-RJK

♦ If thou meanest to enlarge thy religion, do it rather by enlarging thine ordinary devotions than thy extraordinary.

-Jeremy Taylor

◆ Things work out best for the people who make the best of the way things turn out.

-Coach John Wooden

******

Out of Ashes

Astronaut Richard Gordon told a fifth grade class that failure was one of the best teachers they could draw from. Gordon was with the space program (Gemini project) when it was in its infancy in trying to put a man on the moon. He later served as the command module pilot for the Apollo 12.

Gordon admitted that those pioneers of the space program learned the most from their failures. Granted, it was humbling and in some cases tragic, but those involved with the incredible task came out the wiser for it. The truth is without failure there is no character to be developed or wisdom to discover. Failure is that connecting link between what is real and what will prove to be useless in the end. It is that fiber or cord that becomes stronger as each lesson that is learned develops a stronger tie to discovering the unknown with the possibilities of successfully scaling the heights of what can be.

In today's politically correct society, failure is not even considered. In a sense, we are told everyone is a winner in spite of the dismal results and consequences of unproductive lives and activities. In such an environment excellence is never obtained and everything becomes shrouded in a gray mediocrity that once you are past the nonsensical rhetoric of it there is an emptiness that reveals that in the end it will all amount to nothing.

To those who are willing to scale the heights of their dreams, face the mountainous terrain of their aspirations, courageously face the despair of their failures, bravely forge the wide rivers of opposition and skepticism, and push through the unpredictable storms of uncertainty, such mediocrity will not do. They will not allow the defeat of complacency to justify quitting nor will they allow the hard way to stifle the development of their character. They will forge on because to them to give into what they consider to be the cesspool of mediocrity is to give way to the greatest type of defeat, the defeat that comes out of a wasted life that never discovers its purpose, talents, or the heights of its character.

We have a good example of something that appeared to be a source of utter failure, but in the end it rose out of the ashes of death and the grave into a dawning of a new day for mankind. The defeat I am talking about is the cross of Christ. What appeared to be heaven's greatest failure became man's greatest point of hope, salvation, and victory.

When it comes to God, failure always proves to be an opportunity to rise out of that which is lifeless to discover that which is eternal. The ashes may reveal the limitation of our abilities but in the end it becomes an opportunity for God to do the impossible by rising up that which is possible.

For this reason I choose failure as a teacher that will lead me to greatness. I refuse to sweep it under some vague carpet so that I can feel good about myself. I want to avoid from falling into a cesspool that will reveal the foolishness and vanity of not being willing to face what is, so that I can influence and change the face of what appears to be the earmark of failure.

To appoint unto them that mourn in Zion, to give unto them beauty for ashes, the oil of joy for mourning, the garment of praise for the spirit of heaviness; that they might be called trees of righteousness, the planting of the LORD, that he might be glorified (Isaiah 61:3).

♦ I'm perfectly sure God's story never ends with "ashes."

-Elisabeth Elliot

♦ Usefulness for God. Think of it! This is why we are here on this sin-torn planet! To be useful for Him. To advance His kingdom. To become conformed more and more into the image of Christ. For what end purpose? To bring God glory. This is the Christian life. Why aren't we living it?

-E. A. Johnston
(NTB, pg. 31)

♦ It is folly to hold blindly on to something the Lord gave us twenty years ago—or even last year. We must live in today, and hold on to God. It is the present relationship that is vital.

-Watchman Nee
(WN, Jan. 21)

♦ The Christian life is a learned life. It all comes down to learning what will please God, what is acceptable to Him, and what is honorable before Him. As we learn this life and apply it in practical ways, we will be conformed to the very image of Christ.

-RJK

Come unto me, all ye that labour and are heavy laden, and I will give you rest. Take my yoke upon you, and learn of me; for I am meek and lowly in heart: and ye shall find rest unto your souls (Matthew 11:28).

♦ A true Christian will be sensitive to the sin in their life and it will lead them to brokenness and genuine confession, but the person who says they are a Christian and are not sensitive to sin, it does not lead them to confession, a person who is that way is not a Christian.

-Paul Washer

♦ For every look at self—take ten looks at Christ.

-Robert McCheyne

♦ The Christian life is a *holy* life. Do not substitute the word *happy*; happiness is a consequence of holiness.

-Oswald Chambers
(DL, Jun 20)

♦ Joy is an eternal virtue that never ceases regardless of the circumstances. Granted, I must choose to enjoy a matter, but the state of joy is an anchor that I must let down into the depths of my character. I must choose to visit such a state when fear knocks at my door, uncertainty haunts me, insecurity torments me, and unbelief tempts me. In order to visit such a state, I must follow the line of this anchor and come to the state of joy. Clearly, this joy is found in the presence of God. It leads to peace and rest in the Lord.

-RJK

♦ What is the only foundation for a sound character? Reverence for God; and when that is gone the foundation of character is gone.

-R. A. Torrey
(RA, pg. 37)

Prayer: Lord, give me those who are rocks (character and faithfulness) any day, instead of those who are like festive, enthusiastic balloons because they will eventually blow with the self-serving winds of doctrines and personal piety. Amen.

♦ What we think about when we are free to think about what we will—that is what we are or will soon become.

-A. W. Tozer
(AG, Oct. 9)

♦ Agreement in Christianity is not just a mental agreement where one says: "I agree with you." True agreement also is the alignment of attitude that will change behavior. Ultimately, it will lead to the manifestation of true godliness in one's life.

-RJK

♦ In the life of faith, humility has a far deeper place than we think. It is not only one among other virtues, but it is the first and chief need of the soul. It leads us to know the absolute and entire inability in ourselves to do any good.

-Andrew Murray

******

An Apostle of Love

Have you ever heard of a man name Robert Chapman? He was from a rich family, but he lived a most modest life in order to be rich in faith. He started a work in Barnstaple, England. Out of his work local bodies of believers took root and grew as vibrant fellowships. He walked and preached on the streets of England, as well as established places of refuge and rest, where servants of God received both physical and spiritual refreshment. He was an evangelist who not only walked the byways of England, but traveled the roads of Ireland and Spain as well. In his way of thinking, if he only preached to one person, he would declare that he had a large congregation that morning. To him a receptive heart constituted a large congregation. Chapman would walk the roads of his different mission fields because he wanted to be able to share one-on-one the Gospel with those he encountered. In fact, it was against the law of Spain for him to share the life saving message, but he was more concerned about obeying God than the laws of the land. His example caused others to follow in his footsteps in regard to international missionary work.

Great men of faith such as George Muller, J. Hudson Taylor, and Charles Spurgeon had great respect for Chapman. It is said that both Muller and Taylor sought out this man for wisdom and prayer, knowing full well that his wisdom and intercession in prayer was part of the spiritual strength of Muller's orphanages in Bristle and Taylor's China Inland Mission. Chapman also corresponded with the prime minister of England, W. E. Gladstone and knew Samuel Wilberforce, a prominent Anglican clergyman whose famous political father, William Wilberforce, had fought the slave trade in England that led to emancipation in 1833. Spurgeon summarized the character of Chapman by referring to him as, "the saintliest man he ever knew."

Chapman's theology had its roots in the whole Bible. He perceived that the Christian life began at the cross of Christ, and contemplation of it was important to a proper walk before God. Subsequently, obedience to Scripture was preeminent to Chapman. He never got caught up with denominational causes, became limited by a particular school of religious thought, or was detoured by popular doctrinal emphasis. He thought there was much ink and pulpit time being devoted to too much interpretation about spiritual matters that were nothing more than speculation. To him such conjecture was taking away time and energy from other essentials of the Christian life. A man by the name of Henry Dyer likened Chapman's ministry of the Word to an eagle taking flight into the heavens, he was above the clouds; therefore, one could only catch sight of him occasionally. Dyer added, "Robert Chapman in his preaching distributed nuggets of gold...These nuggets the hearers had to beat out for themselves, and the more they were beaten, the more was seen in them."

Chapman was a man who did not like to see divisions among the servants of God that often occurred over doctrinal differences. He worked tirelessly to bring reconciliation when such schisms occurred. He knew the difference between the essential doctrines of the Christian faith and those which were not essential to salvation. He did not allow his ego to defend nonessential, inferential doctrine at the expense of unity. Subsequently, he became famous for his exceptional love, grace, and truth. Such virtues caused others to rightfully label him as "an apostle of love."

There was one story about Chapman that showed the extent of his godly love. Chapman did much street preaching in his community. In one instance the man who owned the local grocer became upset with his message of sin and repentance and actually spit on him. Later one of Chapman' relatives came to visit him. The rich relative wanted to understand why Chapman had chosen such a different life than wealth could offer him. When the relative arrived he found that the conditions may have been modest, but it was what was needed and sufficient for someone who chose to seek God for all of his needs. When the relative asked if he could purchase groceries for him, Chapman gladly assented, but stipulated that he must buy the food from a certain grocer. It is easy to conclude the grocer was the antagonist that had spit on Chapman and opposed his preaching. The relative purchased many goods from the grocer and when the grocer found out that it was to be delivered to Chapman, he commented that the relative must have made a mistake in choosing his shop. However, Chapman's relative assured him that he had come to the right shop because Chapman has specified it. The grocer broke down in tears and eventually came to Chapman's house to ask forgiveness, at which time he also yielded his life to Christ.

Even though Chapman displayed great wisdom and insight about spiritual matters, he refused to leave a record of it. He often destroyed any physical record of those things he expounded. However, his letters to others left a written record of his insight, and one book of his sayings did emerge because someone else collected them to preserve a written witness of his spiritual insight.

Chapman lived to be a century old. His disciplined lifestyle was his way to ensure the quality of his temple. His business on earth was simple: he wanted to please God. He once wrote, "The present times are the best for all of us; since our lot is cast in them, there is abundant grace to enable us to fully please God."

It was clear that he lived his whole life to please God. But, in his desire to please His loving Creator, he himself experienced a satisfying life. He wrote this to a man who asked his permission to name his youngest son after him, "Let prayer and reading the Word so settled as to become a golden chain that no craft or power of Satan can ever loose or break. By treading this path from my youth upwards, I am now, in my ninety-sixth year, spending my days in pleasure."

He delivered his last sermon at the age of 98. At 100 years of age he traveled to a community near his home to encourage Christians. He returned home in fine health but a few days later he suffered a slight stroke which rendered him physically helpless. He only lasted in this state for ten days when the door of heaven finally was opened to him to forever be in the presence of the One he had so loved and faithfully served in his life.

Before he passed into eternal bliss, he dictated this statement to be read at an annual fellowship meeting, "I bow to the sovereignty of God my heavenly Father; I have no will but His. We know that God is love, and if, with love of which there is no measure, there be conjoined wisdom which makes no mistakes what becomes us, His children, but to be full of thankfulness. We have the whole heart of Christ; it is all ours."

By this shall all men know that ye are my disciples, if ye have love one to another (John 13:35).

♦ When a person has this immoral fixity of character (like Herod), his waywardness will be arrested by God, not by the Devil. This is an awful and terrible truth, one to which many people will not readily listen.

-Oswald Chambers
(DL, Sept. 6)

♦ The only real life is to live in the light of eternity—to use all we possess for the promotion of God's glory and with an eye to the everlasting mansions. This, and only this is life in earnest.

-C. H. Mackintosh

♦ It is easy to console ourselves that we are not how we used to be, but the real crux is whether we are where we need to be in our relationship with the Lord.

-RJK

♦ It is possible to engage in service in connection with the gospel according to methods which may appear attractive and successful, but which are not in conformity to the will of God. The Lord gauges our service, not by its success, but by our faithfulness to Him.

-W. E. Vine

♦ I am convinced that life is 10 percent what happens to me and 90 percent how I react to it...we are in charge of our attitude.

-Charles Swindoll

♦ To efface one's self is one of a preacher's first duties. The herald should be lost in his message.

-Alexander Maclaren

♦ The greatest need of my people—is my personal holiness. Take heed to yourself. Your own soul is your first and greatest care. Keep up close communion with God. Study likeness to Him in all things.

-Robert McCheyne

Prayer: Lord make me as holy as a pardoned sinner can be!

-Robert McCheyne

♦ Discipling converts for Jesus Christ is the chief characteristic of a mature Christian!

-Oswald Chambers
(DL, Sept. 13)

♦ In living, daily experience, are we within the veil? Of course, we are there positionally, as believers; but often there is such a difference between our *practice* and *position;* our state and standing, our life up there in the heavenlies, and our life down here on the earth.

-Herbert Lockyer
(MP, pg. 465)

♦ There are three types of offenses that occur. When one breaks the Law, God is offended. When truth cuts through our desired reality, offense will take place in us towards the eternal truth that cut against our personal reality. And, when our pride is not placated properly, we become offended that we are not correctly being recognized or honored. The first offense results in judgment, the second one will bring us to a point of decision, while the last one will either leave us bitter or better depending on how we respond to it.

-RJK

Prayer: Lord, Your life will assure the headway and peace we all desire. Help me to realize how You use the winds and storms of my life to make personal headway in my character and walk. So be it.

♦ Christ will have nothing of the culture of the brain, at the expense of the culture of the character.

-George H. Morrison

♦ True Christianity aims at having the character of Christ formed in us. Then in our most ordinary activities and relationship with people, it will be second nature for us to act like Him. All this is possible because Christ Himself lives in us.

-Andrew Murray

♦ Nobody made a greater mistake than he who did nothing because he could do only a little.

-Edmund Burke

♦ Brokenness is one of the finest elements of a strong character. It doesn't take any discipline to be unbroken. But what self-control is required to be Christ-like when very natural instinct rebels against it!

-William MacDonald

♦ The Christian life does not fall upon us; rather, it is developed in us according to the way we allow it to be worked in our character, and the way in which we walk it out in our daily lives.

-RJK

******

New Every Morning

I don't know about you, but much of my life seems like drudgery. It seems like I am hemmed in by the same old daily routine. There are times I just want to break out of the mode or get off the merry-go-round.

As I consider my life, I realize that the matters of the world are what often prove to be tedious and repetitious to me. The world causes my life to replay itself in many different ways. It is always presenting me with the propaganda that I must try the latest fashion, gadget, or activity in order to find excitement and purpose. The truth is that the things of the world may start out new and exciting, but eventually they lose their newness and become part of the drudgery. A good example of this pattern is leftovers.

In our household Jeannette uses every bit of the leftovers. They end up in the delicious soups she prepares, or in stir-fry, salads, casseroles or as fillings for omelets or crepes. However, they are always tasty whether they are presented the second or third or fourth time around. But, to many in our

197

society leftovers can be a dirty concept. They like the new, the fresh, and the unexpected. This is brought out in the following story.

Three wives were bemoaning their husbands' attitudes towards leftovers. "It gets rough, "one said. "My husband is a movie producer and he calls them *reruns*."

If you think you have it bad," was the reply. "Mine is a quality control engineer and he calls them *rejects*."

"That's nothing compared to me," said the third lady. "My husband is a mortician. He calls them *remains*."

It is obvious that after something ceases to be new, the world can only offer reruns, rejects, and remains. So many times it has to repackage the old because there are no new ideas. Or, its attempt to ride on the success of something of the past ends, which ends up being a disappointment and rejected. In the end, much of what the world tries to do end up as remains, ready to be discarded in its various dumps.

It is for this reason that we also have the tendency to seek the world to find some type of means that will bring newness and excitement to our lives, but eventually it all ends up becoming leftovers that can become unpleasant or unacceptable to our extravagant taste buds.

However, when I consider my Christian life, I realize that everything in it is new and refreshing on a daily basis. The grace I was allotted yesterday flows into a new vein of grace for today that will be appropriated to me with His merit based on where I am in my life. The mercy that was shown to me yesterday, is not carried forward, but is new and capable of meeting me in my personal challenges of today. The compassions that warmed my heart the day before are not extended to me today; rather, they are made fresh to meet me in my present needs.

Clearly, in God's kingdom there are no leftovers. What He gives yesterday was complete and what He gives me today is new and fresh and will prove to be complete for the present, and what I face tomorrow will be met with that which freely flows from the throne of God.

Are you tired of the world's leftovers? In God's kingdom you will never have to settle for what was; you can learn what it means to have the glorious flowing virtues of Christ gracing your life on a daily basis.

This I recall to my mind, therefore have I hope. It is of the LORD's mercies that we are not consumed, because his compassions fail not. They are new every morning: great is thy faithfulness (Lamentations 3:21-23).

♦ The real test of discipleship is not so much a fast start as a faithful ongoing.

-Oswald Chambers
(DL, Oct. 25)

♦ The more often we feel without acting, the less we will be able ever to act, and, in the long, run, the less we will be able to feel.

-C. S. Lewis

♦ We admit that there is One who lies beyond us, who exists outside of all our categories, who will not be dismissed with a name, who will not appear before the bar of our reason...this requires a great deal of humility, more than most of us possess, so we save face by thinking God down to our level, or at least down to where we can manage Him.

-A. W. Tozer

♦ It is always easy to identify the tares in regard to humanity. They are the ones who insist on standing taller than the wheat that has been humbled by its fruit of eternal life.

-RJK

Prayer: Lord, You are my hope and stay. I pray You show me mercy in my logic, for I see myself as being wise. In my religion, I see myself as okay, and in my good deeds, I see myself being acceptable. Lord, all of these things prove I can easily be deluded about myself. Help me to have integrity and discernment in all matters. Amen,

♦ There are many who preach Christ, but not so many who live Christ. My great aim will be to *live* Christ.

-Robert Chapman
(RC, pg. 29)

♦ Nearly all men can stand adversity, but if you want to test a man's character, give him power.

-Abraham Lincoln

♦ Perhaps the time will come when less attention will be paid to the scholarly qualifications of a graduate, and more to the qualifications of character, for entrance and matriculation.

-Clarence Edward Macartney

♦ The man or woman who sets the will of God as his or her goal will reach that goal not by self-defense but by self-abnegation.

-A. W. Tozer

♦ Our lives are to be fruitful. They should taste sweet to those who need to be edified, salty to those who need healing, and bitter to those who are in rebellion.

-RJK

******

Life is a Reflection

The life I reflect has a lot to do with what I come into agreement with. The truth is until I come into agreement with something I will be like a tossed wave on the ocean, being driven by anything that comes along that takes captive my fancy. In such a state I will not have any idea where I will land until I hit the rocky shoreline.

Obviously many people are looking for a place of agreement in which they can confidently land. They are hoping something will attract or alert them to some type of purpose or place of significance. Once they come across such an attraction, they will fling themselves towards it in abandonment.

However, when it comes to the kingdom of heaven this abandonment rarely happens. The extraordinary Christian life that reflects the excellences of heaven comes out of extraordinary devotion. It is birthed by the power of the unseen, the incredible, and the unimaginable. Such devotion is also bathed in love, enfolded by the Spirit, highlighted by heavenly wisdom, touched by a bit of eternity, and marked by the very likeness of Christ.

When you consider what has been made available in Christ, every base has been covered in regard to our lives. Yet, there are many Christians who are not content and are restless waves on the ocean of life. They live in the mire of regrets, wallow in the pigpen of self-pity, and lament in the cesspools of "woe is me." They cry over the spilt milk of the past, while ignoring the precious moments of the present, allowing the hope of the future to slip through their fingers.

The truth is most people are missing God's blessings while they look for the elusive "carrot" of life according to their fanciful take on it. They want life on their terms without realizing that they will not find life in any of it. It is a fantasy at best and a tormenting nightmare at worst.

There comes a point where even God's people must choose to add faith to what they know about Him to find His abiding peace in a matter. The situation may not be void of conflict, but it will be standing sure on the promises of God in light of an eternal peace.

This brings us back to our need to possess devotion. Genuine devotion is grounded by disciplines that keep it sharp when challenged by compromise, steadfast when shaken by uncertainties, and enduring when faith is being tested by the dark cloud of unbelief.

Such devotion will not be easily moved from the Rock it is standing on because it is disciplined by the Spirit and the Word of God. It is focused on the Lord, and as a result, is sure about its foundation. Ultimately, it will not allow itself to be moved away from the path of righteousness as the individual presses forward to reach the heights of the Lord's revelation, wisdom, and glory.

As a Christian, I must properly discern the devotion that is present in my life. Without true devotion, restlessness can begin to take my soul captive. Only Christ can give my life meaning and purpose. He alone satisfies, but I must come into a place of sincere devotion that leads to agreement with my Lord. It is only by exposing myself to Him with unfeigned faith that I will be able to take on His likeness.

Therefore, the prisoner of the Lord, I beseech you that ye walk worthy of the vocation wherewith ye are called, With all lowliness and meekness, with longsuffering, forbearing one another in love (Ephesians 4:1, 2).

A Matter of Carnality and the Profane

~

The World's Concept of Greatness

The world's concept of greatness is to look for great men. The reason for this is because it is great men that make the world appear grand. Granted, the world must provide the arena in which the "idea" of greatness can be exalted. For example, consider how athletes make a particular sport or event desirable and great to the masses. People pay to see the athlete they admire most, or the team that has earned their loyalty.

It is the idea of greatness that makes the things and activities of the world attractive and glorious to the onlooker. The world rewards such greatness with titles and trophies, because without displays of greatness there would be no real attractions to entangle people into a false idea of what constitutes real accomplishments of importance. Without the greatness or distinction of people in certain arenas, the world would have no contrast or means to offer the masses any form of prominence that could be found and admired by them.

The world's presentation of greatness is nothing more than an image that will fade into the temporary, an empty vanity of what can never be since the things of the world are not enduring. What was great will fade into the background as the world's greatness must be once again repackaged in some person or event that can create the appearance of sensationalism to keep the people's interest and attention.

Greatness in the kingdom of God is opposite than the world. It is not based on an idea, but a disposition. It is not based on titles, but inner character and resolve to not compromise what is true. It is not based on physical abilities or talents, but on humility that not only recognizes what is worthy and great, but is always ready to give way to it for the sake of others.

We clearly see the excellence of greatness in God's kingdom through genuine sacrifice, the authority of it in character, and the power of it in submission. We see that in the end it is gentleness that will be regarded as great and meekness will be what actually inherits all that God has for a person.

...Ye know that the princes of the Gentiles exercise dominion over them, and they that are great exercise authority upon them. But it shall not be so among you: but whosoever will be great among you, let him be your minister; And whosoever will be chief among you, let him be your servant (Matthew 20:25b-27).

♦ When we think of the contrast between light and darkness, there is no greater one than this: God so loved the world, He gave His Son as light, hope, and salvation, but man so loves darkness that he prefers to remain lost in it to hide his evil deeds from the righteous, holy God.

-RJK

♦ Casual Christianity leads to causalities.

-Pastor Phil Skoog

♦ We live in the days of a revolting revival of paganism. Men excuse every sort of impurity as "natural," and not to be held in check. Scripture well describes such as behaving like "natural brute beasts" (2 Peter 2:12-13), and solemnly declares that such "will receive the wages of unrighteousness."

-H. A. Ironside

♦ For any man to gain the whole world at the cost of forfeiting his soul would be a bad bargain. If one could get the whole world by forfeiting his soul, it would be an idiotic exchange.

-R. A. Torrey
(RA, pg. 103)

♦ Let us put our pride under our feet and admit frankly that our sins are not big nor mighty nor noble...There is nothing romantic about sin. It is a sordid and shameful thing practiced by moral cads so weak that they take advantage of God's kindness to defy Him and so cowardly that they run whining to Him for help when trouble comes.

-A. W. Tozer
(AG, Aug. 24)

Prayer: Lord, we are so limited in what we know, yet we often fail to strive to come higher to gain Your perspective. Forgive us for accepting our nominal understanding that sees everything from the point of self, the flesh, and the world. Amen.

♦ False teachers of religion are deceiving thousands of people by bending the gospel to suit their own purposes. And in this regard, the human mind is ready to be deceived. If you can teach someone how to ignore sin, he will listen to you. If you can tell him how to ignore the possibility of judgment for his wrongdoing, he will listen to you. This is why the cults of deception are so popular—not because they are true, but because they alter the truth to suit the carnal desires of mankind.

-Oswald Chambers
(DL, Sept. 7)

♦ The world rules too much in the lives of Christians. The "world offers only the lust for physical pleasure, the lust for everything we see, and pride in our possessions"—all this robs the heart of its desire for that true self-denial necessary for receiving the Holy Spirit.

-Andrew Murray
(AP, Jun. 26)

Prayer: Lord, so many of us are on a ship, trying to hold on to our old life. However, You have already passed judgment on it. May we let it go so we can grab a hold of the only true Lifesaver. Amen.

♦ The flesh is absolutely no good. It is not improved one iota at the time of conversion. It is not improved by a lifetime of consistent Christian living. In fact, God is not trying to improve it. He has condemned it to death at the Cross and wants us to keep it in place of death.

-William MacDonald
(ODT, Jan. 6)

♦ Remember this, that you cannot commit some loved sin in private, and perform the work of the ministry in public, with facility and acceptance.

-Warren W. Wiersbe
(PCK, pg. 57)

♦ Where there is uncleanness, unconfessed sin, something contrary to God's will indulged in, there can never be true inward peace with God. Sin suspends the sweetness of communion.

-Herbert Lockyer
(MP. Pg. 495)

♦ How dare anyone think that a world ripening for judgment can be rescued by Christians working together in political/social activism with followers of all religions, along with humanists and atheists. God is the only one who can rescue people from the worldly destruction that is taking center stage. But, first they must seek His help on bended knee and in the utter desperation, knowing that there is no other solution.

-RJK

******

204

Silenced For Evermore

In 1973, one of the greatest tragedies occurred in this nation. Our highest court legalized a holocaust that is now haunting us as a nation in ways we cannot imagine. In 2011, this holocaust claimed 333,964 deaths which worked out to an average of one innocent life every 94 seconds. It was an increase of 4,519 from 2010. It is a money-making venture that receives $542.4 million in government grants and reimbursements. This includes "payments from Medicaid managed care plans." These figures were taken from CNS News. If you do not know what the face of this holocaust looks like by now, it is the abortions that are taking place under the hypocritical guise of human rights, when it is in fact a way to get rid of people. The following poem was written to mark the tragic, wicked milepost of the Supreme Court decision of Roe vs. Wade.

The sentence pronounced!
Death it will be.
Some mourned in despair,
Others wailed in sorrow
As others rejoiced.

In the name of rights run amuck,
Generations doomed by lies,
A holocaust begins,
In the balance a nation once standing tall,
Now frayed by injustice, collapsing as sanctity tumbles and falls.

On the altars of empty possibilities,
Legalized murder touts of open season
On the innocent, the pure, the brightest,
Causing wombs to become the place of execution,
Destroying legacies that will never be.

On the altar of greed
With calculated coldness,
Sworn to uphold life,
Now becoming the executioners,
Refining cruel methods untold.

Victims, victims, shattered lives everywhere,
Sacred lives discarded like useless tissue,
Tender souls crushed by emotional wounding,
Tormented consciences and broken hearts,
Left in the wake of sheer sorrow and ruin.
Hidden behind a veneer of insidious lies,
Millions sacrificed for no good cause,

Opening the floodgates of judgment and death,
Tis' now forty years a nation tried and tested,
Tasting the gall of bitterness.

Silent cries of the sacrificed,
Now being heard with the indictment of rolling tides.
Wading through the debris of moral decay,
Innocence gone, righteousness rejected,
Sanctity all but gone.

Moral fiber vanished, consumed by senselessness,
A nation falling apart, marching to a requiem,
Who will speak, who will stand for what was?
Erie quietness settles on the land,
Alas, silenced forever more, the innocent, the pure, the brightest.

-RJK

Woe unto them that call evil good, and good evil; that put darkness for light, and light for darkness; that put bitter for sweet, and sweet for bitter (Isaiah 5:20)!

♦ Instead of sitting in the presence of God, we give our children clowns and wonder why our youth has no vision.

-Donna Skoog

♦ Natural man is a fallen creature, he is morally corrupt, and he is Hell-bent on autonomy or self-government. He hates God because God is righteous, and he hates God's laws because they censor him and restrict his evil. He hates the truth because it exposes him for what he is and troubles what is left of his conscience. Therefore fallen man seeks to push the truth—especially the truth about God—as far from him as he can possibly remove it. He will go to any extent to suppress the truth, even to the point of pretending that there is no such thing as truth, or that if it does exist, it cannot be known or have any bearing on our lives.

-Paul Washer

Prayer: Lord, we are kept by Your power. It does not matter how much we try to maintain our own self-sufficiency, the storms of life reveal we are indeed corks on the ocean of life. Without Your power, we would not survive to tell of our spiritual adventures in this world.

♦ Obsession is a terrible thing. To lie is to deceive others, knowing one is lying. To be obsessed is to have deceived oneself; to lie, and not know it; to have moved beyond reach of conscience to the point where the light that is in us is darkness. It is, in short, to have shut out the truth. This state is reached by the simple choice of darkness.

-Watchman Nee
(WN, Dec. 16)

*****

A Matter of the Mind

The mind is an interesting instrument. It has such potential to dream the impossible, to scale the heights of great possibilities, and to explore beyond this present world. However, there is one problem with the mind; it is in a fallen state. Granted, the mind may be able to dream, but it has no power to bring a matter about. It may scale heights in its imagination, but it still is subject to the lowlands of vanity. It might want to explore new worlds, but it has no means of getting launched from its pinnacle of overinflated arrogance. After all, it perceives itself as always reaching the ultimate heights of its understanding.

Such a mind is referred to as a carnal mind. The carnal mind surely prefers the world. It is tainted by its philosophies, perverted by indoctrination, and defiled by its practices. Its preference is driven by the lusts of the flesh, is being perpetually consumed by selfishness, and is made mad by the indifference and cruelty of pride

It is for this reason that the Bible is clear: the carnal mind is at odds with God. It thinks itself to be too intelligent to believe in the unseen, too superior to be bothered with simplicity, and too wise to trust in something that does not confirm its own sense of justice and worth. It cannot imagine the best coming out of that which seems childlike, the excellent coming out of self-denial and sacrifice, or the most prized possession coming out of loss.

For to be carnally minded is death; but to be spiritually minded is life and peace (Romans 8:6).

♦ What makes the tragedy of Judas' defection so awful is that he had all the privileges and opportunities of the rest and he threw them all away because of covetousness and worldly ambition.

-H. A. Ironside
(CBO, Jul. 30)

♦ Never keep a list of others' "wrongs" while keeping a list of your "rights".

-Jeannette Haley

♦ Christian thinking today is "man-centered". Its focus is on improving, empowering, and enlarging one's base of operation. Its "center" is oneself. Basically, it is humanism wrapped in sermons and printed in best-sellers with topics driven with "purpose" and egocentric teachings, wrapped up in a "feel good" type of Christianity.

-E. A. Johnston
(NTB, pg. 91)

♦ People who turn Christianity into a cause run the risk of confusing violence for obedience.

-Extreme Devotion
(ED, pg. 76)

♦ Three considerations should destroy pride forever within our breasts: the majesty of God, the enormity of our sins and the wonder of Christ' redeeming death. But so tenacious is the root of Adam that we are often proud even of our want of pride.

-A. W. Tozer
(AG, Oct. 10)

♦ As humans we want our worlds to be in order, but God wants to bring order to our lives. Many times He uses the chaos in our worlds to bring His order to our existence. However, the truth is if God does not step on the scene, eventually everything established by man will collapse in complete ruin. It will be buried by the dust of vanity, lost in a maze of ineptness, marked by the ash of decay and death, and forgotten as the sands of time erase away all memories of its existence.

-RJK

Prayer: I give myself...my life, my all, utterly to Thee, to be Thine forever.
-Betty Scott Stam

♦ That is where sin begins—in a desire to be independent of God, in a desire to have our own way, in a desire to do as we please.

-R. A. Torrey
(RA, pg. 77)

♦ All the decisions you make...how many of those decisions are based on you doing simply what's right in your own eyes, and how many times specifically have you gone to Scripture looking for the answer, with regard to anything?

-Paul Washer

******

The Unhitched Rudder

The one member of our body that will give us away the most is the tongue. Often proving to be an undisciplined, unruly, unyielding, and unmanageable rudder that is running amuck, it reveals the most about our inner character.

Many have written about the folly and destruction of the tongue. Herbert Lockyer Sr. stated that backbiting is a malicious defamation of man behind his back. A 16th century Biblical expositor, Richard Turnbull described the tongue in this way, "That scorpion hurteth none but such as he touched with the tip of his tail; and the crocodile and basilisk slay none but such as either the force of their sight, or strength of their breath reacheth. The viper woundeth none but such as it biteth; the venomous herbs or roots ill none but such as taste, or handle, or smell them, and so come near unto them; but the poison of slanderous tongues is much more rank and deadly, in that it can spread far and wide." (DP, pg. 53)

The tongue is behind the greatest types of attack against righteousness which comes by way of gossip and slander. Such ways are cursed; however, the wicked can do nothing more than their father, Satan. They cannot help but lie. Their goal is to kill decency and destroy any real testimony of righteousness. This destruction is often inspired by jealousy and comes in a subtle way.

Innuendos dropped in the imaginations of the vulnerable, hurtful impressions left to create a mire of suspicions in the weak, a flow of tears of self-pity to start a wave of sentimental nonsense with the emotional, and so-called "noble gestures" to cover up the hate and wickedness from the masses. However, to God such attempts are profane. Regardless of the reality that is created by these people, it is void of truth. It is self-serving and destructive. It ultimately leads nowhere, but death.

Once again, as believers we must keep in mind that these people can do nothing outside of the low ways of Satan. He also accuses the saints on a daily basis. How he must weary the courts of heaven with his onslaught of lies.

And the tongue is a fire, a world of iniquity: so is the tongue among our members, that it defileth the whole body, and setteth on fire the course of nature; and it is set on fire of hell (James 3:6).

♦ We are too quick to be tolerant towards the unholy aspects and practices of our lives. We are not fierce enough about righteousness and holy agreement. As a result, the leaven of perversion is often allowed to grow in our lives, causing spiritual dullness.

-RJK

♦ In discussing how leaven was put out of the Jewish home during the Passover, H. A. Ironside made this observation about the subject. "The disciples were warned against the leaven of the Pharisees which is hypocrisy and self-righteousness, and the leaven of the Sadducees which is false doctrine, also of the leaven of Herod, which is worldliness and political corruption. The Corinthians were warned against the leaven of immorality, which, if unchecked would leaven the whole church, and the Galatians were warned in the same way against the leaven of legality." (CBO, Jun. 6)

******

The Christ is in Court today;
The World and the Flesh deride Him,
Mankind is jury and judge,
And the right of appeal is denied Him.
Who are His witnesses? Whom will He call
To answer for Him in the judgment hall?

The Christ is in Court today.
The World and the Flesh will try Him,
Mankind is jury and judge,
Shall those He hath loved deny Him?
We are His witnesses, ours is the call,
To speak for our Lord in the judgment hall.

-Annie Johnson Flint
(1866-1932)

The world cannot hate you; but me it hateth because I testify of it, that the works thereof are evil (John 7:7).

♦ The central citadel for the Devil's attack on Jesus was the same as for his attack upon us—'my right to myself.' He tempted Jesus to do God's work in His own way. Likewise even when a soul is sanctified, the Devil attempts to get the saint to do God's work in his own selfish way. He will do anything to dethrone the Lord as Lord!

-Oswald Chambers
(DL, Dec. 28)

♦ The hypocrite has, much angel without, more devil within. He fries in words, freezes in works; speaks by ells, doth good by inches. He is a stinking dunghill, covered over with snow; a loose-hung mill that keeps great clacking, but grinds no grist; a lying hen that cackles when she hath not laid.

-Thomas Adams

♦ All the vices of fallen angels and men have their birth and power in the pride of self, or I may better say, in the atheism and idolatry of self. Self is both atheist and idolater. It is atheist because it is had rejected God. It is an idolater because it is its own idol.

-Andrew Murray

Prayer: Lord, Your yoke will keep the burdens of life light upon my shoulders. Help me to come into step with Your yoke so that I can endure the burdens of this present world. Amen.

♦ Banish our worldliness, help us to ever live with eternity's values in view.
-Lucy R. Meyer

♦ Flesh touches God's glory in order to pervert it,
The world defiles God's glory in order to dull its majesty,
While man's religion puts a twist on it to adjust it to its self-serving ways.
-RJK

♦ Dogmatists could even find fault with Jesus Himself. He ought not to have trembled in Gethsemane. But life, even religious life, is not concerned with dogmas. It pursues its own course, and that course seems foolish to reason.

-Richard Wurmbrand

♦ By all which it appears that a Christless person is a most helpless and shiftless creature in the day of trouble.

-John Flavel
(RR, pg. 198)

******

The Reality of Wickedness

As a people, we are clearly reaping the misfortune of experiencing firsthand the consequences of what happens when a nation becomes complacent towards righteousness, ignores the responsibilities of righteousness, or compromises righteousness to live in peace with any form of wickedness. We now can see that in such a state of sin, foolishness replaces wisdom, folly mocks sobriety, insanity trumps reason, ignorance rejects truth, and lawlessness and rebellion rage against justice.

To spiritually overcome the wickedness that has taken center stage in this nation, we must choose the ways of righteousness. But, we must remember that there is nothing nominal, complacent, or indifferent about righteousness. It is wise enough to see that to be silent when evil reigns is suicidal, to be complacent when wickedness tears at the moral fiber of what is right is to sign a death warrant, and to lay down when righteousness demands you to stand against the tidal wave of injustice is to prove that one is not courageous or worthy to know or experience the goodness that will naturally flow from what is right, just, and honorable.

In the way of righteousness is life; and in the pathway thereof there is no death (Proverbs 12:28).

♦ Fleshly pursuits will always make us indifferent to the move and work of God in our midst. These pursuits produce the ways of wickedness. Wickedness grows when the standard of righteousness is not being lifted and offered up. God's people were set apart to be a moral compass in the midst of abominable practices. They were to bring the contrast between the holy and the profane. Today, it appears as if some of God's people are sliding into the pit of immorality and coming into agreement with the abominable. Such agreement will show utter contempt towards God.

-RJK

Prayer: Lord, we seek so many vain, useless avenues to keep going. We seek the dead-end ways of self to find purpose, the vanity of the world to find happiness, man's religion to find meaning, and the philosophies of the world understanding. However, You are the only One who can satisfy our lives. Forgive us for our useless, vain pursuits. Amen.

♦ But believe me, O you earthly, sensual, carnally minded professors, however little you may think of Christ now, or however industriously you may strive to keep him out of your thoughts, by pursuing the lust of the eye, the lust of the flesh, and the pride of life, yet there is a time coming, when you will wish you had thought of Christ more and of your profits and pleasures less.

-George Whitefield
(GW, pg. 84)

♦ There are different classes of sinners and different forms of sin. There is sin that is coarse, and there is sin that is refined. There is sin that is low and vulgar, and there is sin that is genteel and elegant. But all sin is alike in essence. It is man seeking to be independent of God, man seeking to have his own way; that is where sin begins, that is the very essence of sin.

-R. A. Torrey
(RA, pgs. 77, 78)

♦ Sadly, people do not want to win, they just want to slide by, slide into home, and somehow make it through life by stealing bases without ever hitting the ball. Therefore, it is sad to see the condition of people. They are not prepared to stand for what is right. They want their life in Christ handed to them without paying the price to know God or how to obtain their life in Him.

-RJK

******

What Can You Offer Heaven?

I heard a funny story in church about man who was bound and determined to take his worldly treasures with him when he died. When he finally passed from this life to the next he managed to take some gold with him. When Peter met him at the pearly gates, he asked him what he had with him. The man told him he had brought some gold. Peter's reply was, "Why did you bring pavement with you?"

Heaven's streets will be paved with gold. It is amazing how heirs of salvation are so bound by those things that will prove to be either dust or pavement in the kingdom of God. There is no real lasting value to what the world prizes. Therefore, it is vital that as believers we treasure that which is eternal in our hearts.

We must be rich in faith and not be caught up with the worldly riches that are temporary and vain. We must be determined to take the glorious reality of Christ with us and not that which could not even hold a candle to the Lord's heavenly light.

Hearken, my beloved brethren, Hath not God chosen the poor of this world rich in faith, and heirs of the kingdom which he hath promised to them that love him (James 2:5)?

♦ When you take what has been ordained by God or consecrated to Him for His glory, and make it common or insignificant, you will profane it.

-RJK

♦ Nervous and emotional disorders arise from materialism, not from walking with God by faith.

-William MacDonald
(TD, pg. 115)

♦ Man, made more like God than any other creature, has become less like God than any other creature. Created to reflect the glory of God, he has retreated sullenly into his cave—reflecting only his own sinfulness.

-A. W. Tozer
(AG, Oct. 20)

♦ Vanity brings its own bondage. It promises, but all it can do is torment. It offers purpose, only to prove to be fleeting. It shows itself in a false glory that quickly gives way to emptiness. It has no form; therefore, there is no real order to be found in any of it.

-RJK

♦ Wherever celibacy is a matter of ecclesiastical compulsion, the danger of impurity and immorality is great.

-William MacDonald
(TD, pg. 81)

Prayer: Lord, before You will speak to the winds and waves of this present world, You must first speak to the storms that are raging in my soul. This is the only way I will be able to receive Your solution, comfort, and encouragement. Amen.

♦ When it came to the war between the old man of the flesh and the new man of Christ in us, John Rusk made this statement, "And here also the new man suffers—humility is opposed by wretched pride—meekness by a hard heart—love by enmity—faith by unbelief—hope by despondency—peace by bitterness—love to God by a love to idols—zeal for truth by carelessness and indifference.

♦ The greatest war rages inside of man. He seeks rest, but it eludes him. He seeks purpose, only to encounter emptiness. He seeks meaning only to become more confused. Nothing makes sense but God. This is why each of us must be restored back into a relationship in Christ with God to have inward peace.

-RJK

◆ Oh Christian! Take heed of a lazy slothful spirit, or a vain and earthly heart, which will easily suffer the duties of religion to be jostled aside, and put by for every trivial occasion; especially beware of slight, formal, superficial, and dead-hearted performances of duty, which are little better than the intermission of them; they may indeed prevent the scandal, but can never give thee the comfort of religion.

-John Flavel
(RR, pg. 206)

◆ Externalism has taken over. God now speaks by the wind and the earthquake only; the still small voice can be heard no more. The whole religious machine has become a noisemaker.

-A. W. Tozer
(AG, Nov. 13)

◆ It is not unusual to see people stand between two opinions. They want the best of both worlds. They pick and choose between worldly ways and moral values that have been readily accepted by the religious world. They want to be politically correct to display a worldly savvy, while being decent and morally okay to silence their conscience. Clearly, this is a dangerous mixture.

-RJK

******

Let It Be

One of the things that always shock me is that people cannot just let things be. They cannot let people simply live their lives. They cannot let them be content in their present status of being content. They must disrupt and cause the same type of discontentment in others as often drives them.

For example, wicked rulers cannot let righteous moral laws stand as a means of governing people. Such despotic leaders cannot accept the fact that those who are moral can govern themselves with great integrity. Subsequently, upright individuals stand as an epitome of man's potential if he chooses the excellent way of moral character. Because of the empty lawlessness reigning in their own souls, these despots must change what is liberating into oppression by tearing down that which is moral and opening the floodgates of wickedness. These wicked floodwaters disrupt order, and create unrest and confusion, allowing these despots to step in to orchestra their wretched ideology and agendas in the situation.

If you don't have to contend with wicked leaders, you might have to push back someone in your life who cannot let matters be. As I study such people, I can see restlessness in their spirit. These individuals are often not content to let matters be because they are not satisfied with their lives. They swing from one limb of expectation to another in an attempt to find the happiness that they perceive they deserve or would bring them satisfaction.

However, each limb leaves them more dissatisfied, causing them to look around for that which might bring them happiness. Once they focus on a possibility, they pursue it, but each time, they are left with emptiness because no person, event, or situation can bring them purpose, happiness, and life. It is clear that if these restless souls do not possess these virtues within, such virtues will always elude them regardless of where they look. What these individuals leave in their wake in regard to others is a sour taste of frustration, disappointment, and emptiness.

The truth about godly character is that it finds contentment in whatever state it is in. Even though those who possess godly character know their place in Christ, they will never settle for mediocrity. Their integrity never allows them to just get by with the "status quo," for they are forever striving to reach heights of personal excellence as a means to be enlarged in their inner being. This enlargement allows them to embrace challenges, face adversity, and walk through valleys of uncertainty.

The solution to all matters is Jesus. He is the only one who can fill our lives with contentment, but we first must deny ourselves of the right to find the happiness we think we might deserve from this present age. We must let go of the possibilities of what may await us on the other side of the mountain, accepting that such pursuits are based on fanciful notions. We must exchange the foolish expectations with the expectation promised in the Word of God.

Our real expectation is not of this present age, and our future hope will be realized in the next world to come. It is only by possessing Christ that we can avoid settling for the "status quo" of this present age and discover the true happiness that can only be found in the abundant life promised by our Lord and Savior. He alone is the giver of life and the author and finisher of our faith, a faith that is able to possess the promises of heaven.

But godliness with contentment is great gain (1 Timothy 6:6).

♦ The longer you live for the world the less enjoyment you get out of it, but the tighter its grip becomes upon your shriveling soul.

-R. A. Torrey
(RA, pg. 204)

♦ We must keep in mind that the things of the world will be wiped from our memory; therefore, we must choose to remember all that we hold on to will be tested in the fires of judgment. And, only that which is eternal and true will pass from this world into the next.

-RJK

♦ He who masters his passions is a king even while in chains. He who is ruled by his passions is a slave even while sitting on a throne.

-Epictetus

♦ Wicked men, like wild horses, would run over and trample underfoot all the people of God in the world, were it not that the bridle of divine providence had a strong curb to restrain them.

-John Flavel
(RR, pg. 63)

♦ Taking the side of righteousness might cost us our place in the world, but the wrong side will cost us our souls. The Bible reminds us that we must "count the cost." We cannot possess the world without selling our souls. We cannot properly possess our souls without letting go of the world. This is the reality of the decision that must and will be made by each of us as we come to this time in our lives and in light of our history.

-RJK

♦ Procrastination is a deadly enemy. We mean well. We may know we are prompted by God to do something, but somehow we forget about it. Our lives become busy, and somehow our "good intentions" drop to the bottom of our to-do lists.

-K. P. Yohannan

♦ Witchcraft is somebody trying to get you to agree with his or her reality against your will.

-RJK

♦ In a sense, everyone is mad. Some are mad for money, others for sexual partners. The Communists are mad for power. I wish definitely to be mad for God. Just as one has to work oneself up to the other kinds of madness, one has to work oneself up for this, too. It seems that it is human destiny to become mad.

-Richard Wurmbrand

♦ We are vulnerable because our flesh serves simply as a covering and not as an armor of protection.

-RJK

♦ You love to listen to the very things that nailed your supposed Master to the tree?! Come off of it, man! Become a hellion, give yourself to demons, run wild; but don't come in here saying you're a believer and playing that game! You want to dance with the devil, then dance all night long! But don't come in here dancing with Christ for a moment, and then go back out there and share your love.

-Paul Washer

♦ This world is a raging and boisterous sea, which sorely tosses the passengers for heaven which sail upon it, but this is their comfort and security; "He stilleth the noise of the sea, the noise of the waves, and the tumult of the people."

-John Flavel
(RR, pg. 63)

Prayer: Lord, You are the One who needs to intrude into my present reality and change the rugged terrain of my soul, but often it is the memories that intrude into my present life and justify the ragged and dangerous aspects of my base character. Lord, I want everything to be connected by Your work of redemption. May I remember the work You did on the cross as I consider my present prevailing mood and look forward to receiving a glorious inheritance that will maintain an upright status with You forever. Amen.

♦ It is sad to think that we have a tendency in our fallen condition to hide behind or run back to wicked, unmerciful masters because our deeds are profane. In such a state, we do not want to accept the ownership of Jesus. We want to hypocritically belong to the blessings of heaven while laying claim to the darkness of the world that serves our purpose.

-RJK

♦ Because the human mind has two compartments, the practical and the idea, people are able to live comfortably with their dreamy, romantic conception of Jesus while paying no attention whatsoever to His words. It is this neat division between the fanciful and the real that enables countless thousands of persons to say "Lord, Lord" in all sincerity while living every moment in flat defiance of His authority.

-A. W. Tozer
(AG, Jul. 14)

♦ A little man with narrow view can cause a world of trouble.

-Charles E. Jefferson

♦ Many Americans have been living in a bubble that says their country is too great to fall. However, a country is only as great as its people. And, if the people lose their edge or caliber of greatness, they cannot expect their country to remain great. It will collapse from within, for the substance of greatness that made it what it was no longer exists. It has been ebbed away by indifference and offered up on the world's altars by selfishness and the pursuit of useless pleasure and wicked philosophies.

-RJK

♦ Any doctrine, any experience that serves to magnify Him is likely to be inspired by Him. Conversely, anything that veils His glory or makes Him appear less wonderful is sure to be of the flesh and the devil.

-A. W. Tozer
(AG, Sept. 16)

Prayer: Lord, save me from the world's foolish substitutes. They abound, but there is only one way to know You—by your Spirit. Amen.

♦ As you follow the Lord's ministry and trial, you will see how the kingdoms of the world were used against Him. The educational system of His time was used to try to entrap Him, the economic system was used to try to deem Him as being part of an insurrection, the religious system was used to declare Him guilty, and the system of the government was the tool that ultimately was used to offer Him up as a scapegoat to maintain a veneer of peace.

-RJK

♦ Popularity is the most fearful of all tests.

-Charles E. Jefferson.

♦ He that is good for making excuses is seldom good for anything else.

-Benjamin Franklin

♦ Worry is the *antithesis of trust. You simply cannot do both.

-Elisabeth Elliot

Take therefore no thought for tomorrow: for the morrow shall take thought for the things of itself. Sufficient unto the day is the evil thereof (Matthew 6:34).

♦ Our tongue often proves to be a loose cannon. It is not only used to shoot others full of holes, but we will inevitably turn around and shoot ourselves in the foot with it.

-RJK

♦ The frustrating thing is that those who are attacking religion claim they are doing it in the name of tolerance, freedom and openmindness. Question: Isn't the real truth that they are intolerant of religion? They refuse to tolerate its importance in our lives.

-Ronald Reagan

♦ We should remember that evil once done is evil that will never be undone.
-H. A. Ironside
(CBO, Sept. 22)

♦ The problem with most people is that they see everything from the pinnacle of personal arrogance. What they fail to realize is that they have never left the base ground of self-delusion.

-RJK

Prayer: Lord, from the heights of arrogance it is easy to design our own yoke, but pride will dictate that it must be immense, self will call for it to bring distinction to us, and the world will require it to be ornate with the things of the present age. In the end, it will simply bury me. Lord, replace my yoke with Your yoke. Amen.

♦ A mere knowledge of Christ in the head only leads to pride that stinks in the nostrils of God.
-Hebert Lockyer
(MP, pg. 303)

♦ And where the leaven of self enters in, the loaf of pride rises, which is the primary recipe for works of the flesh.
-T. A. McMahon

♦ Christians who simply get by in their lives will find themselves giving way to the subtle, but deadly, entanglements of the world.
-RJK

♦ Saintliness is not built on admiration for Jesus Christ... The stately beauty of a saint is not a reformed edition of carnality. A saint is the work of our Master Workman, the Lord Jesus Christ... Saintliness is the product of Calvary and Pentecost where our Lord Jesus Christ dug our souls.
-Oswald Chambers
(DL, Jan. 10)

♦ From whichever side a social gospel originates, it is always man-centered. Its basic claim says man needs to fix or improve his condition through social activism, Christian activism, philanthropy, and good works. A social gospel leaves out the preaching teaching that is the primary reason for the problems of our world.
-Brannon Howse

******

Foolishness of the Flesh

When I look back at my life, I can't help but notice how the foolishness of my flesh, the tyranny of my selfishness, and the arrogance of my conceit affected my life. The traits of the old man in me set me up to be wounded by the sword of truth, the darts of indifference, the arrows of arrogance, and the spears of reality. It was obvious that the weaponry of life had the means to knock me off my high horse, cause me to fall off my pinnacle of self-importance, and be pulled from my position as king of my particular molehill. Ultimately, these weapons would be used to bring me down into the dust of failure, the cesspool of need, and the endless pit of ineptness.

William MacDonald stated that, "If we can't face minor difficulties, how can we expect to face major ones? If we buckle under the petty blows of life, how will we bear up under the sledgehammer blows?"

MacDonald went on to comment on Christians who sulk and pout because they have been offended by others. There are also those who turn in their resignation because someone dared to criticize them, and then there are those who easily get their nose out of joint because someone did not go along with their particular idea or cause. Such people display great immaturity, but what is behind it shows a lack of character. It is insidious and will prove to be foolish. It is nothing more than pride that rides on the fragile shirttails of an overinflated ego or the fanciful silliness of vanity.

I realize that what was often wounded by the different weaponry of life was my pride. The smell of wounded pride is atrocious. It reveals how corrupt the ways and works of the flesh are. Only repentance, forgiveness, and reconciliation can wash away the stench left by the rotting decay of this sin.

My wounds stink and are corrupt because of my foolishness (Psalm 38:5).

♦ The reality is that many people have a false confidence in man's flesh. Whether it is upon the governments run by men, the medical societies that are adjusted to embrace the latest drug, the educational system that propagates godless people, or a religious system that turns out religious skeptics, man cannot change the reality of the currents of life that will slam against the resolve of weak flesh.

-RJK

♦ Why does God say that we should have no other gods? Because He knows that men become like the objects of their worship, and false gods lead to depravity.

-William MacDonald

♦ Sunday morning in America is the greatest hour of idolatry in the whole week. Why? Because most people who are even worshiping God, are worshiping a God they don't know. They're worshiping a god that looks more like Santa Claus than the God of Scripture. They're worshiping a god that is a figment of their own imagination. They created a god in their own likeness and they worship the god they've made."

-Paul Washer

♦ When dealing with the superstition of Ireland and the misguided, oppressive religion of Spain, Robert Chapman made this comparison, "Superstition is better than profane irreligion." (RC, pg. 98)

♦ Offense arises from wounded personal opinion. Stumbling arises from following another person you love, rather than following Christ. Most of our "isms" have arisen from following the prescribed limitations of someone's personal convictions, instead of the Lord.

-Oswald Chambers
(DL, Feb. 6)

♦ The world offers what appears to be many exciting slides, but they all lead downward into a place of complete spiritual ruin.

-RJK

******

A Fool By Nature

In 1 Samuel 25, we are told about the character of a man named Nabal. He was the husband of Abigail, and even though she was an honorable woman, he was churlish, an infidel by nature, the epitome of a fool. John Trapp describes such a man in this way, "That sapless fellow, that carcass of a man, that walking sepulcher of himself, in all religion and right reason is withered and wasted, dried up and destroyed."

Such fools do not care if there is a God. They live for the present and have no vision for tomorrow. They do not retain any real knowledge of God; therefore, they are what we would refer to as a classical example of an "atheist."

Herbert Lockyer Sr. made this statement, "Atheism, The Creed of Fools, robs those who embrace it of all nobility of character. They are corrupt. Of this, we are certain; such a Creed is not accepted in Hell.

On earth are atheists many,
In Hell there is not any."

222

The fool hath said in his heart, There is no God. They are corrupt, they have done abominable works, there is none that doeth good (Psalm 14:1).

♦ I have great assurance when I study my own conversion, when I discuss it with other men, when I look over the 25 years of my pilgrimage with Christ; I have great assurance of having come to know Him. But even now, if I were to depart from the faith and walk away and keep going in that direction into heresy and worldliness, it could be the greatest of proofs that I never knew Him, that the whole thing was a work of the flesh.

-Paul Washer

♦ Carnal men and women would rather magnify the idea of the Cross than submit to the humiliation of the Cross. May God get us to the point of submission!

-Oswald Chambers
(DL, Apr. 1)

♦ Each age of the world carries a big shovel with it. In other words, the world has the ability to bury each of us with it various demands, trap us with its numerous temptations, confuse or delude us with its humanistic philosophies, and cause us to succumb to its deadly ways and lies.

-RJK

Beware lest any man spoil you though philosophy and vain deceit, after the tradition of men, after the rudiments of the world, and not after Christ (Colossians 2:8).

♦ This world is compared to "a sea of glass mingled with fire;" a sea of glass, for the brittleness and frailty of everything in it; and a sea of glass mingled with fire, to represent the sharp sufferings and fiery trials with which the saints are exercised here below. The only support and comfort we have against the fickleness and instability of the creature, is the unchangeableness of God.

-John Flavel
(RR, pg. 131)

♦ The profane entices our pride to toy with its deadly fruits, while pride will always set us up to fall into the destructive traps of the unholy.

-RJK

♦ Some people claim to get converted and entirely sanctified at every camp meeting or revival meeting. They receive the Word of God with great joy,

223

but they soon fall back into their old way of living. They are spiritually shallow because they have never had their selfish wills broken.

-Oswald Chambers
(DL, Aug. 8)

♦ We would like to justify ourselves by thinking that if our past was different, we would be a different person as well. The truth is that we presently are who we are because we have chosen to become that individual in our way of thinking and being.

-RJK

♦ Let no man talk of sinless perfection this side of the grave. I can hardly speak a word that is not sinful. I can hardly think a thought that is not in some way unclean. I can hardly do a thing that is not imperfect. I can hardly have a motive that is not stained with selfishness.

-Herbert Lockyer
(MP, pg. 395)

♦ Man is restless and is forever searching to land on some place that will bring satisfaction to his soul. However, he rarely realizes his restlessness is a spiritual matter and not a fleshly pursuit.

-RJK

******

The Misty Flats

In her book, *By Searching,* China missionary, Isobel Kuhn talks about the time she gave up the narrow road of Christianity to live in what she referred to as the Misty Flats of the world. One might wonder why a Christian would lay aside what he or she has known as truth to give way to that which operates in the grayish clouds of speculation, the foggy mist of compromise, the lifeless plateaus of vanity, and the illusive shadows of wishful thinking and nonstop dead ends.

Her detour from the Christian way came by way of higher education. Since her belief was based on her parent's faith, she had no real substance to defend it when a professor at her secular college put her into a headlock with his atheistic so-called "rational logic" about God. He convinced her that his logic was based on intellectual observance and not on some unseen, unproven, silly hope.

The Word tells us that, "faith is the substance of things hoped for (Hebrews 11:1). There is substance in unfeigned faith but it has been established because a person has believed His Word is true in regard to the creed he or she has chosen to live by. In other words, the person possesses it for him or herself. Isobel had not established this matter in her own heart before she went to college. Therefore, she became easy prey.

When Isobel accepted the godless arguments of her professor, she had no idea where such an attitude would lead her. She writes this about the path she discovered she was on, "I had unconsciously stepped off the High Way where man walks with his face lifted Godward and the pure, piney scent of the Heights call him upward, on to The Misty Flats. The in-between level place of easy-going—nothing very good attempted, yet nothing bad either—where men walk in the mist, telling each other that no one can see these things clearly. The Misty Flats where the in-betweens drift to and fro—life has no end but amusement and no purpose—where the herd drift with the strongest pull and there is no reason for opposing anything. Therefore, they had a kind of peace and a mutual link which they call tolerance."

Eventually, Isobel came back to the reality of God. Her detour into the foggy mist of the world turned into a spiritual search. At the end of it she did find the God of her parents, and through her pursuit, she discovered some important truths about God. She records these truths in one of her books. "God is not a puppet. Man may not pull strings and expect Him to perform—not even doctrinally correct strings, such as Balaam tried to pull. God is not man's servant, that a puny atheist may shout a challenge and He is bound to respond. Neither is God a genie, that if man is lucky enough to find the right combination of words, He will suddenly pop out and reveal Himself. God is our Creator, all-powerful and dwelling in light unapproachable. He demands reverence. But He is also willing to be *Father* to such as come to Him by His ordained road, Jesus Christ, and as a Father He tenderly stoops to the immaturity of the babe in Christ."

Looking back on her experience, she had learned that her fleshly pursuit could not bring happiness. That underneath the triumphant pose of happiness and merriment was misery and nonsense. There was no happiness, just a gnawing reality of disillusionment. She made this statement, "But it was necessary that first I drink to the dregs the emptiness of the promises held out by the Misty Flats: only then could I be freed from their lure and subtle call."

I have traveled through the Misty Flats as well. I had to taste its bitterness to understand the poison it cleverly hides behind its so-called "beauty." I had to come to the end of personal dissatisfaction before I honestly admitted this place held nothing of value in any part of it.

Where are you on your journey through this world? Have you taken a detour to explore the Misty Flats? Have you enough of the emptiness and nonsense you have encountered. If so, repentance and confession will put you back on the right path.

Thus said the LORD; Cursed be the man that trusteth in man, and maketh flesh his arm, and whose heart departeth from the LORD (Jeremiah 17:5).

A Matter of Confronting the Unseen

~

The Real Challenge

What does it mean to effectively live the Christian life? We must be willing to confront the unseen to overcome that which is considered fleshly and worldly. The truth of the matter is the unseen affects us more than what we can physically see with our eyes. For example, we cannot see thoughts even though we think them. We know they exist and they may even erect images in our mind, but such thoughts remain unknown to others unless they are express. Our soul and spirit are unseen, yet the spirit will determine our disposition and the condition of our soul will determine our attitude. Both will be expressed in the personality we develop and how we conduct ourselves around others.

The reality of the unseen is that it takes the invisible virtue of integrity to honestly confront it and the resolve of a saint to withstand it, for the unseen represents the greatest battle to be fought by the believer and the ultimate war that will be won by the Lord of lords and King of kings. However, we must be on the right side to confront and overcome the unseen. This is why we have been given armor and told to endure as "good soldiers."

"Good" soldiers will do what they have to do to prove beneficial to Jesus, His kingdom, and His army. It is for this reason Christians must quit playing at being a soldier and become one. They must quit running around on the outskirts of the Christian way, giving the impression that they are part of this great army, and they must soberly find their place in it. They must quit waving flags of victory and actually pick up their weapons to secure it. It is time for the army of God to get rid of the foolishness of their carnal, civilian ways that seem to be evident in their attitudes. They must prepare to go into a battle that will ultimately determine the outcome of souls that are weighing in the balance.

Thou therefore endure hardness, as a good soldier of Jesus Christ (2 Timothy 2:3).

♦ Never mistake blessings for His mighty regenerating work. Never mistake the external blessings of God for entire sanctification. If you want to be saved, you must repent of your sins and ask for God's forgiveness. If you want to be entirely sanctified, you must bind the "sacrifice with cords" to the altar.

-Oswald Chambers

****

What though I stand with the winners,
Or perish with these that fall?
Only the cowards are sinners,
Fighting the fight is all.
Strong is my foe, who advances,
Snapped is my blade, O Lord;
See their proud banners and lances—
But spare me the stub of a sword.

-quoted by Amy Carmichael
(1867-1951)

♦ There is only one remedy to be found to enable us to gain victory over the powers of this world. It is the manifest presence of our Lord.

-Andrew Murray

Prayer: Lord, sometimes we have to leave the place of security to find the place of safety. I pray I will be like a Peter, willing to leave my boat in order to walk with You through the midst of the storms of my life. Amen.

♦ If the authority becomes arbitrarily tyrannical, we have a demonic situation, which means a regime which is not submissive to God. It would be a sin to submit to a diabolic power.

-Bishop Eivind Berggrav

♦ We as Americans are the wealthiest Christians who ever walked on the face of the earth. We are the most protected Christians that ever walked on the face of the earth, and yet we are the emptiest Christians who ever walked on the face of the earth.

-Paul Washer

♦ The day is coming when the universe will be perfected and will no longer be stained by the curse of sin. Yes, as a believer and co-heir with Christ, you are richer than my frail pen can describe, or that your mind, no matter how high your I.Q., can comprehend.

-Marvin Rosenthal

♦ God allows us to be cast upon the rocks of life to tear away the temporary so that we can embrace the eternal.

-RJK

******

These then are three of the primary hindrances to true discipleship, illustrated by three men who were not willing to go all the way with the Lord Jesus Christ.

Mr. Too Quick—the love of earthy comforts.
Mr. Too Slow—the precedence of a job or occupation.
Mr. Too Easy—the priority of tender family ties.

-William MacDonald
(TD, pgs. 27-31)

◆ So much "devotional writing" today is shallow and sentimental and not at all spiritual.

-Warren W. Wierbe
(PCK, pg. 200)

◆ A determination to know what cannot be known always works harm to the Christian heart.

-A. W. Tozer
(AG, Jun. 4)

◆ The truth is I am very needy, and if I do not keep my spiritual plight in perspective, I will set myself up to fall into the abyss of utter despair. After all, life knows how to knock me off of my all-knowing pinnacle of arrogance and sever the all-knowing weak branches of folly.

-RJK

******

Are You A
Religious Shopper?

The children of Israel were not content with the manna from heaven. This attitude is understandable, but when taken to the extent of one becoming a grumbler, it translates into contempt that is born out of familiarity. The truth is the things of God will never grow old to those who have the right attitude towards Him.

It seems that today, there are so many Christians shopping around for their place in Christ, rather than coming to terms with their calling and vision. They give an appearance that they know who they are and where they are going. They do not see their present state as being one of discontent. Rather, they believe that they want more, but they fail to realize it is on a fleshly plane. The real truth of the matter is that these Christians are looking for that arena that will serve their purpose instead of seeking to know God so they will know which direction He is calling them to.

The problem with being a shopper in Christianity is that God can occasionally open the door of desire to the individual. This door will appear as everything the person has been waiting for or looking for, but in the end it turns out to be a door of judgment. What the person thought he or she wanted becomes sour to his or her taste buds and a stench to his or her nostrils. Hopefully, that as Christians, we each learn our lesson, but in most case the tendency for people is to become bitter and disillusioned towards God.

But lusted exceedingly in the wilderness, and tempted God in the desert. And he gave them their request; but sent leaness into their soul (Psalm 106:14, 15).

♦ Many people are caught up with visions. However, visions can prove to be untrustworthy. You may have a great vision, but if other people do not share in it, nothing will be accomplished. Visions of self-accomplishment will prove to be sentimental, unrealistic, and selfish, while visions inspired by the world will prove to be grandiose, self-serving, and lifeless. However, visions that come from above may call for the miraculous, but in the end they will prove to be practical and beneficial not only to the person who has been entrusted with them, but to others.

-RJK

♦ Please don't get so involved in today's trivia that you forget eternity awaits us all.

-K.P. Yohannan

♦ The secret of a holy life is not in imitating Jesus, but in letting the perfections of Jesus be manifested in our mortal flesh.

-Oswald Chambers
(DL, Jan. 17)

Prayer: Dear Lord, I give myself away, 'tis all that I can do.

-Isaac Watts

♦ Jesus is the One who uncaps the Living Water of the Spirit in the soul. This is why He sent forth the invitation to come to Him. The reality is that there is so much in the soul of man that would hinder the flow of these rivers. There are walls of fear, and the boulders of wounds and unforgiveness that block the way. There are barren wildernesses of unbelief that will absorb such water without it making any real impact on people's lives.

-RJK

♦ If we can only learn the folly of living away from God by bitter experience, God let us have the experience.

-R. A. Torrey
(RA, pg. 79)

♦ Never make a principle out of your own experience; let God be as original with other people as He is with you.

-Oswald Chambers

♦ The hustle and bustle of that road drowns out His message of self-sacrifice—few desire to hear that message. The wide road does not lead to a hill called Calvary and to death of the self-life, but to a path lined with amenities that satisfy the self-seeking.

-E. A. Johnston
(NTB, pg. 33)

♦ Christians must be aware of the subtleties of Satan. He is not locked up yet, and he is having a field day within the so-called Church in America.

-Marv Rosenthal

******

Are You A Spiritual Somnambulist?

Do you know what a somnambulist is? It is a word I have recently learned. It is not that I am ignorant of such a condition, but I know it according to another term: sleep-walker. However, to be a somnambulist is to be more than someone who walks in his or her sleep. It is an abnormal, addictive condition where these people will not only walk in their sleep, but they actually perform some type of action. For example, there is a story about Robert Ledrue. In his youth he was one of the foremost detectives of France.

Ledrue was given an assignment to investigate the murder of a man who was shot at night after bathing in the sea. The police were baffled because there was no real motive or reason for the man's murder. However the murderer had left prints in the sand and a bullet in the victim.

After Ledrue investigated the murder, he went to the head of the police and asked to be arrested. The shoeprints, which reveal that the big toe on the right foot was missing, as well as the bullet from a special revolver pointed to him as a murderer. Granted, he could not remember doing such a horrific deed but the evidence could not be refuted.

He asked the police department to keep him permanently under surveillance. Later, while wandering around at night, he shot at another person, completely unconscious of what he was doing. Since his revolver was filled with harmless bullets, no one was injured, but the police discovered he was a somnambulist. He was sentenced to lifelong isolation on a solitary farm under police surveillance.

The problem with sin is that it puts people to sleep. Many become spiritual somnambulists. They do wicked deeds, but have no idea what they are doing. Jesus confirmed this when He stated on the cross that His accusers and executioners did not know what they were doing. Spiritual somnambulists are not only asleep to the hurt they cause others, but they are indifferent to the destructive tide they leave behind. They are blinded by the god of this age and walk in the shadows of denial as they justify their actions as being right and excusable. They have no sense of the reality around them as they walk in the darkness of their own self-delusion.

It is for this reason that we need to discern if we are asleep, unaware of what is taking place in our lives, and around us, and if we are walking in the light of Christ, fully conscious of everything around us that is affecting our lives. After all, as believers we have been called children of the light. As children of the light, we are no longer subject to the ways of darkness.

Ye are all the children of light, and the children of the day: we are not of the night, nor of darkness. Therefore let us not sleep, as do others; but let us watch and be sober (1 Thessalonians 5:5, 6).

♦ I have learned that I am the one who constructs how my memories connect me to my past and define my present. I am the one who will determine how such memoirs ultimately affect the terrain of my disposition, attitude, and behavior. Therefore, I have the responsibility to consider the way in which I handle these recollections when it comes to the attitude that is being developed in me towards life.

-RJK

♦ I want to submit to you tonight that this country is not gospel-hardened; it is gospel-ignorant because most of its preachers are. And let me repeat this: the malady in this country is not liberal politicians, the root of socialism, Hollywood, or anything else; it is the so-called evangelical pastor, preacher, and evangelist of our day. That is where the malady is to be found.

-Paul Washer

♦ When it is dark don't curse the darkness; turn on the lights.

-Unknown

♦ It is hard for people to realize they are preparing themselves for eternity. If people can't stand the truth, how can they stand heaven? If people resent having sin revealed, how can they remain in the light of heaven? If people become anxious over the moving of the Holy Spirit, how will they tolerate His power and presence in heaven?

-RJK

******

Yield not to temptation,
For yielding is sin;
Each victory will help you
Some other to win;
Fight manfully onward,
Dark passions subdue;
Look ever to Jesus,
He'll carry you through.

To him that o'ercometh
God giveth a crown;
Through faith we shall conquer,
Though often cast down;
He who is our Saviour
Our strength will renew;
Look ever to Jesus
He'll carry you through.

-H. R. Palmer
(1834-1907)

♦ Sin before God is of two kinds. One is the sin of refusing to obey when he issues orders; the other is the sin of going ahead when he has issued none. The one is rebellion; not doing what the Lord has commanded. The other is presumption: doing what he has not required.

-Watchman Nee
(WN, Oct. 17)

♦ Condemnation is always the opposite of justification, never the opposite of sanctification.

-Anna Alden-Tirrill
(SP, Jun. 5)

There is therefore now no condemnation to them which are in Christ Jesus, who walk not after the flesh, but after the Spirit (Romans 8:1).

♦ Away from God there is barrenness, away from God is an aching void, away from God is the bottomless abyss of insatiable desire; away from God is woe, woe, woe!

-R. A. Torrey
(RA, pg. 82)

♦ Contrast is necessary. After all, there is a distinct contrast between light and darkness, but not much of a contrast between grays and the twilight of man's soul. For example, in the spiritual realm, grays represent compromise of righteousness, and twilight symbolizes the justification of sin. Both will cast shadows that will ultimately cover the real essence of the darkness that is invading one's soul—that of spiritual ruin.

-RJK

♦ Temptation may best be called "that wild reach of possibility" which stretches one to fame or infamy; and the higher we walk, the more severe the temptation.

-Oswald Chambers
(DL, Apr. 5)

♦ The Christian is engaged in warfare as long as he lives on this earth. But his role can be compared to that of a military physician. He has to give medicine and comfort to the wounded on both sides.

-Richard Wurmbrand
(AWG, pg. 41)

******

How Am I Faring?

In the fall we have feathered visitors. Once at this time of the year in our previous house a family of five turkeys paraded around our place. The tom stood as a watchman while the mother and the five offspring enjoyed the goodies that the ground provided for them.

As I watched these creatures, a smile came to my lips as I remembered a story our landlord's wife shared with me about an incident that happened at the house before we resided there. She was sitting on the deck as her husband was doing odds and ends jobs around the place. She heard a commotion. She looked around to see a procession coming around the corner of the house. The scene she beheld could have come out of the pages of a comic book. Leading the procession was her small dog that appeared close to hysteria. Behind the dog were wild turkeys running at high speed. Behind the turkeys was her small grandson with his play bow and arrow in hand. He was chasing right behind the turkeys as if he was after some game for the dinner table.

I am sure you can imagine such a sight. But, as I consider myself, I wonder how my armor and weapon is faring in my spiritual battles. Is my armor paper-like and does my weapon appear as if it is just a toy? It is something that I must honestly examine for there are great battles before me, and I must be prepared to stand at all times with my weapon drawn.

Prayer: Lord, we can take on all kinds of battle poses as we flex our muscles, but when it finally comes, the only thing that will ensure our endurance through it is the armor You provided for us. Lord, help me to make sure I have it in place every day. Amen.

♦ The unjust sinner can no more go to heaven than the justified sinner can go to hell.

-A. W. Tozer
(AG, Apr. 14)

♦ What most people fail to realize is that evil is not an intellectual issue. Granted, we may have the intelligence to recognize evil, but evil is a moral and spiritual problem. Therefore, it cannot be confronted on an intellectual front. It must be addressed on a spiritual front.

-RJK

♦ We shall have all eternity to celebrate the victories, but we have only the few hours before sunset in which to win them.

-Amy Carmichael

♦ Egyptian and Babylonian, Grecian and Roman philosophy had trained men to think about unseen things. The whole spirit of the world tempted Christians to be content with the first elements of salvation and not to press on to the life in which the world, with its wisdom and its pleasure, had to be entirely sacrificed before Jesus Christ could take possession of the heart and rule the whole life.

-Andrew Murray
(AP, Oct. 22)

******

A Christmas Miracle

Even though there is much we contend with in the physical world, we must be aware that it is greatly affected by the unseen world. If we only consider the physical aspect of a matter, we will eventually end up in utter despair. We must believe and know that there is much that we cannot see or know because of the providence that governs the unseen. After all, it is the unseen that speaks of the miraculous. It is the unseen that gives us glimpses into the arena of that which inspires hope and allows us to walk in assurance when all seems hopeless.

I recently read about such a matter in a church newsletter. It was a story about tasting the bitterness of the physical, only to be given hope by that which had no real explanation. At such times one must concede that some type of miracle took place, even if it took on a physical form to bring it about. This incident took place around Christmas.

It was December 23, 1910 in eastern Czechoslovakia. A plague of diphtheria had hit the tiny village of Velky Slavkov.

A lone man walked against the wind in the shadow of the High Tatra Mountains with a can of black paint. The inevitable was about to happen again. He would have to mark another door with a black "X."

Inside the marked house a distraught woman was kneeling at her doorpost, weeping and praying in Slovak. The woman's name was Suzanne. Her sorrow went deep into the recesses of her soul. She and her husband Jano were now childless. Their five-year-old daughter had succumbed to the dreaded disease a week prior, but now she had to face two new coffins that would be the final resting place for their two precious sons who had also become the latest victims of diphtheria. They would be laid to rest in the frozen ground right beside their sister.

Tomorrow was Christmas Eve and the house would be silent even though haunting memories of what was would echo through the empty vacuum. Clearly, the house had become a tomb that was marked by the seal of death.

Jano was also weak from the illness. He mentioned that he might not see in the New Year. All seemed hopeless as the jaws of doom gripped the couple's sorrowful hearts.

However, the silence of the tomb was interrupted by someone knocking at the formidable door. Suzanna opened the door. An old woman appeared on the other side of it. Suzanna warned her of the deadly plague that had laid claims on the home. In spite of the warning, the old woman stepped into the house. Her instruction was simple. She held out a jar of kerosene oil. She instructed Suzanna to take a white cloth, wrap it around her finger and put it in the kerosene. Then she was to swab out her husband's throat, and then have him swallow a teaspoon of the oil. The old woman told Suzanna that it would cause him to vomit the deadly mucous. Otherwise, he would die. Upon her instruction, the woman exited the house to disappear into the cold night

236

True to the old woman's word, upon following her instructions, Jano retched up the deadly phlegm and his fever broke. The curse of death was broken from the house and there was rejoicing that reached into the air towards heaven.

That Christmas there were no Christmas presents under the tree, but the jar on the window represented a gift of life for generations to come.

Jano and Suzanna shared the miraculous ingredients in the jar with others. Jano eventually immigrated to America and Suzanna later joined him with their eight children. They settled near the steal mills of Johnstown Pennsylvania. It was this couple's great granddaughter who wrote this Christmas story that was put into publication for others to marvel at the grace shown by the unseen hand of Providence.

Be not forgetful to entertain strangers: for thereby some have entertained angels unawares (Hebrews 13:2).

******

♦ Even though darkness can prove to be great upon our souls, we know that Christ serves as the anchor in our spirits.

-RJK

♦ Oh, how many men grow careless, grow worldly, grow sinful, grow indifferent, because somebody has inoculated them with the pernicious error of eternal hope. How many men there are alive now, once earnest in the service of God, who are indifferent about the condition of the lost, the worldly, and the careless, because they have read some books undermining, or trying to undermine, the doctrines of Jesus and the Apostles.

-R. A. Torrey
(RA, pg. 122)

******

The Luxury of Ignorance

There is a certain luxury in being ignorant, due to the fact that one is not responsible for what he or she does not know. In America we have had the opportunity to live in such ignorance when it comes to the struggles of others. We can imagine, on a very limited basis, some of the living conditions that much of the world struggles beneath. To them surviving the harshness of life is a 24/7 battle that eventually will be lost.

I recently read a book about this struggle, titled, *No Longer A Slumdog*, by K.P. Yohannan. I had some knowledge of the depravity that is plaguing what is known as the 10/40 window. Within the 10/40 window includes South Asian countries, but I was overwhelmed by the figures of just how far- reaching it is.

The bondage of these people exists in their thinking. There are those in America that talk about class warfare, but in reality they have no idea the depth of it because it is not practiced on a national basis such as being practiced in South Asia. In countries in South Asia, each individual is put into a caste that is determined by birth. In other words, it does not matter what kind of talent, intelligence, or ability you may have to make a difference, you will be prevented from ever reaching your potential because you were born to a lower caste.

This oppressive way of thinking began around 1500 B.C. with the arrival of the Aryans in India, who thought themselves to be of a superior race. In their arrogance, they devised a cruel system to keep from being "contaminated" by the indigenous people. This also was their way of controlling the population. They used the mind-bending tool of the caste system to bring separation between the people. The system put into practice actually used the present idolatry, and taught that people were born from different parts of the body of their god Brahma and thus had differing value. Their means of indoctrination cleverly twisted how the people began to look at each other, as well as themselves.

The caste system divided society based on roles or jobs. Those born in a lower caste had no hope of advancing. And, with the indoctrination of generations this perverted view became accepted by the people without being rationally questioned. Of course, their belief system entangled them more into a destructive loop.

According to their belief system, everyone's present lot is based on their previous life. Because of their karma or past deeds, their lot was cast and established by the position in which they were born. As a result, regardless of how oppressive their lot may be, they have to accept their position because there is no way out of the cycle of what is known as reincarnation, except coming to a point of utter nothingness, where life ceases altogether.

The four categories in the caste system are as follows: Brahmins (priests and teachers), Kshatriyas (rulers and soldiers), Vaisyas (merchants and traders), and Sudras (laborers and servants). Within these four categories are countless sub-castes that further divide and categorized the Hindu population. At the bottom of the bottom are the Dalits, which are also known as the "untouchables." The Dalits can barely survive and are often cruelly taken advantage of by those in a higher caste. According to figures, only five percent of the "Brahmins," make up those who dominate the country's political, social, and economic arenas. Dalits and OBCs (Other Backward Castes), make up more than 60 percent of India's population which is equal to the population of Europe. This means every 10 people alive today on the planet earth are either a Dalit or an OBC.

The greatest victims in this wicked, caste system are the children of the Dalits. The figures are astounding. There are 1.2 billion children who make up one part of the 10/40 window. More than 300 million children, one-fourth of the 10/40 window live in the South Asian countries of India, Bangladesh, Myanmar, and Sri Lanka. The population of these children would be as large as the United States.

Even though there are child labor standards that have been established by the United Nations, many of these children are still being exploited. Innocence is taken away from them at an early age. Sixty percent of these child laborers are 11 years or younger. More than 50 million children are in "hazardous work" involving long hours; physical or sexual abuse, and exposure to toxic environments.

Every year, an estimated 1.2 million children become victims of trafficking. Nepal women and girls as young as nine years old, amounting to 10,000 to 15,000 per year, are sold into India's red-light district. Sri Lanka is known as a pedophile's paradise with up to 40,000 child prostitutes, mostly boys, trafficked to serve tourists. The final figure is that 300,000 children worldwide are currently trafficked as child soldiers.

The Bible is clear that man has a sin problem. Different aspects of civilization can use all the laws they want to try to protect the less fortunate, but those who are users are forever figuring ways around them, and continue to play on the circumstances, ignorance, and indoctrination of others. The reason why is because man has a bent towards sin. He is established by pride that has been conditioned with prejudices. Until this blinding veil is taken away from the hearts and minds of the people, grave cruelties will be justified by the arrogance of others. There will be no conscience or display of conscience from such people.

As Christians we know that God is not a respecter of persons. There are no classes or differences to Him when it comes to societies. However, we must make sure that we do not hold to such arrogance and prejudice. We must remember that the cross of Christ is a big equalizer for everyone. We all need to be saved and we all need to be forgiven. And, praise God, He has made salvation available to all who will come, regardless of their status.

But if ye have respect to persons, ye commit sin, and are convinced of the law as transgressors (James 2:9).

♦ What difference is there between the king on the throne and the beggar on the dunghill, when God demands their breaths? There is no difference, my brethren, in the grave, nor will there be any at the day of judgment.

-George Whitefield
(GW, pg. 242)

♦ When people are busy, they are not prepared to receive. For Christians, this means receiving instructions, encouragement, or direction. For this reason many Christians are becoming lost, confused, or burned out. We are running when we need to be listening. We are weary when we need to be running the race. We are complacent when we need to stand.

-RJK

♦ Often God has to shut a door in our face, so that He can subsequently open the door through which He wants us to go.

-Catherine Marshall

♦ The wisdom and love of God hath built an house for a refuge and sanctuary to believers in tempestuous and evil times, containing many comfortable and pleasant chambers prepared for their lodgings, till the calamities be overpast; three of them have been already opened, viz, the power, wisdom, and faithfulness of God.

-John Flavel
(RR, pg. 130)

♦ So much that impacts change is hidden from sight, but it either reaches down into the deep canyons of testing or it reaches upwards to the heights of revelation, but it remains unseen until it breaks forth in the dawning of a new day of hope. This dawning only occurs because the best of the day is first prepared in the obscurity of darkness. In the end, its fruit will speak of the depths it plummets to and the heights it has reached in light of the glory of heaven.

-RJK

♦ Anyone can retire into a quiet place, but it's the shutting of the door that makes the difference. Solitude is a time for stripping away everything to focus on God.

-Unknown

♦ The evidence that you truly repented long ago when you said you did is because you're still repenting now and even to a greater degree. The evidence that you believed a long time ago is that you're still believing now and ever more believing in greater and greater degrees.

-Paul Washer

♦ But what it means to perish in all the eternal outworkings of a depraved character, what it means to perish in that endless vista that lies ahead of us, no human language can describe, no human fancy can conceive.

-R. A. Torrey
(RA, pg. 157)

♦ Feelings often mean you are grasping at straws. We often feel with our fingers because we cannot see the certainty of the future. Many times our conclusions and aspirations turn out to be nothing more than wishful thinking.

-RJK

♦ One single devil whom we have pitied can destroy a paradise. One day of softness and a nation can lose overnight its happy institutions built up through generations of struggle...When occasion demands, tell a devil in a high position that he is a devil.

Richard Wurmbrand
(AWG, pg. 42)

Prayer: Lord, we think we are so clever trying to keep one toe in the Living Water while bathing in the contaminated waters of the world. We then wonder why the bitter taste of vanity is welling up in our mouths and we come out smelling of the filth of the world. We cannot serve two masters or walk in two directions. I want to be in Your flow going the direction of righteousness. Amen.

♦ The person condemned is the one who insists on saving himself, instead of trusting Jesus to save him. Be careful my friend! You may have a good testimony, a spotless record, and yet be condemned at the end of it all. Like Judas, you may have been with Jesus Christ for three long years, night and day; you may have been used of Him; but you may be exposed, expelled, and condemned by Him.

-Oswald Chambers

♦ We never reach the innermost room in any man's soul by the expediencies of the showman or the buffoon. The way of irreverence will never lead to the Holy Place.

-John Henry Jowett

♦ Devotion without discipline can become shallow mysticism.

-Warren W. Wiersbe
(PCK, pg. 111)

♦ The problem with most people is they are more interested in appearing clever when it comes to the things of the world, than being wise about the matters that really count in light of eternity.

-RJK

Prayer: Lord, it is foolishness to cling to my take of things, stupid to insist on it, and suicidal if You give it to me. Help me to cease from foolishness, flee the stupid ways of self, and bow out of committing spiritual suicide over nothing more than the vanity of the world. Amen.

******

Have You Calculated the Miraculous?

I have always marveled at Jesus feeding the 5,000 people plus with a couple of fish and five loaves of bread. But, have you ever thought about how much manna had to fall from heaven to maintain the Israelites in the wilderness? In his book, *All the Messianic Prophecies of the Bible,* Hebert Lockyer gives some idea as to the proportions that entailed feeding the Hebrews based on a family made up of four members. Each man would have to gather an average of six quarts of manna a day. If 500,000 men gathered this amount, the daily supply must have been 93,500 bushels. If you compute this finding based on 40 years in the wilderness, the children of Israel would have consumed *one thousand three hundred and seventy millions, two hundred and three thousand, six hundred bushels.* Regardless of the numbers or the circumstances, provision is nothing to God. Imagine, we occasionally become concerned about our Lord providing us with our daily needs! No wonder the Lord said to His disciples, "O' ye of little faith!" (MP, pg. 304)

Prayer: Lord, we display little faith because we look at the circumstance instead of You. Help me to fix my eyes upward instead of fixing them on the terrain and elements that surround me. Amen.

******

We are in a battle, and God has provided the armor and weapon that is necessary to be triumphant. In his book, *True Discipleship,* William MacDonald lines out what it takes to be victorious in the unseen battle. Here is an outline of his points.

War demands:
Austerity and sacrificial living
Suffering
Obedience

Knowledge of the enemy and of his strategy
Undistractedness
Courage in the face of danger

MacDonald pointed out what others have previously made reference to, "that the armor of the Christian soldier in *Ephesians 6:13-18* makes no provision for the back and therefore no provision for retreat."

Put on the whole armour of God, that ye may be able to stand against the wiles of the devil (Ephesians 6:11).

******

♦ We want to be Christians without being involved in battle.
-Richard Wurmbrand
(AWG, pg. 59)

♦ If God has really done something in Christ on which the salvation of the world depends, and if He has made it known, then it is a Christian's duty to be intolerant of everything which ignores, denies, or explains it away.
-James Denney

♦ Man is what his "will" makes him, and sin's seat of operation is in the human will. A person's attitude toward God depends on the simplicity of a personal choice.
-Oswald Chambers
(DL, Jan. 11)

♦ Many people see the promises of God from a far off, but they will not leave their old ways behind in order to be prepared to walk towards, and in, those promises.
-RJK

♦ In regard to temptation, A. W. Tozer pointed out that the faithfulness of God can deliver us from temptation. He then goes on to say, "God's faithfulness is the way out, because it's the way up, you can be sure of that." (AG, Jun. 19)

But every man is tempted, when he is drawn way of his own lust, and enticed (James 1:14).

♦ Live near to God—and all things will appear little to you in comparison with eternal realities.
-Robert McCheyne

♦ Unless you meet God at the altar, He will never alter you.

-Oswald Chambers
(DL, Mar. 15)

♦ There is a lack of sincerity about committing the eternal soul to God and holding back the mortal life—professing to give Him the greater and withholding the lesser.

-R. A. Laidlaw

♦ No matter how dark and long the valley of distress appears, we can be assured that in due time the penetrating light of the Morning Star (Jesus) will break through and provide us with the wings for our souls to once again soar on the currents of expectation.

-RJK

♦ (God's) holiness and hell are two fires that are never quenched.

-Hebert Lockyer
(MP, pg. 383)

♦ The greatest act of judgment that God can pour out on a people is being poured out on America, and it is this: He's taken away the knowledge of God, and He's closed the mouth of those who are supposed to be speaking for Him. So that little boys lead us with their silly little ideas and we like it that way, because we really do want our best life now.

-Paul Washer,

♦ It is easy to follow some great person or cause in light of expectation, but once darkness comes between the zeal and the expectation of a matter, that is when people will determine if something is worthy of their consideration and commitment.

-RJK

♦ The glory of light cannot exist without its shadows. Life is a whole, and *good* and *ill* must be accepted together.

-Sir Winston Churchill

♦ Satan can imitate the Holy Spirit in everything but one. Experiences? The Devil will give you thousands of them. But he can never produce the result the Holy Spirit produces—a holy character that glorifies Jesus.

-Oswald Chambers
(DL, Apr. 25)

♦ As Christians, our eyes must not mirror this present world, but reflect the glory of the next.

-RJK

******

Forms of Darkness

If you are going to understand the extent of darkness in this present world, you must come to terms with the light that has been given that can penetrate the darkness. For instance, there are different types of darkness. There is the darkness of the night, the darkness of the age we live in, and the dark night of the soul. But, God has provided the light in which we can see what we need to see to walk through each type of darkness.

For example, the world we live in has its own natural darkness. However, God has provided the light of the moon and the stars to shine through the natural darkness to highlight the terrain or landscape around us. In the age we live in the darkness is caused by sin and death, but God has provided His Son to penetrate the darkness of the present age with His light of truth. In the dark night of the soul He has provided His Spirit to bring comfort and His Word to guide our steps.

As Christians, we have the abiding light with us at all times. However, we must let Him provide the light by seeking Him in times of darkness.

For ye were sometimes darkness, but now are ye light in the Lord: walk as children of light (Ephesians 5:8).

The Reality of Church And Religion

~

The Power of the Church

When we think about the Church, we usually associate it with a building, denominations, and religion. However, the true Church is not a lifeless building, a theological school of thought, or a set of religious rituals and rules. Rather, the true Church of Jesus Christ is a living organism, a many-membered body, and a universal habitation that is marked by the seal of the Spirit and set apart by a heavenly glory that manifests itself in righteousness and godliness.

We know that the Church is established on the eternal Rock of ages. It is aligned to the Cornerstone of Zion, and it must grow up in the head of the Lord of lords in order to realize its high calling in this world. This universal body has also been endued with the power of the Holy Spirit and serves as fruitful garden that offers the eternal waters from the everlasting fountain of heaven.

The Church has been endued with such power that hell will not be able to prevail against it. However, there is another point in which the Church is able to experience such power. It is a point that is not always greatly emphasized in the right way, for it is often ignored by those with their only agenda. It has to do with oneness.

The Church is to be one body, bound by one Spirit and an unchangeable truth. There is no real schism in the real body, but due to man's religious influence, divisions occur among those who are immature and carnal. In such a state, doctrinal elitism and burdensome practices have caused self-righteousness to flourish. Such elitism does not call for excellence but submits to the base ways of being critical and unteachable.

Not everyone in the body of Christ will have the same conclusions about spiritual matters just as the various members of the physical body will have different functions. If an eye could hear what the ear hears, it would not be an eye. It the arm could do what a leg does, it would not be an arm. The diverse spiritual conclusions of the different members of the Church vary, not because of division, but because the callings, experiences, and responsibilities vary. Each member must walk according to his or her own path. Since each member will walk a different path, he or she will also see different terrain. Once again the difference paths do not constitute division in the body.

The power of this oneness was brought out when an atheist attended an underground meeting in Russia. The Christian preacher asked the atheist before he exited the meeting, "How many do you think were here?" The reply of the atheist was a hundred. The preacher told him that is what he saw, but actually what he really saw was a body of one, which functioned as one soul and one heart.

The preacher went on to make this declaration, "We are one person who bears the name 'hundred.' We are one who soars toward heaven, and heaven inclines toward us with all its beauties. If you could feel for one moment the rapture of this oneness, not only with our fellowmen but with the whole creation and with God, you would leave everything in the world for it."

Jesus talked in His prayer about the power there is in His Church being one. He stated this truth, *"That they all may be one; as thou, Father, art in me, and I in thee, that they also may be one in us: that the world may believe that thou hast sent me. And the glory which thou gavest me I have given them; that they may be one, even as we are one: I in them, and thou in me, that they may be made perfect in one; and that the world may know that thou hast sent me, and hast loved them, as thou has loved me" (John 17:21-23).*

And I say also unto thee, That thou art Peter, and upon this rock (Jesus) I will build my church; and the gates of hell shall not prevail against it (Matthew 16:18). (Parenthesis added.)

******

♦ The true Gospel has been a casualty in the present religious environment. The light of it (Christ) has been alleviated by unbelief and compromise. The warning of it (repent and flee the wrath of God upon all sin), has been done away with, and the hope of it (resurrection) has been exchanged for wishful thinking. In essence, the glass of the Gospel has been fragmented by compromise, broken by heresy, and clouded by unbelief. It is time for the mirror to be reestablished in its completeness so men can hear the message and flee the wrath to come on all unbelief and disobedience to the Gospel.

-RJK

♦ It is not until a man finds his faith opposed and attacked that he really begins to think about implications of that faith. It is not until the church is confronted with some dangerous heresy that she begins to realize the riches and wonder of orthodoxy. It is characteristic of Christianity that it has inexhaustible riches and that it can always produce new riches to meet any situation.

-William Barclay

♦ The church is in trouble—that's what they say anyways. The problem is most of what they call the church is not the church, and the church is not quite as in trouble as everybody thinks. As a matter of fact, the church today is absolutely beautiful—she's glorious, she's humble, she's broken, and she's confessing her sin. The problem is what everybody's calling the church today isn't the church. Basically, by and large, what's called the church today is nothing more than a bunch of unconverted church people with unconverted pastors.

-Paul Washer

♦ There are thousands of Christians, men and women, today whom one would not, for the world, un-Christianize—but whose Christianity is puny, weak, infirm, hopeless, complaining, fretful, miserable; of whom you cannot think as "good soldiers of Jesus Christ. " Soldiers! They are more fit for a hospital than a battlefield. They have no joy, no peace, no testimony; they are victims of the world, the flesh, and the Devil, almost without resistance; and the whole secret of it is this, they starve their "souls"... They have neither time nor inclination—or if they have inclination they have not the time, and if they have the time they have not the inclination—to seek for, and feed upon, the Bread of Life through those channels which God has provided for its reception.

-Unknown

Prayer: Lord, so much of what I see in Christendom appears to be like that of the vision Ezekiel had of the valley of dead bones. However, You can breathe on the dead bones and they will be quickened and rise up with new life. Lord, send Your Spirit. Amen.

♦ The Presence of God is meant to be more than just an occasional event during Sunday morning worship. We are meant to live in God's Presence all the time! God is omnipresent, and His Presence is always with us.

-Anna Alden-Tirrill
(SP, Mar. 20)

♦ Easy chair Christianity has no place on the narrow road.

-E. A. Johnston
(NTB, pg. 19)

♦ The price the pastor fails to pay, the sheep end up paying.

-Donna Skoog

♦ Formality and hypocrisy in any religious exercise is an abomination unto the Lord. And to enter his house merely to have our ears entertained, and not our hearts reformed, must certainly be highly displeasing to the most high God, as well as unprofitable to ourselves.

-George Whitefield
(GW, pgs. 127, 128)

******

Keeping My Spiritual Edge

Through the years I have noticed an important pattern occurring in God's Church. Jesus will always call His people to follow Him, and when He turns His back to lead His sheep, the wolves will come in to attack, devouring and taking away vulnerable sheep.

It is hard for God's people to realize that when it is time for them to follow Jesus, they are the most vulnerable. If they linger behind or stop to graze on bits of grass, they will find themselves falling prey to wolves.

Jesus is clear that all disciples must first deny themselves of the luxury to linger a bit longer, crucify the tendency to graze on that which has no substance or purpose, and become serious in following Him up the path of righteousness.

In my years of ministry I had to learn the hard way about heeding the voice of Jesus. After all, the voice of a wolf may be perverse, but it can be enticing and destructive. To keep my spiritual edge I must remain within hearing distance of my Lord and Shepherd.

To him the porter openeth; and the sheep hear his voice; and he calleth his own sheep by name, and leadeth them out...And a stranger will they not follow, but will flee from him: for they know not the voice of strangers (John 10:3, 5).

♦ Tertullian's remark that the blood of the martyrs was the seed of the church, inexplicable though it might be, has proved to be true. People apparently wanted something more than pleasure and profit. Only firmly held convictions worth dying for could make life worth living.

-Dave Hunt

♦ It certainly is true that hardly anything is missing from our churches these days—except the most important thing. We are missing the genuine and sacred offering of ourselves and our worship to the God and Father of our Lord Jesus Christ.

-A. W. Tozer

(AG, Nov. 14)

♦ Christ's last command to evangelize the world is our first command.

-Marvin Rosenthal

♦ Every religion, except Christianity, reveres the past. Christianity alone makes the best in the past seem poor, compared to the present—and the present seem poor, compared with what is yet to be.

-Oswald Chambers

(DL, Apr. 12)

******

The Commission

How important is it for Christians to fulfill their commission to share the Gospel with the lost, and to serve as a living, walking example of Christ? Its importance was brought home to me years ago. A young man was brought to me for ministry. He looked innocent enough, but I found out that he was organizing a group of 50 high school students to wreak havoc on the community in which I lived.

This young man received Christ, but imagine if he had carried out his plans? Perhaps one of my friends, family members, or myself might have been directly affected in a traumatic way.

There is another story where a weary pastor expressed his concern because of a missed opportunity to convert people to Christ. It had come to the attention of this pastor that a young member of Romania's Communist Youth Organization was once arrested and unmercifully beaten by a "self-proclaiming" Christian police officer. The young man who was beaten became a ruthless dictator of the Communist nation of Romania. His name was Nicolai Ceausescu. He was responsible for the torture of countless Christians, which included this pastor.

We never know who we will eventually come face-to-face with down the line. Personally, I do not want to face someone as an enemy that I once missed the opportunity to share my life in Christ with them.

We possess a message that can change not only a course for one person, but many. The domino affect of our action or inaction will not be fully realized in this world, but we must remember we will come face to face with it in the world to come.

Also I heard the voice of the Lord, saying, Whom shall I send, and who will go for us? Then said I, Here am I; send me (Isaiah 6:8).

♦ Let us never forget that the presence of the Lord is more important than the vessels of the Lord.

-Herbert Lockyer
(MP, pg. 468)

♦ Let me add, that any religion that is not saving you from the power of sin today will not save you from the consequences of sin in eternity. There is a lot of religion in this world that is absolutely worthless.

-R. A. Torrey
(RA, pg. 74)

♦ Christianity rests on three great pillars: the Incarnation, the Crucifixion, and the Resurrection of the Lord Jesus Christ.

-H. A. Ironside
(CBO, Dec. 25)

♦ It is not unusual to discover that after the dust settles on much of the activity surrounding religion, that nothing has been settled in light of eternity because such activities were a matter of carnality.

-RJK

Prayer: Lord, Your Word is clear; we must not think so highly of ourselves that we end up judging You. In such arrogance we may believe we are right, but in due time Your Word will prove how wrong we are. Bring us up to the snubbing post of humility and break us in our stiff-necked ways. Amen.

♦ This holy and fervent flame in the soul awakens the interest of heaven, attracts the attention of God, and places at the disposal of those who exercise it, the exhaustless riches of divine grace. The dampening of the flame of holy desire is destructive of the vital forces in church life. God requires to be represented by a fiery church, or He is not in any proper sense, represented at all. God, himself, is all on fire, and His Church, if it is to be like Him, must also be as white heat.

-E. M. Bounds

♦ In the last century the Church throughout the world has sadly dropped the ball of discipleship and has deflated its true meaning to fit current ideologies of comfortable Christianity. We are willing to "commit" to Jesus, but unwilling to "surrender" to Him.

-E. A Johnston
(NTB, pg. 1)

♦ How does the Church reach her goal? Only by traveling the pathway from pressure to enlargement, from poverty to enrichment.

-Watchman Nee
(WN, Jan. 25)

♦ The church has lost the opportunity to win the *proletariat to its side. We have given them into the hand of the Communist because we preferred a comfortable life. We were not ready to fight in order to win souls.

-Richard Wurmbrand
(AWG, pg. 58)

♦ We may indeed depend on the broken reed of an external profession; we may think we are good enough, if we lead such sober, honest, moral lives, as many heathens did. We may imagine we are in a safe condition, if we attend on the public officers of religion and are constant in the duties of our closets. But unless all these tend to reform our lives and change our hearts and are only used as so many channels of divine grace—as I told you before, so I tell you again, Christianity will profit you nothing.

-George Whitefield
(GW, pg. 269)

Not every one that saith unto me, Lord, Lord, shall enter into the kingdom of heaven; but he that doeth the will of my Father which is in heaven (Matthew 7:21).

♦ Toleration of false teachers in the church of God is treachery to Christ.

-H. A. Ironside

♦ When Jesus Christ comes back, it is not the liberal politicians who ought to be trembling, it's the pastors...because so many men have built their 'ministries' on the dry dead bones of unconverted church members.

-Paul Washer

♦ Everything that we possess is a sacred stewardship from God. All that can be called our own are the fruits of our diligent study and service here, and the rewards of faithful stewardship there. If we have not proved dependable in handling God's property, then we cannot expect to enter into the deep truths of God's Word in this life, or to be rewarded in the next.

-William MacDonald
(TD, pg. 38)

♦ This pulpit has never been belittled by the petty treatment of small and vulgar themes.

-John Henry Jowett

♦ The future of the Church and the world depend on today's education. The Church may be seeking to evangelize unbelievers but is giving up her own children to secular and materialistic influences.

-Andrew Murray
(AP, Jun. 14)

Prayer: Lord Jesus, have mercy upon Your Church. Give, I pray You, the Spirit of prayer and supplication as of old, that Your Church may prove what power from You rests upon her to win the world to Your feet. Amen. (AP, Nov. 6)

-Andrew Murray

♦ No man preaches well who has not a strong and deep appreciation of humanity.

-Phillips Brooks

♦ A preacher who is spiritually anemic, or intellectually impoverished, or morally depleted, will wish often for a juniper tree.

-Charles E. Jefferson

♦ Today in pulpits across America a "new brand" of the gospel has been foisted on congregations. It is "Jesus loves you!" "Come to Jesus. He loves you. He will bless you if you come to Him. God is a God of love. He loves the sinner and hates the sin." Actually my Bible states that, "God is angry with the wicked every day" (Ps. 7:11) and "The way of the wicked is an abomination unto the Lord" (Prov. 15:9). God hates sin. Yielded Christians are obedient Christians. Today in America, believers and the lost world around us think of God only as a God of love. They have forgotten that God hates sin!

-E. A Johnston
(NTB, pg. 38)

♦ We live in a culture bound by sin like bands of iron. Moral stories, quaint maxims, and life lessons shared from the heart of a beloved pulpiteer or spiritual life coach have no real power against such darkness. We need preachers of the gospel of Jesus Christ who know the Scriptures, and by God's grace face any culture with the cry, "Thus saith the Lord!"

-Paul Washer

♦ In the history of the Church, times and a man have always seemed to come together...and...God generally finds the man where men are not looking for him.

-G. Campbell Morgan

But God hath chosen the foolish things of the world to confound the wise; and God hath chosen the weak things of the world to confound the things which are mighty (1 Corinthians 1:27).

♦ Not one of a thousand would seem entitled to share in the rule of the heavenly kingdom, did the title hang upon walking in the Spirit...In John 17 Christ...does not distinguish between one measure of obedience and another, among the children of God; He only makes mention of the unspeakable difference between the world of (unbelievers) and those that are born from above....The title to share the glory and dominion of the Lord in His kingdom...hangs upon sonship, oneness with Christ, not on the measure of obedience.

-Robert Chapman
(RC, pg. 174)

******

Some want to live within the sound
Of church or chapel bell;
I want to run a rescue shop
Within a yard of hell.

C. T. Studd

♦ Most people today in our churches are lost, and they demonstrate that they are lost because their entire Christianity is nothing more than, "They made a decision."

-Paul Washer

♦ The church today, including both the adult and teenage generations, is in an era of rampant biblical illiteracy.

-Barry Shafer

Behold, the days come, saith the Lord GOD, that I will send a famine in the land, not a famine of bread, nor a thirst for water, but of hearing the words of the LORD (Amos 8:11).

♦ "To abide in something" means to continue, dwell, endure, be present, remain, and tarry. We must abide in the doctrine of Christ. This means we must *continue* in obedience to it. It also means we must *dwell* in it so it will *dwell* in our beings as truth. We must *endure* all challenges and attacks against His doctrine to maintain its integrity. It must be ever *present* in our thinking and living. When challenged to deny it, we must *remain* standing. Ultimately, we must *tarry* in His doctrine until all has been fulfilled in His kingdom.

-RJK

♦ Abiding or remaining with Christ goes beyond just our devotional times or quiet times with Him. It means cultivating an on-going sense of His Presence with us throughout the day.

-Anna Alden-Tirrill
(SP, Jan. 28)

♦ When the church loses her doctrine, she also loses her dynamic.

-Herbert Lockyer
(MP, pg. 407)

♦ We are not sent into the world to make our converts, or to fund our movements, or to conserve our beliefs.

-Oswald Chambers
(DL, Nov. 16)

♦ There has been a tendency throughout church history that continues today to deal with biblical correction when it is presented by "shooting the messenger" rather than heeding the message and repenting. Although the messages have been true to the Scriptures, a common ploy in rejecting the message has been to dodge the convicting biblical subject by diverting attention to God's less-than-perfect messengers, who thus become vulnerable targets.

-T. A. McMahan

♦ But, sadly, we are only building bigger buildings for our own comfort and ease in our earthly Zion, which we have created from a watered-down gospel message that is popular rather than penetrating. A. W. Tozer used to call it the "Apostolic Standard."

-E. A. Johnston
(NTB, pg. 20)

♦ The disgrace of the Church in the twenty-first century is that more zeal is evident among suicide bombers and cultists than among Christians.

-William MacDonald

♦ Many things have accumulated in heaven because God has not yet found his outlet on earth; the Church has not yet prayed.

-Watchman Nee

♦ The members of the redeemed Church should be bound into a bundle of love with the Holy Spirit. The truth is that God never fathered His Church apart from the Holy Spirit. We should be anointed with the Spirit. We are led of the Spirit. We are taught by the Spirit. The Spirit, then is the medium, the divine solution, in which God holds His Church.

-A. W. Tozer
(AG, Aug. 10)

From whom the whole body fitly joined together and compacted by that which every joint supplieth, according to the effectual working in the measure of every part, maketh increase of the body unto the edifying of itself in love (Ephesians 4:16)...And hope maketh not ashamed; because the love of God is shed abroad in our hearts by the Holy Ghost which is given unto us (Romans 5:5).

♦ A real Christian? You know there are two kinds—professing Christians and real Christians. Now I will admit that there are a great many people in the world that call themselves Christians, who have just enough religion to make themselves miserable. They are holding to the world with one hand, generally the right hand, and to Jesus Christ with the other.

-R. A. Torrey
(RA, pg. 148)

♦ God's covenant. I mean the new covenant; this is a great consolation; for though everything at times to us appears to be in confusion, yet God's covenant stands fast with Christ—confirmed by His oath, and ratified also and established by the death of our Lord Jesus Christ—ordered in all things and sure. A covenant of mercy, which regenerates us—a covenant of life, which quickens us—a covenant of grace, which pardons us—a covenant of peace, which reigns in our hearts—and a covenant of wedlock to unite us to the Lord Jesus.

-John Rusk

♦ There may be a lot of Christians who do nothing, but there are no Christians who have nothing to do.

-Church Newsletter

♦ The Lord Jesus Christ must be presented to sinners. The Spirit of God will guide you, as you rely on Him, to the presentation of Him that is required for each sinner. But if you attempt to enclose Jesus Christ into neat little doctrinal packets, one marked "salvation," another marked "sanctification," another marked "the baptism in the Holy Ghost," you will fail to convince sinners that they need Him. In every case, we need to rely on the Holy Spirit.

-Oswald Chambers
(DL, Sept. 4)

******

A church that has no heavenly vision will find itself lost.
A church that operates apart from its holy status will simply become a social
 club.
A church that has no concern for truth will be apostate.
A church that has no vision for the lost has become disobedient to its high
 calling.
A church that lacks the Holy Spirit is void of life.
A church that is legalistic can only regurgitate dead-letter doctrine that will lay
 stagnant and bitter in the hearts of thirsty, seeking souls.

-RJK

♦ The church of today, the Christian of today, is impressed more by the
 "book of the month" with its latest man-centered philosophy that brings
 the world into the church than he is concerned with the "books" of the
 Bible which provide nourishment for the age. If we as Christians make our
 diet one of false fruit we will die of spiritual starvation.

-E. A Johnston
(NTB, pg. 77)

♦ A very great portion of modern revivalism has been more a curse than a
 blessing, because it has led thousands to a kind of peace before they
 have known their misery; restoring the prodigal to the Father's house, and
 never making him say, "Father, I have sinned." How can he be healed
 who is not sick, or he be satisfied with the bread of life who is not hungry?
 The old-fashioned sense of sin is despised... Everything in this age is
 shallow... The consequence is that men leap into religion, and then leap
 out again. Unhumbled they came, unhumbled they remain in it, and
 unhumbled they go from it.

-C. H. Spurgeon

♦ I believe a lot of churches in America are not churches.

-Paul Washer

♦ For the confession of our Lord's divinity is the rock upon which he builds
 his church. Was it possible to take this away, the gates of hell would
 quickly prevail against it. My brethren, if Jesus Christ be not the very God
 of the very God, I would never preach the gospel of Christ again.

-George Whitefield
(GW, pg. 85)

♦ As Christians, I believe we must do all we can to alleviate pain and
 suffering in those around us. This sort of concern for others is a natural

fruit of the Gospel. But we must never minister to someone's physical needs at the expense of preaching Christ.

-K. P. Yohannan

For though I preach the gospel, I have nothing to glory of: for necessity is laid upon me; yea, woe is unto me, if I preach not the gospel (1 Corinthians 9:16).

♦ A sermon of the right sort gets itself up. If I supply the soil and the seed and the sun and the rain, the sermon will come up of itself. My soul is a flower-garden. My business is raising sermons.

-Charles E. Jefferson

♦ The chief danger of the Church today is that it is trying to get on the same side as the world, instead of turning the world upside down. Our Master expects us to accomplish results, even if they bring opposition and conflict. Anything is better than compromise, apathy, and paralysis. God, give to us an intense cry for the old time power of the Gospel and the Holy Ghost.

-A.B. Simpson

♦ The church in general, and youth ministry in particular, has demonstrated more of an appetite for goose bumps than for God's truth, more interest in how our young people feel than how they think...But where are Christian teenagers learning basic tenets of the Christian faith? And if they don't understand those basic truths or doctrines...then how does that impact their long-term faith? I'm concerned that too much of our teaching is reduced to what can...be communicated by a worship band, illuminated by stage lighting and well-placed candles.

-Duffy Robbins

♦ The difficulty with most men is not so much that they have not a refuge, as that they have a false refuge, a refuge that will fail them in the hour of crisis and need...a "refuge of lies." Religion is a refuge of lies. Religion never saved anybody. You say, "What do you mean?" I mean just what I say—religion never saved anybody. Trust in religion is one thing; trust in the personal Christ is another thing. There is many a man who trusts in his religion and yet he is not saved. You go to men, and they say, "Yes, I am religious; I go to church every Sunday; I read my prayer-book, and say prayers regularly every day; I read my Bible; I have been baptized; I have been confirmed or united to the Church; I have taken the Sacrament regularly, and that is what I am trusting in." Is it? Then you are lost.

-R. A Torrey
(RA, pgs, 112, 126)

♦ The Great Commission does not involve exerting a Christian influence upon society. We are not to "change society" but to "convert individuals.".... We must denounce sin, call for national repentance, and preach the gospel in convicting power...The church must be indicted both for its lack of social concern and for its heresies and failure to preach the truth. We must denounce the destructive false teachings that abound. It is hypocritical of the church to protest the world's sins while tolerating and even honoring within its ranks those who preach a false gospel and are the enemies of the cross.

-Dave Hunt

♦ We have taken the glorious gospel of our blessed God and reduced it down to four spiritual laws and five things God wants you to know, with a little superstitious prayer at the end; and if someone repeats it after us with enough sincerity, we popishly declare them to be born again. We've traded regeneration for decisionism.

-Paul Washer

******

A Cheap, Easy Christianity

What does it cost to be a Christian? I grant freely that it costs little to be a mere outward Christian. A man has only got to attend a place of worship twice on Sunday, and to be tolerably moral during the week—and he has gone as far as thousands around him ever go in religion. All this is cheap and easy work—it entails no self-denial or self-sacrifice. If this is saving Christianity and will take us to heaven when we die—we must alter the description of the way of life, and write, "Wide is the gate and broad is the way that leads to Heaven!"

But it does cost something to be a real Christian, according to the standard of the Bible. There are . . . enemies to overcome, battles to be fought, sacrifices to be made, an Egypt to be forsaken, a wilderness to be passed through, a cross to be carried, a race to be run.

Conversion is not putting a man in a soft armchair, and taking him pleasantly to Heaven. It is the beginning of a mighty conflict, in which it costs much to win the victory. Hence arises the unspeakable importance of "counting the cost."

True Christianity will cost a man...his self-righteousness, his sins, his love of ease, and the favor of the world. A religion which costs nothing—is worth

259

nothing! A cheap, easy Christianity, without a cross—will prove in the end a useless Christianity, without a crown!

-J.C. Ryle
(1816-1900)

Strive to enter in at the strait gate: for many, I say unto you, will seek to enter in, and shall not be able (Luke 13:24).

♦ How dare we, all these stupid evangelists walking around telling men after they've made some little prayer that they need to write their name in the back of their Bible, and put the date and if the devil ever comes to them, they need to show him that. That is Roman superstition, it is not the gospel of Jesus Christ. You see, we've turned the gospel into a flu-shot.
-Paul Washer

♦ Herbert Lockyer tells why the gates of Hell will not be able to prevail against the Church. It has a faith that looks back to Calvary, a hope that looks forward to His return, and a love that looks upward to Him with gratitude and a sincere desire to please and obey Him as its members await Jesus' Coming.

♦ True Christianity is far removed from the hurdy-gurdy entertainment of modern Christendom. It is not to be confused with the luxury-living and pleasure-seeking that are so rampant today. Rather, it is a struggle to the death, an unceasing conflict against the forces of hell. No disciple is worth his salt who does not realize that the battle is drawn and that there is no turning back.
-William MacDonald
(TD, pg, 61)

♦ Many things in Christianity have become too cheap today, but there is no easy shortcut to spiritual worth.
-Watchman Nee
(WN, Aug. 3)

♦ This is evangelicalism today: sensual, carnal, unconverted people that have just enough deceptive religion to drive them straight into Hell! Are you that kind of person? Or do you have new affections?
-Paul Washer

♦ Tragically, the evangelist is a dying breed, and what has replaced him are motivational speakers who are nothing more than worldly cheerleaders trying to stir up the masses to some type of emotional insanity that will cause them to swing from one emotional branch of hype to another.

Sadly, these poor souls do not realize that there is no real net in which to catch them when it all comes crashing down.

-RJK

♦ The servant of the Lord Jesus must be instant in season and out of season, knowing that he is the Lord's messenger to every one with whom he has to do, and ever learning of the Lord; seeing that he is to be continually ministering to others, he must be receiving all channels. Meditation on the Word and prayer should occupy the chief part of his time. In his public ministry and in his private conversation he should aim at hearts and consciences, seeking in every way to magnify Christ and abase the creature. In short, he should set the Lord always before him, and so walk in His steps as to represent Him to every eye.

-Robert Chapman

Preach the word; be instant in season, out of season; reprove, rebuke, exhort with all longsuffering and doctrine (2 Timothy 4:2).

♦ Anytime we try to take a short cut in dealing with souls, God leaves us alone!

-Oswald Chambers
(DL, Oct. 9)

♦ Think yourself empty, read yourself full, write yourself clear, pray yourself keen—then enter the pulpit and let yourself go!

-W. H. Griffith Thomas

♦ I would rather win souls than be the greatest king or emperor on earth; I would rather win souls than be the greatest general that ever commanded an army.

-R. A. Torrey

♦ The power of the Roman Empire was nothing in the presence of the power that the Church wielded in prayer.

-Andrew Murray

♦ Nothing is so hurtful to a Christian life as play-acting, nothing so blessed as when our words, our prayers, our very demeanor, all become a spontaneous expression of the life of Christ our wonderful Lord.

-Watchman Nee
(WN, Sept. 15)

♦ Every man feels instinctively that all the beautiful sentiments in the world weigh less than a single lovely action.

-James Russell Lowell

♦ The accent in the Church today is not on devotion, but on commotion.

-Leonard Ravenhill

♦ Any objections to the carrying on of our present golden-calf Christianity is met with the triumphant reply, "But we are winning them." And winning them to what? To true discipleship? To cross carrying? To self-denial? To separation from the world? To crucifixion of the flesh? To holy living? To nobility of character? To hard self-discipline? To love for God? To total commitment to Christ?

-A. W. Tozer

And he received them at their hand, and fashioned it with a graving tool, after he had made it a molten calf; and they said, These be thy gods, O Israel, which brought thee up out of the land of Egypt (Exodus 32:4).

♦ Preaching that costs nothing accomplishes nothing.

-John Henry Jowett

♦ The pulpit is not meant to exalt personal causes. As ministers of the Gospel, we have been commissioned to preach the Gospel and not personal causes that involve non-essential theology that has nothing to do with salvation. It is the Gospel that will penetrate the soul, while causes, regardless of how strong the passions are, will fall flat at the door of religious stagnation.

-RJK

♦ We have been accustomed to look upon holiness as a virtue, upon humility as a grace, upon love as a gift to be sought from God. But the Christ of God is *himself* everything that we shall ever need. Let us unhesitatingly draw upon him.

-Watchman Nee

♦ All the religion of the natural man turns the bible upside down; it begins with works and then leads man to hope for mercy, whereas the Bible begins with the pardon of sin and then enjoins obedience.

-Robert Chapman
(RC, pg. 174)

♦ The difference between a *servant* of God and an *instrument* of God is brought out in *Matthew 7:21-23*. An *instrument* is a person whom God uses, whether that person is right or not. God will bless His Word, whether a saint or a sinner preaches it. But the *servant* of God lives in the fullness of His Spirit, evidencing the life of obedience.

-Oswald Chambers
(DL, Oct. 3)

♦ Many a man in the ministry fails, not because he is bad, but because he has a genius for blundering.

-Charles E. Jefferson

♦ The Church should seek above everything to cultivate the power of an unceasing prayerfulness on behalf of those without Christ...It is when Christians cease looking for help apart from God and aim at being bound together to the throne of God, that the Church will put on her strength to overcome the world. This comes by continuously asking for power of God's Spirit.

-Andrew Murray

♦ A pastor is not a maker of sermons but a maker of saints.

-Richard Wurmbrand

♦ We have had so many legal and so few-free-grace preachers, for these many years, that most professors now seem to be settled upon their lees, and rather deserve the title of Pharisees than Christians.

-George Whitefield
(GW, pg. 162)

♦ The man who belongs to the world but not to his time grows abstract and vague, and lays no strong grasp upon men's lives and the present causes of their actions. The man who belongs to his time but not to the world grows thin and superficial. . .Truth and timeliness together make the full preacher.

-Phillips Brooks

♦ Materialism and wealth are hindering the flow of spiritual power in the Church today. Revival will never come while believers are reigning as kings.

-William MacDonald

And he said unto them, Take heed; and beware of covetousness; for a man's life consisteth not in the abundance of things which he possesseth (Luke 12:15).

♦ The business of the Church of God. She is purest when most engaged with God and she is astray just so far as she follows other interests, no matter how "religious" or humanitarian they may be.

-A. W. Tozer
(AG, Jan. 20)

♦ I am the little servant of an illustrious Master.

-J. Hudson Taylor

♦ More is said from our pulpits in favor of sin than against it.

-John Flechter

♦ No longer is the thundering message of the prophet of God heralded from the sacred pulpit, warning against the wrath of a holy and just God against sin.

-Wesley Duewel

♦ Formerly the heretics were manifest, but now the Church is filled with heretics in disguise.

-Cyril of Jerusalem

******

The Religious Pose

I came across an interesting statement that is *apropos for the challenges of today, "The problem with some servants of God trying to keep a godly balance according to the intent of God's Word is that they are considered too conservative for the liberals and too liberal for the conservatives."

It seems that the lines of righteousness have either been adjusted to liberalism or the truth of righteousness causes others to appear unbending. It is clear that there is a line being drawn between these two camps that will not be erased. The problem is not the difference between the two, but the spirit that is motivating each camp. There is such a separation that there is no real place for agreement. As a result, unsuspecting believers can find themselves in a crossfire, where they receive fire from both camps.

I can relate to this precarious place. That which drives the religious liberals insane is the holiness of God. He will never cease to be holy in His ways or approach to a matter. Regardless of how narrow and unbending His holiness may be, its righteous standard will never be brought down to man's best which is considered filthy rags. In the end, His holiness will bring an indictment against those who refuse to believe the complete Gospel, which declares we are dead in sin and must be raised up in newness of life according to the righteous, perfect ways of God.

On the other hand, what drives some of the conservatives crazy is the Holy Spirit. He cannot be boxed in by rules, controlled by religious rituals, or corralled by doctrine. It is the Spirit who brings life to God's people to truly pursue their life in Christ, as well as putting life into their religious ways and activities. For the liberal, they end up missing Christ altogether, but for the conservative, they fail to breathe in and out the life of Christ. Ultimately, their life becomes cluttered with dead-letter beliefs and useless activities bringing leanness to their souls.

Sadly, we live in a time that much of the visible church is beginning to walk the broad path of liberalism. They tout that the rigid ways of conservatism do not work or are obsolete. Granted, it appears for the most part that the liberals' attempts are all quite religious, but the reality is that they are man-centered. These people's presentation of salvation is nothing more than humanism. Their presentations are void of any real awareness that redemption is the work of God, and that it addresses the utter despotism of the unregenerate human disposition. It calls for complete repentance by fleeing the wrath of God to come. It challenges quasi-religious environments, indifferent pious poses towards God, a worldly attitude, and a lack of passion for souls.

Today these two camps of conservatism and liberalism still exist, but on the liberal side, some camps take on a militant pose that proves cruel and mean-spirited. Regardless of the pose liberals take on, they are enlarging their path to embrace the very ways of hell.

The only way to heaven is narrow, and it does not embrace any other way but the way of redemption.

Having a form of godliness, but denying the power thereof: from such turn away (2 Timothy 3:5).

♦ In the Church of God the teacher's error is the people's trial.

-Vincent of Lerins

♦ The security and growth of the churches of God depend upon their obedience to His Word.

-H. A. Ironside
(CBO, Sept. 23)

♦ One vital test of all religious experience is how it affects our relation to God, our concept of God and our attitude towards Him. God being who He is must always be the supreme arbiter of all things religious.

-A. W. Tozer

♦ Religion is nothing else than doing the will of God and not our own. Heaven or hell depends on this alone.

-Susannah Wesley

♦ Prayer links the King on the throne with the Church at His footstool.

-Andrew Murray

♦ It is the weaklings and not the giants, who neglect their people. It is the Pagan and not the Christian who shines in public and leaves undone the private duties which belong to him as an ordained steward of the Son of God.

-Charles E. Jefferson

♦ All God's giants have been weak men, who did great things for God because they reckoned on His being with them.

-J. Hudson Taylor

♦ A man speaks about the sufferings of a poor God and yawns. No wonder the audience yawned too. Pastors and flocks are fed up. They are also fed up with good sermons. They are too wise. Fools for Christ are needed.

-Richard Wurmbrand
(AWG, pg. 13)

♦ In regard to Alexander Whyte, Warren W. Wiersbe wrote this, "Here is a great preacher's philosophy of pastoral work, God makes a man; the man makes a ministry; the ministry makes a church." (PCK, pg. 171)

******

Religion that is:
Fleshly is paganism,
Man-centered is humanism,
Metaphysical is New Age,
Pursuing hidden knowledge is occultism,
Operating according to Spirit and truth is Christianity.

-RJK

Pure religion and undefiled before God and the Father is this, To visit the fatherless and widows in their affliction, and to keep himself unspotted from the world (James 1:27).

He suffers, and hence the Doctrine of Atonement.
He pleads, and hence the Doctrine of Spirit Influence.
He rises from the grave, hence the Doctrine of
    Resurrection and Glory.
Our Lord came down from Heaven, not so much to
teach the Gospel as to be Himself the Subject of it,
leaving the Spirit to be the chief Interpreter. We study,
therefore, the Law in the Gospels; the Gospels in the
Epistles; and all in Christ.

-Augus

♦ A local church will only be as great as its conception of God.

-A. W. Tozer
(AG, Jan. 29)

♦ Unity can be practically exemplified in the work of the kingdom. Intercession in the Spirit can bring true unity. When we as believers learn the meaning of our calling as a royal priesthood, we will see that God is not confined to our limited spheres. He invites us to pray for all who believe or can yet believe. By intercession, the Church of Christ will be bound to the throne of heaven as never before.

-Andrew Murray
(AP, Nov. 14)

But ye are a chosen generation, a royal priesthood, an holy nation, a peculiar people; that ye should shew forth the praises of him who hath called you out of darkness into his marvelous light (1 Peter 2:9).

******

The Identifying Mark
Of Christianity

I have been thinking about how Christianity is often being presented. In a way the presentation of the Christian life has brought much mourning to my soul. Some professed Christians make it about doctrine, others about religious affiliation, rituals, or good works, and some even identify it with a church pew that bears their invisible names. However, none of these points of association identify a person as being born again with the life of Christ and truly being a member of His Body, the Church.

As I think about these different points of identification, I realize that each mark can reveal the type of gospel that people are hiding in. For those who see doctrine as their savior, they are hiding in a gospel that may be moral, but has no life. When it comes to those who are religious, their gospel is one of self-exaltation in personal piousness. Those who are looking to rituals can end up with an anti-Christ gospel that serves as a substitute for real faith towards God. Those caught up with good works can succumb to a social gospel that will make people comfortable in their doomed state, and for those who see their pew as their ark of safety, they will eventually hear destructive storms slam against the doors of their lives, threatening their well-being.

The one identifying mark upon the lives of God's people is their desire to do His will. In order to do God's will, I must believe who He is, trust His intentions towards me, and obey His Word.

Jesus saith unto them, My meat is to do the will of him that sent me, and to finish his work (John 4:34).

Shelah

~

You see the word, "shelah" in the Psalms. It simply means a "pause" or a "place for meditation." As Christians we need to pause from various activities and simply meditate about where we are in our relationship with the Lord. We have to consider whether we have applied the lessons and principles of God to our walk to ensure a touch of heaven upon our lives. We need to test our attitude towards matters to determine if we are displaying the mind of Christ. We have to honestly consider our conduct and see if it can be traced back to God as the One who has inspired or instructed it as so.

We are taking a pause at this moment to give the reader a chance to possibly enlarge his or her understanding about the kingdom of heaven. This pause is meant to add a bit of fun to the following exercises, but the subjects have merit and are meant to challenge and enlarge our understanding.

******

Declaration and Songs

The Jews have a great confession of faith. It is called the "Shema". Jesus made this declaration as well. See if you can unscramble the words in the following statement to find out what their declaration of faith is.

reha, O elasir; het dolr uro ogd is eon lrdo.

As Christians we have a confession of faith. See if you can unscramble the words to bring clarity as to the believers' confession of faith. The correct answers to the following puzzles can be found on page 285.

ouht rat het tricsh, eth nos fo the gilvin ogd.

Below are hymns that have touched generations for many years. See if you can unscramble each song to discover what it is.

1. magizan carge
2. slebesd racsunase
3. eht dol gudreg srocs
4. who raget uoht tar
5. ni the danger
6. sutj a losecr kalw hiwt ehet
9. ta lavcary
10. ogd si os dogo
11. susej velos eht tiltle hiedrncl
12. sujt sa I ma
13. Foltsy dan lyendret
14. alnneig no the relavesgint mars

269

7. twese rouh of yarrep
8. ti is lewl thiw ym losu

15. rethe is perow ni teh dolob
16. shi yee si on eth warpros

****

Who Am I?

It is easy for Christianity to become cheap and non-essential when Christians do not understand the history or price that was paid for them to have such a legacy passed down to them. Below are those who make up a great cloud of witnesses. Some of their names may not be known, but their works have followed them in some way.

See how well you know some history of the Christian Church. The answers to the following descriptions can be found on page 285.

1. Winston Churchill as a young boy was brought to visit this saint who was also known as the "Patriarch of Barnstaple."
2. This great man of God served as the president of the Methodist Conference and of the Free Church Council in the 1920s.
3. This famous pastor of St. Peter's Church in Dundee, Scotland died when he was only 30.
4. Due to his studies in Germany, this founder of the Bible Institute of Los Angeles (BIOLA) was able to confront German higher criticism and theological liberalism.
5. Abraham Lincoln visited this Chicago evangelist/preacher's school and commended his work.
6. Before his conversion and challenging work to bring forth a reference Bible, this former drunken legislature and U.S. Attorney for Kansas received the Cross of Honor for bravery at Antietam while serving with the Confederate Army.
7. This famous preacher and author lived during the time of Moody. He was known as a "militant mystic" and was described as being "velvet steel" because he was gentle.
8. This man who was knighted in 1909, and edited weekly journals and magazines, along with many scholarly books which included, *The Expositor's Bible* and *The Expositor's Greek New Testament*. As a result, he was considered to be the father of modern religious journalism.
9. His famous father wanted to see him take over his pulpit. Eventually, he did come back to England after his father's death from his work for the Lord in New Zealand to take over his father's position in the church. As it was so graciously written about this minister of God, that in the end he proved that he was not to be an echo of his father, but a voice for God.
10. This pastor shepherded the Westminster Chapel in London during both World War I and World War II.

11. This man served as pastor to Carr's Lane Church in Birmingham, London and the prestigious Fifth Avenue Presbyterian Church in New York City in the early 1900s.
12. This popular Scottish pastor of the late 1800s and early 1900s made over one thousand visits to his sheep in an average year.
13. This missionary spent all of her 60 years in the harvest field of India without ever going home on furlough.
14. This man's wife, Gertrude (Biddy), was an expert stenographer. As a result, all of his teachings were preserved and compiled into various books.
15. This former Salvation Army officer, famous preacher, and author was thought to be dead when he was born. It was an hour after his birth that the nurse felt his pulse and he was completely revived after being plunged into a hot bath of water.
16. This pastor was born out of wedlock into great poverty, but he filled the pulpit of Edinburg's leading church and one of Scotland's most important places of ministry for forty years.
17. This minister, who was born in England, served as pastor of Moody Memorial Church in Chicago from 1953-1962.
18. This preacher was convinced that preaching like an apostle, without joining together those who are awakened, and training them up in the ways of God, is only begetting children for the murderer.
19. This godly servant and author of a famous hymn, described himself in this way, "I was a wild beast on the coast of Africa, but the Lord caught me and tamed me; and now you come to see me, as people go to look at the lions in the Tower.
20. She became one of England's most able and intrepid advocates for Sunday School. In fact, she published a number of books that were suited to help Sunday School teachers.

******

The Moral of the Story

Every great story has a message that can benefit us. The following story contains many names of places that can be found in the Bible. These names may be known and obvious, or they may be unknown by the reader and hidden in words or the contents of the sentence. The names might even be disrupted by spaces, grammatical punctuation, or extended to the next line.

There are 34 names of Biblical locations in this story. See how many you can identify without referring to the answers. Without actually looking at where the names are located in the story, you can consider the names of the places you have not yet found that will be listed above the following story on pages

285-287 along with the answers, and see if you can locate them before conceding.

*****

There were some friends who decided to take a journey to the Holy Land. They wanted to walk where Jesus walked. These friends included Beth Ellis from Philadelphia, Jeri Kidron from Calvary, Ada Ekron of Athens, and for protection purposes, Beth's brothers, Ed, Adam, and Caleb from adjoining communities.

Admittedly, these six individuals seemed like unusual companions. For the enthusiastic traveler, Beth, she meshed such groups together in the past without much incident. However, this group had an unusual mixture that she perceived might be a bit challenging.

Each person wanted to go to different places. Granted, they had aired out their differences and all came to the same conclusion that they wanted to see places such as Jerusalem, Bethlehem, and the Sea of Galilee. However, to mix up the pot, Jeri choose the sights of Egypt as a must, while Ada' curiosity about Petra, located in Jordan seemed a bit eccentric even to Beth. On the other hand, the idea of possibly seeing the ruins of Capernaum caused Ed to so dominate the negotiation that he came across as a spoiled baby, longing and striving to get complete control of those around him. Even Caleb, a non-committal person in most matters became somewhat upset about Ed's attitude. If possible Caleb wanted to see such sights as Masada, but could see that his desire would be completely ignored if Ed had his way. Since Adam's sense of humor made him a ham, mathematically, he tried to figure out how everyone could fit their preferences into the schedule in a comical way. He used a deadpan face to communicate his desire to visit the Dead Sea, while being aware that Beth also wanted to see Nazareth. Regardless of how they tried, Adam advocated that six could not be equally divided into nine, vehemently pointing out that there must be compromise or agreement if they were going to be successful in their upcoming trip.

To Beth, any time she could find people to journey back into historical lands was to add an array of depth to what she considered her small world. She was especially excited to visit the Holy Land. She wanted to stand as close as she could to Golgotha, the place of the cross where redemption had been secured. The idea of not being able to enjoy it because of conflict between her traveling companions, made her melancholy. At that time, Beth said a silent prayer, knowing the Lord had always been her anchor.

After her silent prayer, Ada said she would reconsider Petra if necessary. Adam, as custom to his easy-going personality, said that he did not have to visit that which was dead, for he realized that Christ pointed to that which was alive. Jeri came down on her enthusiasm in seeing the Pyramids in order to give Ed a chance to stop at go, land emotionally, and become reasonable in his attitude. Caleb calmed down to once again become non-committed in his attitude.

Each person waited quietly for Ed to concede some of his passion. However, the question remained, would he? Bronzed in appearance, it appeared as if he was not about to melt, but a miracle was taking place underneath the surface. Ed was remembering what the journey was about. It was a spiritual journey that was to bring each of them to a place of personal identification by walking where Jesus walked. The man who spoke of love, unity, and fellowship came to bring reconciliation, not conflict and division. At that conclusion, he naturally had to concede to that which was greater in purpose. Shiloh, a place of rest was in order instead of Armageddon. It was time for him to back down and come together with the rest in an attitude of reason. Perhaps, they could all see their desired attractions. It was simply a matter of listening to one another and making the necessary plans.

Ed omitted the details as to what changed his position, but Beth knew. She knew that the Lord had reminded him that the real journey in life is a spiritual one. This journey entails character that must be balanced by mercy, compassion, grace, and love towards others. Such character reaches the heights of excellence in disposition, attitude, and conduct. Beth also knew that she had already experienced a bit of the Holy Land. The Lord came in their midst because of prayer, interceded because of mercy, and revealed His grace through a miraculous and incredible way, unveiling a bit of His heavenly power and glory in the heart of one man.

Bits And Pieces From the Past and Present

~

The Reality of Life

When you think about life, it is made up of bits and pieces. You have the cultural, political, educational, and religious influences that greatly influence your worldview and philosophies. Therefore, it is natural for people to take bits from one arena and pick up pieces from another to establish some semblance of life. Eventually these bits and pieces become a mosaic in their minds, but when it comes to the presentation of this assortment, it can come across as confusing and abstract to others.

As I consider that which has influenced my life, I can see how my views have been defined or discarded by what has captured my heart and imagination. My hope is that my view about life in general and the type of person I am becoming is influenced by the wisdom, righteousness, sanctification, and redemption of heaven itself.

Casting down imaginations, and every high thing that exalteth itself against the knowledge of God, and bringing into captivity every thought to the obedience of Christ (2 Corinthians 10:5).

******

♦ None who have always been free can understand the terrible fascinating power of the hope of freedom to those who are not free.

Pearl S. Buck
Author

******

The Repeat of History

George Santayana stated, "Those who cannot remember the past are condemned to repeat it." Sadly, we can see history repeating itself generation after generation. In September of 1662, 400 Presbyterian ministers were being driven from their churches. Hugh McKail delivered the last sermon that was to be preached to these ministers in the High Church of Edinburg. Speaking of the persecutions of the Church he dearly loved, McKail said, "She has suffered from an Ahab on the throne, A Haman in the State, and a Judas in the Church."

Today, we can relate to McKail. So much that has been considered decent in this nation has been perverted by the various Ahabs who have sat in high places of government, while the second rate, wannabe "Hamans" have planned and devised opportunities to build gallows to silence righteousness, and the Judases have looked for opportunities to betray all that is true for 30 pieces of silver.

May it never be said of any of us who call upon the name of the Lord that we have helped an Ahab, conspired with a Haman, or agreed with a Judas. It is true that we might be tested as we taste the foolishness and consequences of Ahab, the wrath of Haman, and the betrayal of Judas, but we will be assured that upon our resurrection we will be able to stand in assurance before our majestic Savior, Lord, and King.

The poet William Cowper (1731-1800) put it best:

'Tis my happiness below
    Not to live without the cross;
But the Savior's power to know,
    Sanctifying every loss.

Trials make the promise sweet;
    Trials give new life to prayer;
Trials bring me to his feet—
    Lay me low, and keep me there.

Did I meet no trials here—
    No chastisement by the way—
Might I not, with reason, fear
    I should prove a cast-away?

Bastards may escape the rod,
    Sunk in earthly vain delight;
But the true-born child of God
    Must not—would not, if he might.

****

A Bit of History

I am sure that most Christians have heard of names like George Whitefield, John Wesley, Isaac Watts, Jonathan Edwards, and John Newton. They were part of a great move of God which is known as the 18th century revival.

Whitefield and Wesley were associated with the revival that took place in England. Both of these men along with Edwards were part of the revival that took place in America. In his book, *Portraits of the Great 18th Century Revival,* Paxton Hood made this statement, "How impossible it is to do more than merely mention the names of men, every action of whose lives was consecrated, and every breath an ardent flame, all helping on and urging forward the great work of rousing a careless world and a careless church."

When you study the history of this revival, you will find that the great preachers of that time experienced persecution from the clergy as they denied them access to their pulpits, as well as the clergy also hiring rebels to disrupt the services. Like the scattering of the first century Christians during persecution, these preachers were driven out into the streets and fields where they would at times preach to thousands of people, resulting in many conversions.

However, there are other names associated with this revival that are not as well known such as Roland Hill and John Nelson. However, the one name that is constantly mentioned during this time is Anne Hastings, the Countess of Huntingdon. She promoted such men as Whitefield and Wesley to the aristocrats of her time. When many of the aristocrats rejected them, she went to the poor. This godly woman had her own church which often became the starting point for many of the great preachers during this powerful move of God. She also provided training for those who felt called to the great harvest fields of the world.

In his book, Paxton wrote this summation about the life of the Countess of Huntingdon. "In 1791, in the eighty-fourth year of her age, died the revered Countess of Huntingdon; her last words, 'My work is done; I have nothing to do but to go to my Father!' No chronicle of convent or canonization, nor any story of biography, can record a more simple, saintly and utterly unselfish life."

Out of this revival came people with vision. Robert Raikes started the first Sunday school in England which became the pattern for those who followed. William Wilberforce became a relentless force in the Parliament to stop slavery, and William Carey became a missionary to India. It was also during these times that missionary societies were established to support missionaries on the foreign mission fields.

The revival also proved to be far reaching beyond the borders of England. David Bogue used his eloquent intelligence to produce the admirable work, *The Divine Authority of the New Testament.* This was sent to Napoleon who was exiled at St. Helena by the Viscountess Duncan. After the former Emperor's death, the work was returned to the author full of annotations. These annotations brought astonishment and clarity as they gave insight into the soul of the exiled leader.

It seemed that many found their calling including a man by the name of Silas Told. Like the Quaker, Elizabeth Fry, he became one of those who went into the prisons of England. However, those he was called to minister to were of a particular group of people. They were those poor souls that were on death row. He led many to the Lord and even walked with them to the gallows to comfort and encourage them.

The sad reality is that there was not much justice when it came to the English justice system at the time of the revival. Perhaps the environment made hearts tender and desperate towards the just Creator. The system was so chaotic that it was not easy to know why people were on death row. Some were on it because they sold some property, while there were those who had been falsely accused, but there was no proper investigation to confirm matters. And, there were also those who had committed terrible crimes. Therefore, Silas ministered to many different people who were innocent or accused of crimes that would be considered minor, but they each faced the same future. It is hard to say how Silas' message, compassion, and prayer affected the outcome of people's lives.

There was one story about Silas, which involved a time when he walked to the gallows with two men. Apparently, one was a believer, but the spiritual status of the other one was not recorded. After their dead bodies were taken down to dispose of them, sailors from a ship came demanding the body of one of the men. Apparently they had served with the man on the high seas and had come to try to intervene before his demise. The sailors were instructed where to locate those who had already taken the corpse. With great swiftness, they managed to locate the body and apparently carried it off to an unknown destination. However, the men became tired of carrying such a dead weight. They decided to leave it on the doorstep of the first home they came to.

Needless to say it was a frightful surprise for the female owner of the house to discover a dead body on her front steps. However, to her surprise, she discovered that it was the body of her son. She arranged a proper burial for him with some semblance of closure.

It seemed like the last three centuries have had great moves of God taking place. It was true that England provided us with spiritual giants such as

Whitefield in the 18th century, but in the 19th century America reciprocated by sending Dwight L. Moody. The Lord used him to start a revival in England that eventually swept parts of America. The 19th century also witnessed the renowned Charles Finley.

In the early 20th century there were revivals as well. Some of those who were part of the great move of God were not just men, but women as well. Even though their names are not mentioned as much, there are books that reveal how God used these unlikely instruments.

We are now in the 21st century. There are those who prophesize there will be another revival, but it is hard to say. It seems like everything is winding down to the second advent of Jesus. I believe there could be revivals, but I do not know to what extent they will reach. Instead of a revival that sweeps a large area, it could be pockets of revival.

For me I know I need a personal revival. In many cases revival does not simply quicken the spirit, but it restores or produces a new vision for God's people. When God's people lose sight of their calling, they become dull and ineffective. They must be raised from a state of spiritual slumber, self-sufficiency, and complacency to once again possess a burning passion, an urgency that will not lift until all the heirs of heaven have come into the fold of Jesus Christ.

For thus saith the high and lofty One that inhabiteth eternity, whose name is Holy; I dwell in the high and holy place, with him also that is of a contrite and humble spirit, to revive the spirit of the humble, and to revive the heart of the contrite ones (Isaiah 57:15).

♦ The past is not an anchor to drag us back but a rudder to help guide us into the future.

-Warren W. Wiersbe
(PCK, pg. 8)

♦ Our national drift is seen in the incivility that is becoming pervasive. Incivility is behavior that seems inconsequential to the doer, but is rightly perceived as coarse and inconsiderate by others.

-Dr. Larry Spargimino

♦ No one will begrudge us when we are doing our best, but when we strive to be the best is when we lose focus of what is important, thereby, becoming lost in a current of vanity, foolishness, and failure.

-RJK

- Efficiency is doing things right; effectiveness is doing the right things.

-Peter F. Drucker

- We often overstate our problems and underestimate our ability to bear up under them.

-Extreme Devotion
(ED, pg. 335)

******

The Devil's Ideology of Social Justice Among all

In Communist countries, farming has been collectivized. No man possesses a hundred sheep anymore. Who cares if one is lost? It is state property. Fathers don't have inheritances to impart to *profligate sons. When they get into trouble, there is no one who possesses swine who might hire them. They must be state employees, and they would not be free to leave their job to return to the father. Kings cannot arrange marriage feasts for their sons anymore; they have been dethroned. Beggars can no longer hope for alms at the door of rich men. The capitalists have been expropriated, deported to some slave labor camps. They would be willing to beg for a piece of bread themselves, but for a situation epitomized in a little joke:

What is the difference between a pessimist and an optimist? The optimist says, "With this regime, we will all become beggars," to which the pessimist replies, "But from whom will we beg?"

-Richard Wurmbrand
(AWG, pg. 54)

Prayer: Lord, Your justice will win out. The wicked will not live to declare any substantial victory. They will be cut off to be remembered no more. Lord, I am thankful that I am on Your side. It places me on the side of eternity that guarantees me of an eternal inheritance. Praise Your Holy Name. Amen.

- He who fails to distinguish between "thine" and "mine" has not learned the first principle of integrity in human relations. There is no communism sanctioned by the Bible except that voluntary sharing which at the beginning of the Christian era was practiced for a time by the persecuted believers in Christ. . .Respect for the rights of the individual and the recognition of the sacredness of property lie at the base of all reputable governments.

-H. A. Ironside
(CBO, Oct. 23)

♦ The one thing I am glad for is that my real heritage is not of this world. It cannot be taxed by wicked governments, taken away by despotic leaders, or squandered by the foolish.

-RJK

♦ I am not afraid of an army of lions led by a sheep; I am afraid of an army of sheep led by a lion.

-Alexander the Great

♦ You cannot teach what you do not know; you cannot lead where you do not go.

-O. L. Clark

♦ If you want total security go to prison. There you're fed, clothed, given medical care and so on. The only thing lacking…is freedom.

-Dwight D. Eisenhower

♦ Liberals claim to want to give a hearing to other views, but then are shocked and offended to discover that there are other views.

-William F. Buckley

******

Paraprosdokians

Have you ever seen such a word as "paraprosdokians"? It almost seems like a made-up word, but the truth is it is a figure of speech in which the latter part of a sentences or phrase is surprising or unexpected. These figures of speech are frequently used in a humorous situation. Winston Churchill loved them. Here are some examples of paraprosdokians.

o Where there is a will, I want to be in it.
o Light travels faster than sound. This is why some people appear bright until you hear them speak.
o If I agree with you, we'd both be wrong.
o We never really grow up, we only learn how to act in public.
o War does not determine who is right – only who is left.
o To steal ideas from one person is plagiarism. To steal from many is research.
o Nostalgia isn't what it used to be
o Change is inevitable, except from a vending machine.
o You're never too old to learn something stupid.
o Where there's a will, there's relatives.

******

◆ A friend is just a gift from GOD wrapped up in a wonderful package. It's wrapped in paper of understanding and sharing, is the ribbon on top. But caring, is what's deep inside, like GOD, who cares for us.

-Bill Moore

◆ Freedom is not constituted primarily of privileges but of responsibility.

-Unknown

◆ Without the proper influence of God upon the hearts and minds of each generation, the generation will slide into the quagmire of lawlessness and hopelessness. It will become lost in the culture of death, the suffocating hypocrisy of liberalism, the skepticism of humanism, and the ridiculousness caused by the insanity of it all.

-RJK

◆ Which tent are you in: contentment or discontentment.

-Church Sign

◆ The thing that goes the farthest toward making life worthwhile, that costs the least and does the most, is just a pleasant SMILE.

-Church's Newsletter

◆ A friend is one of the nicest things you can have, and one of the best things you can be.

-Douglas Pagels

◆ In every generation the number of the righteous is small. Be sure you are among them.

-A. W. Tozer

******

Manny

Pierre didn't know where it came from, he only knew that it came and it helped in oh-so-many ways. The money always arrived with a small short note that simply said, "Keep up the great cause, we will prevail," and was simply signed, "Manny."

Pierre didn't know who Manny was - nobody did! Not then anyway, we do now. But this was during World War II when the Black Horror was sweeping

Europe. That's what Manny called it, The Black Horror, and of course he was referring to the Nazi plague that was taking over most of the continent.

Pierre was a leader of the French Resistance, commonly called the underground. He fought with groups of French citizens in the best way he could, by living within main society and leading bands of armed resistance against the Germans in *clandestine activities. They would ambush German patrols, blow up German installations, and sabotage Nazi operations in any way they could.

The Allies were good at providing arms and weapons, but the underground also needed money. That was a commodity that was very hard to come by during the war, especially when your country is completely occupied by an invading military force.

And that's where Manny came in. He sent money, and he sent a lot of it. Manny was Emmanuel Goldenberg, born a Romanian Jew, who was now living in America. Manny had done very well in his life and he knew only too well what kinds of horrors were going on in his native Romania and the rest of Europe. Jews and others were being gassed and killed by the millions and he had to do something.

One thing he could do was use his good fortune to help the war effort. He had tried to join the Armed Forces, but he didn't qualify, so he did what he could. He sent money to where it was needed the most—to the resistance as I said, Pierre was one of the leaders of the resistance. There were many, but Pierre controlled the action around the area of Normandy. He and his people were very instrumental in assisting the Allied invasion on D-Day by sabotaging, redirecting many Nazi forces moments before the actual invasion. Much of this was possible because of the money that arrived every month. Month after month for two years money arrived for Pierre and his cause from Manny. It never failed! It literally saved the day. No, Pierre never knew who Manny was, only that he sent money for food, clothes, gasoline, and many other important things.

But years later, we know who Manny was, that silent guardian angel of the French underground. So do you. He was one of the biggest stars in Hollywood, and a fine gentleman. It's a Little Known Fact that a very important part of the success of the French underground came from a source they never knew: Emmanuel Goldenberg, or as you knew him, the very fine actor Edward G. Robinson.

P.S. Not many know that Robinson was a famous actor in the Yiddish theater before he became a movie star.

******

The End of All Matters

Did you know that before the election of 2012 that there are 545 human beings who were overseeing 311 million lives in America? These 545 individuals were made up of one president, nine Supreme Court justices, one hundred Senators, and 435 members of the House of Representatives. When we consider the condition of our country we have to give our leaders a failing grade, but yet it appears that thousands will put up with the insane politics of Washington D. C. Clearly, the agenda has nothing to do with maintaining the integrity of this country; rather, it points to something that is sinister and wicked.

The question is why do the majority of the people put up with such insanity? The main reason is they are sheep, easily persuaded. In fact, they are more prone to be persuaded by lies than truths. Lies allow for fantasy, while truth requires action.

Leaders simply mirror the moral temperature of the people. Notice, I used the word "temperature" of the people. You could even call it "climate" of the people. There can be moral people but if they are asleep or prefer to remain ignorant towards the moral character of leadership, the climate of the nation will be one of compromise. If a people can only be roused by sensationalism, you will have people who can be entertained into a lethargic state in regard to that which does not catch their attention. If people are self-serving, they will sell their vote for a cell phone.

President James A. Garfield issued this warning during his presidency, "Now more than ever before, the people are responsible for the character of their Congress. If that body be ignorance, reckless, and corrupt, it is because the people tolerate ignorance, recklessness, and corruption. If it be intelligent, brave, and pure, it is because the people demand these high qualities to represent them in the national legislature."

Clearly, the past generations of Hitler and Stalin have proved that people prefer to be sheep, even if they are being systematically led to the slaughter. They want to be lied to about what is really going on and just where it is leading them. They do not want the responsibility of getting too involved. It might require them to take a stand against what is popular and have to make some type of sacrifice. They tend to go with what they want to hear, rather than honestly face what is.

As a result of people being vulnerable in relationship to their preference and reality, there is much that is vying for their hearts and minds. However, the reason for this has to do with power, control, and influence. Individuals who have power, or who are in places of authority often want to control or influence others towards their reality. However, there is a chain of command in place. At the top of this chain is the god of this world, Satan. The real motive is to rid the world of the God of the Bible and all associated with Him. It is for this reason *Psalm 55:23* makes this declaration, *"But thou, O God, shalt bring them down into the pit of destruction: bloody and deceitful men shall not live out half their days; but I will trust in thee."*

The rally cries of these different groups vary. It seems the higher the place of power the greater the evil that is present to deceive, mock, and consume. Those who dare to be moral and decent often find themselves on the lower part of the chain, being flipped around and ramrodded. Subsequently, these individuals often feel isolated and powerless because of the propaganda and lies that seem to have captured and enfolded the masses.

God laughs at the attempts of the wicked. Granted, He will give the wicked a season to do their damage. However, the reason for such a season is to allow evil to come to maturity so that He can judge it. Although those who are wicked believe they are now in a position to bring forth their wicked agenda, they will ultimately fail to bring it to complete fruition. The Bible tells us that when the wrath of God finally manifests itself, these wicked fools will call for the rocks to fall on them to hide them from facing the inevitable.

Let's consider how this chain works.

Satan over the world systems,
World Planners over nations,
Dictators and despots over the masses,
Communists over the revolutionaries,
Revolutionaries over the fanatics,
Fanatics over the liberals,
The liberals over the moderates,
The moderates over the conservatives,
The conservatives over the decent folk,
The decent folk over the dissenter.

However, when all is said and done, the Bible tells us that it is the meek who will inherit the earth.

Blessed are the meek: for they shall inherit the earth (Matthew 5:5).

Declarations and Songs
(Answers)

Shema: Hear, O Israel: The LORD our God is one LORD (Deuteronomy 6:4).

Thou art the Christ, the Son of the living God (Matthew 16:16).

1. Amazing Grace
2. Blessed Assurance
3. The Old Rugged Cross
4. How Great Thou Art
5. In the Garden
6. Just A Closer Walk With Thee

7. Sweet Hour of Prayer
8. It Is Well With My Soul

9. At Calvary
10. God Is So Good
11. Jesus Loves the Little Children
12. Just As I Am
13. Softly And Tenderly
14. Leaning On The Everlasting Arms
15. There Is Power In the Blood
16. His Eye is on the Sparrow

Who Am I
(Answers)

1. Robert Chapman
2. Samuel Chadwick
3. Robert Murray McCheyne
4. R. A. Torrey
5. Dwight L. Moody
6. C. I. Scofield
7. F. B. Meyer
8. W. Robertson Nicoll
9. Thomas Spurgeon
10. G. Campbell Morgan
11. John Henry Jowett
12. George H. Morrison
13. Amy Carmichael
14. Oswald Chambers
15. H. A. Ironside
16. Alexander Whyte
17. Alan Redpath
18. John Wesley
19. John Newton
20. Mrs. Sarah Trimmer

The Moral of the Story

Bethel	Jericho	Nineveh
Philadelphia	Egypt	Bethany
Kidron	Ur	Addan
Calvary	Jordan	Golgotha
Ekron	Capernaum	Shiloh
Athens	Sodom	Bethsaida
Bethshemesh	Babylon	Damascus
Ai	Lebanon	Golan
Jerusalem	Hammath	Hebron

Bethlehem   Dead Sea   Hena
Sea of Galilee   Nazareth   Edom
Armageddon

(You can find these names in Smith's Bible Dictionary.)

There were some friends who decided to take a journey to the Holy Land. They wanted to walk where Jesus walked. These friends included Beth Ellis from Philadelphia, Jeri Kidron from Calvary, Ada Ekron of Athens, and for protection purposes, Beth's brothers, Ed, Adam, and Caleb from adjoining communities.

Admittedly, these six individuals seemed like unusual companions. For the enthusiastic traveler, Beth, she meshed such groups together without much incident. However, this group had an unusual mixture that she perceived might be a bit challenging.

Each person wanted to go to different places. Granted, they had aired out their differences and all came to the same conclusion that they wanted to see places such as Jerusalem, Bethlehem, and the Sea of Galilee. However, to mix up the pot, Jeri choose the sights of Egypt as a must, while Ada' curiosity about Petra, located in Jordan seemed a bit eccentric even to Beth. On the other hand, the idea of possibly seeing the ruins of Capernaum caused Ed to so dominate the negotiation that he came across as a spoiled baby, longing and striving to get complete control of those around him. Even Caleb, a non-committal person in most matters became somewhat upset about Ed's attitude. If possible Caleb wanted to see such sights as Masada, but could see that his desire would be completely ignored if Ed had his way. Since Adam's sense of humor made him a ham, mathematically, he tried to figure out how everyone could fit their preferences into the schedule in a comical way. He used a deadpan face to communicate his desire to visit the Dead Sea, while being aware that Beth also wanted to see Nazareth. Regardless of how they tried, Adam advocated that six could not be equally divided into nine, vehemently pointing out that there must be compromise or agreement if they were going to be successful in their upcoming trip.

To Beth, any time she could find people to journey back into historical lands was to add an array of depth to what she considered her small world. She was especially excited to visit the Holy Land. She wanted to stand as close as she could to Golgotha, the place of the cross where redemption had been secured. The idea of not being able to enjoy it because of conflict between her traveling companions, made her melancholy. At that time, Beth said a silent prayer, knowing the Lord had always been her anchor.

After her prayer, Ada said she would reconsider Petra if necessary. Adam, as custom to his easy-going personality, said that he did not have to visit that which was dead, for he realized that Christ pointed to that which was alive. Jeri came down on her enthusiasm in seeing the Pyramids in order to give Ed a chance to stop at go, land emotionally, and become reasonable in his attitude. Caleb calmed down to once again become non-committed in his attitude.

Each person waited quietly for Ed to concede some of his passion. However, the question remained, would he? Bronzed in appearance, it appeared as if he was not about to melt but a miracle was taking place underneath the surface. Ed was remembering what the journey was about. It was a spiritual journey that was to bring each of them to a place of personal identification by walking where Jesus walked. The man who spoke of love, unity, and fellowship came to bring reconciliation, not conflict and division. At that conclusion, he naturally had to concede to that which was greater in purpose. Shiloh, a place of rest was in order instead of Armageddon. It was time for him to back down and come together with the rest in an attitude of reason. Perhaps, they could all see their desired attractions. It was simply a matter of listening to one another and making the necessary plans.

Ed omitted the details as to what changed his position, but Beth knew. She knew that the Lord had reminded him that the real journey in life is a spiritual one. This journey entails character that must be balanced by mercy, compassion, grace, and love towards others. Such character reaches the heights of excellence in disposition, attitude, and conduct. Beth also knew that she had already experienced a bit of the Holy Land. The Lord came in their midst because of prayer, interceded because of mercy, and revealed His grace through a miraculous and incredible way, unveiling a bit of His heavenly power and glory in the heart of one man.

******

Bibliography

(AP): The Best of Andrew Murray on Prayer (Daily Devotion), © 2000 by Barbour Publishing, Inc.

(MP): All the Messianic Prophecies of the Bible, © 1973 by Herbert Lockyer, Zondervan

(DL): Devotions for a Deeper Life, Oswald Chambers, © 1986 by God's Bible School

(DP): A Devotional Commentary Psalms, Herbert Lockyer, Sr., © 1993 by Kregel Publications

(CBO): The Continual Burnt Offering, H. A. Ironside, © 1994 by Loizeaux Brothers

(ED): Extreme Devotion, © 2001, The Voice of the Martyrs

(ODT): One Day at a Time, © 1998, William MacDonald, Gospel Folio Press

(AG): Tozer on the Almighty God, A. W. Tozer, © 2004 by Zur Ltd.

(RR): The Righteous Man's Refuge, John Flavel, Old Paths Gospel Press

(SP): The Secret Place, God's Invitation to Intimacy, Anna Alden-Tirrill, © 2012 by White Cottage Publishing Company.

(TD): True Discipleship, © 2003 by William MacDonald, Gospel Folio Press

(WN): A Table in the Wilderness, Daily Meditations, Watchman Nee, © Angus I. Kinnear

(GW): Sermons of George Whitefield, © 2009 by Hendrickson Publishers Marketing, LLC

(RA): Revival Addresses, R. A. Torrey, © 1903 by Fleming H. Revell Company

(DW): The Drummer's Wife and Other Stories from Martyr's Mirror, Joseph Stoll, © 1968 by Pathway Publishing Corporation.

(PCK): 50 People every Christian Should Know, © 2009 by Warren W. Wiersbe

(RC): Robert Chapman, A Biography by Robert L. Peterson, © 1995 Robert L. Peterson

(AWG): Along with God, Richard Wurmbrand, © 1999, The Voice of the Martyrs.

(PGR): Portraits of the Great 18th Century Revival, Paxton Hood, © 1997 Ambassador Productions Ltd.

(KM): Knothole Glimpses of Glory, F. Ellsworth Powell; © 1963 by Osterhus Publishing House

(NTB): No Turning Back, E. A. Johnston, © 2005, Gospel Folio Press
Tongues of the Prophets, © by Robert St. John, Country Life Press

By Searching, Isobel Kuhn, American Edition © 1959 by China Inland Mission, (Now known as the Overseas Missionary Fellowship)

Glossary

adumbration: to foreshadow vaguely, to present a sketchy representation or outline.

anathema: a ban or curse by excommunication, a denunciation of something that is now accursed.

antithesis: opposition, contrast the rhetorical contrast of ideas by means or parallel arrangements of worlds, clauses, or sentences.

apropos: at an opportune time as in something being relevant.

arduous: steep, difficult , hard to accomplish, marked by great effort.

clandestine: secretly, akin to hide.

mould: It is the same as the word "mold" something into shape.

profligate: completely given up to dissipation and licentiousness, wildly extravagant.

proletariat: the lowest social or economic class of a community, the laboring class.

propagate: to continue or increases.

tutilege: an act or process of serving as guardian or protector.

vitiated: to make faulty or defective often by addition of something that impairs, to debase in moral or aesthetic status.

wont: to dwell, accustomed, inclined, habitual way of doing.

Most of the above definitions were obtained from the Webster's New Collegiate Dictionary, © 1976 by G. & C. Merriam Co.

About the Author

Rayola Kelley, an ordained minister of the Gospel, was born again and saved out of a cult in 1976 while serving in the U.S. Navy. Her spiritual journey continued through extensive discipleship, before following the Lord's call upon her life into full-time ministry 35 years ago, when, with Jeannette Haley, founded Gentle Shepherd Ministries in 1989.

Through the years, Rayola's gift of teaching the Word has opened many doors for her to teach adult Sunday school, oversee a fellowship for over 15 years, hold evangelistic meetings in churches, conduct seminars, and speak at retreats. She has served in jail ministry, and is well known for her gift of spiritual insight and counseling. Upon being called to be a missionary in America, Rayola, along with Jeannette Haley established different fellowships where intense Bible Studies and discipleship training were conducted to equip believers for the ministry. These different mission fields in America entailed working in various churches as well as working with other cultures such as Korean and Hispanic nationalities.

Rayola, along with co-laborer Jeannette Haley, (professional artist, author of Christian novels, Bible Studies and stories for children) began sending out a monthly newsletter containing articles for the Body of Christ in 1997 which continues to grow. Ms. Kelley has authored over 50 books, and numerous Bible Studies including an advanced Discipleship Course (available in both English and Spanish) that is being used in countries such as Africa, Bulgaria, Israel, Ireland, India, Cuba, and Pakistan. Among her many books is *"Hidden Manna"* which deals with destructive cycles in people and relationships, and *"Battle for the Soul"* which presents a clear picture of the battle that rages in the soul. She has written six in-depth devotional books, including both the Old Testament and New Testament devotional study which takes the reader through the entire Bible in one year. All of her books are hard-hitting, bottom-line spiritual food for the hungry and thirsty soul to "chew" upon in order to *"grow strong in the Lord, and in the power of His might."*

Rayola currently resides in Oldtown, ID and continues to fulfill Christ's commission to make disciples through teaching, spiritual counseling, and writing.

Please visit Gentle Shepherd Ministries Web Site at: www.gentleshepherd.com for further information, and to access her challenging and informative audio sermons.

Volume Seven: Discovering True Ministry
From Prisons and Dots to Christianity
So You Want To Be In Ministry

Devotions
Devotions of the Heart: Books One and Two
Daily Food for the Soul: Books One and Two

Gentle Shepherd Ministries Devotion Series:
Being a Child of God
Disciplining the Strength of our Youth
Coming to Full Age

Nugget Books:
Nuggets From Heaven
More Nuggets From Heaven
More Heavenly Gems
Heavenly Treasures

Gentle Shepherd Ministries Series:

The Christian Life Series
What Matter Is This?
The Challenge of It
The Reality of It
The Leadership Series
Overcoming
A Matter of Authority and Power
The Dynamics of True Leadership

Other Books By:
Jeannette Haley
Books co-authored with Rayola Kelley:
Hidden Manna (original)
The Many Faces of Christianity (Volume 6)
Discovering True Ministry: Volume 7
Post to Post 3: Meditations Along the Way
Other Books:
The Pig and I
Reflections of Wonder (Devotional)
Children's Books:
Little Stories for Little People
Traveler's Tales
The Adventures of Zack and Mira
The Adventures of Paul and Dana
(A House on the Beach)
The Monster of Mystery Valley

www.ingramcontent.com/pod-product-compliance
Lightning Source LLC
Chambersburg PA
CBHW031241090426
42742CB00007B/270